Sparks (44-23329) 4-26-65

THE ROAD TO SALEM

THE ROAD
TO
SALEM

BY ADELAIDE L. FRIES

Chapel Hill

THE UNIVERSITY OF NORTH CAROLINA PRESS

PRINTED IN THE UNITED STATES OF AMERICA
AMERICAN BOOK-STRATFORD PRESS, INC., NEW YORK

PREFACE

THE STORY OF ANNA CATHARINA IS TAKEN FROM HER AUTOBIOG-raphy, filed in manuscript in the Salem Moravian Archives, elaborated with information gained from diaries and other records kept by leaders of the Moravian Church in Georgia, Pennsylvania, and North Carolina.

It is not fiction with a background of history, but a recital of things that really happened. Every man, woman, and child actually lived and acted as presented, and with very few exceptions their real names are used, four or five being disguised for obvious reasons.

Especially should it be noted that Catharina is not a composite character. Her life was her own, and if it were desirable, line and page reference could be given for each item, even such trivial matters as the nonsense rhymes of Henry Antes and Gottlieb Reuter's fear of snakes. Catharina happens to have been an unusual woman, with varied contacts and responsibilities, and it is doubtful whether any other Moravian of her day saw life from as many different angles.

The Unitas Fratrum or Unity of Brethren, commonly called the Moravian Church, was founded in 1457 by followers of the Bohemian reformer and martyr John Hus. During the first dramatic period of its existence it endured many persecutions, spread through Bohemia and into Moravia and Poland, grew vigorously, preached the Gospel, established schools, printed books, and attained prominence and wide influence. In the anti-reformation of the seventeenth century it was almost annihilated, but in the third decade of the eighteenth century, descendants of the Ancient Unity emigrated from Moravia into Saxony, where the Unity was resuscitated on the estate of a young nobleman, Nicholas Louis, Count Zinzendorf.

v

From that center the Unity spread into many parts of Europe, to England, and to America. In 1732 Moravian missionaries went to the West Indies; in 1735 Moravian colonists came to Georgia; in 1740, to Pennsylvania; in 1753, to North Carolina.

Anna Catharina was born in Pennsylvania, and as a bright, observant child she noted conditions in that colony and their effect on her father, who was a rather prominent man in his locality. When Spangenberg came up from Georgia and became her father's friend, she was just at the age to be attracted by his kindliness and fascinated by the accounts of his adventures and of the attempted colony in Savannah. As a teen-age girl she was pulled two ways by her father's interest in the founding of Bethlehem and by the criticisms currently hurled at Count Zinzendorf and the Moravians. When she joined the Moravian Church as a young woman, she threw herself heartily into its activities in Pennsylvania; then, with her first husband, she moved to North Carolina, where the rest of her life was spent.

The Wachovia Tract, the 98,985 acres bought by the Moravian Church for the North Carolina settlement, covered about two-thirds of the modern county of Forsyth, in the piedmont section of the state. Salem, the chief Moravian town, has united with her hundred-year-younger sister to form the present city of Winston-Salem. The old Moravian villages of Bethabara and Bethania still exist, as do the country congregations of Friedberg, Friedland, and Hope, now supplemented by a number of urban and rural Moravian churches founded since Catharina's day.

Contemporary manuscript records of the short-lived Moravian colony in Georgia and of the permanent settlements in Pennsylvania and North Carolina are preserved in the Moravian Church Archives in Bethlehem, Pennsylvania, and in Winston-Salem, North Carolina, and give accounts of many more things which Catharina saw but which cannot be included within the scope of this book.

ADELAIDE L. FRIES

CONTENTS

ILLUSTRATIONS

THE ROAD TO SALEM

"Something Concerning My Journey through Time"

"I have indeed long wished to write something concerning my journey through life, as it seems remarkable to me. It has been written piecemeal, and now when I can no longer write well, I am putting it together. It is badly written, and whether any one can read it I do not know, but to the glory of the Saviour I must bear witness that out of lost sinners He can make blest men, and on the 24 of April, 1786, I also was ordained a deaconess by Brother Johannes."—*Literal translation of the introductory paragraph of Catharina's autobiography, written in 1803.*

MY CHILDHOOD

―――――

"PLEASE, GRANDMOTHER!"

"When you have finished one more round on your needles."

"But, Grandmother—"

"No."

When Grandmother Antes spoke in that tone, I knew better than to argue, but I pouted as she picked up the dropped stitch and put the interminable gray stocking back into my hands. "Now, Anna Catharina, stop looking out of the window and put your mind on your work," she admonished, "and you will soon be through." This was true enough, for thanks to her teaching I could knit rather well for a five-year-old.

Grandmother was a very busy woman, but as often as she could she sat down with me during the knitting lesson. "Please tell me a story, Grandmother," I would beg, and sometimes my coaxing had the desired result. Naturally I cannot remember just when she told me what, but I grew up knowing that I was named for her, and that my father, Henry Antes, looked like a certain Baron of Mainz, about whom many legends seem to have gathered. Just how far up the family tree the Baron grew, I never knew, but Grandmother spoke of him often. "They say he was tall and strong, like your father, with light hair and blue eyes, a daring, brave man, popular with his friends and respected by his enemies." This description fitted my father (except that he had no enemies), and so the legendary baron and my pioneer father merged into one in my mind.

When my father was nineteen, that is, in 1720, he accompanied his parents on the long tedious journey from the Palatinate to the New World. Emigration to Pennsylvania was still in its infancy, but farms were being begun in the country west of the Delaware River, and Grandfather and Grandmother Antes decided to build an inn in Frederick Township, on the road which began at Philadelphia and Germantown and ran westward toward the Blue Mountains, serving the settlers and the traders who dealt with the Indians. There were many Indians of various tribes composing the Six Nations, and their camps were scattered all over the western part of the Colony. In times of peace they gave little trouble, but when war came they were a serious menace to the white settlements.

The Antes inn was a large, well-built, two-story log house, with two chimneys placed toward the middle. In the public room there was a large fireplace, and in cold weather travelers gathered eagerly around the big fire blazing there. In the kitchen there was another fireplace, even larger, and on its raised hearth were the covered pots and long-handled pans used in cooking, with larger pots hanging from the crane.

Grandmother and Mother each had a smaller fireplace in her room; and there were others upstairs, though they were seldom used, as the guests were quite content with good straw beds and the ample supply of quilts that were provided.

Usually Father helped his parents in the inn, but now and then, when the Baron in him demanded action, he would don his deer-skin suit, leggings, breeches, hunting shirt, and cap, take his gun from the rack, and go into the forest for a day or a week or longer. My mother (Christina Elisabeth De Wees by birth) used to worry when his absence became prolonged, fearing that he had met with some accident or had been murdered by treacherous redskins, but he always returned safely, loaded with game, and met her reproaches with some laughing reference to the Baron, who would have feared the Indians as little as he did the banditti of his day. Father was an excellent shot, but sometimes game was hard to find. When friends commented on his wonderful luck his reply was, "When I go hunting, I stay until I get what I went for," and this answer probably explained much of his success in life.

I was born on November 19, 1726, and was the eldest child; so I had a good deal to do besides learning to knit. "Anna Catharina, come and amuse Margaret." "Anna Catharina, come and pick up John's blocks." "Anna Catharina, come and rock the cradle." So it went for most of the day. Margaret was a good child, seldom in mischief and easy to amuse; but John's chief aim in life was to throw down his blocks as fast as I could pick them up, and try to climb out of his cradle when he was supposed to go to sleep. If he hurt himself, I was blamed, for it was my duty to take care of the baby, and if I failed I suffered. Father was a kind man, but strict, and he expected and secured obedience. Mother followed his lead, and I was trained to do as I was bid or take the consequences.

But in spite of all this, I spent many happy hours out of doors in the shade of our favorite tree, which grew near enough to the inn so that Mother could keep an eye on us and call me if she needed me. To this tree, Susel Barunt, the hostler's daughter, and I ran whenever we could, and there we played the games which children invent with sticks and moss and stones. From there, also, we watched the passing on the road—long hunters, with their guns, going to or coming from the forests; a settler who had been to Philadelphia and was returning with his purchases loaded behind him on his horse; a farmer and his wife, riding double; a trader with his packhorses, going out to the Indians, or coming back with a load of furs; perhaps a family who had been able to purchase a two-wheeled cart and in it were taking their possessions to the place where they planned to build a home. Best of all was a peddler, who was almost sure to stop at the inn to display his goods, for then Grandfather was likely to make some small purchase for me, and add something for Susel.

Whoever came brought with him the news of the outside

world. Perhaps another ship from Rotterdam had docked at Philadelphia, bringing relatives of some of our neighbors, lured to the
New World by the descriptions sent home by the families already
here. Perhaps an English ship had arrived, and there had been
many present to see whether they could pay the passage of one or
another redemptioner and secure his services for a term of years.

Or the gossip might be personal. Governor Patrick Gordon
was promoting trade with the West Indies, Spain, and Portugal, as
well as with Great Britain. Mr. Thomas Penn was becoming un-
popular because he was so cold and distant. Mr. Benjamin Frank-
lin was about to establish a library in Philadelphia and fifty persons
had agreed to support it.

Such talk as this meant nothing to Susel and me, but it was of
great importance to my father, who was keenly interested in all
that went on in the Colony.

When I was about seven years old, Father decided that it was
time for me to have some schooling. There was no school near;
so Father engaged a tutor to teach me and several of the neighbor
children, whose parents were glad to take advantage of the opportunity. The tutor lived in the inn, and there was no difficulty
about attending classes. As I was quick enough when I cared to
try, I easily learned to read and memorized the Shorter Catechism
during the first winter. Father also bought a clavier for us, and I
was fascinated by the black keyboard with the ivory-faced keys
for the halftones. We were taught to sing by note, and the singing
lessons gave me much, much joy.

It was about this time that my father began to take an interest in religious matters. Grandmother was a strict member of the
Reformed Church, and when some Seventh Day Baptists moved
into the neighborhood, she feared that Father might be moved to
join them and was severe in her criticism of their doctrines. Father
answered her only with rhymes, which he sang to her, and I
promptly picked up the rhymes and sang them over and over,
though I knew little of their import.

In my tenth year, Father built a mill on a branch of the

Perkiomy Creek, a tributary of the Schuylkill River. The mill was of logs, and contained several living rooms besides the mill-room proper, and we lived in the mill until the stone dwelling house was finished. When we moved into the stone house, the rooms in the mill were occupied by the miller and his wife, and were used, too, by people who must stay overnight while their grain was ground. I rejoiced that the mill was only one mile from the inn, so that I could see my grandparents often. Father also began to farm the land around the mill.

Our house was always open to the neighbors, and my life began to broaden. At the inn we children were not allowed to mingle with the guests, who were sometimes rude and uncouth, but this was different, and we ran in and out, bringing fresh water, a glass of cider or a plate of apples, while Father discussed life with the visitors and won their liking by his intelligence, uprightness, and friendly ways.

At the mill, too, I saw more of the boys and girls of the neighborhood, who came on horseback, alone or with their parents, bringing wheat and rye to be ground. This so aroused my desire that I finally summoned courage to ask my father, "Don't you think it would be a good thing for me to learn to ride?"

"What put that into your head?" asked Father quietly. This was encouraging, for I had feared a flat refusal.

"All the boys and girls of my age ride," I said, feeling that this was not a very strong argument, since we did not have to go a distance for our flour as the others did.

Father looked me over thoughtfully, eyeing me from head to foot as if measuring me. Then he delighted me by saying, "You are not very tall, but I believe you could ride the little bay mare. Ask your mother to help you make a riding skirt, and then I will teach you myself." He must have seen my surprise at his ready consent, for he added, "Every man and woman, every boy and girl, should be able to ride and drive, and the time to learn is when you desire it. You will need the ability all your life." This was true, though at the time I realized only the keen pleasure it gave me to have my stalwart father teach me carefully and take me with him whenever he could, so that I came to feel quite at home on a horse. Later in life, both in Pennsylvania and in North Carolina, the ability to ride stood me in good stead many times.

The making of the riding skirt led to new employments. Mother had already taught me to sew a straight seam, to hem a towel, and the like, but now she began to trust some of the family sewing to me, and I found it much more interesting to make garments than to sew just for the sake of practice. We dressed very simply, with the same kind of dress for Grandmother, Mother, and me, but many stitches were required. We used homespun linen in the summer and linsey-woolsey in the winter, and I began with the former, since it was easier for young fingers to manage. The long, full skirt must be tucked from the waist half way to the bottom; the apron of calico or of linen must be neatly hemmed. The waist with its elbow sleeves was easier to make than the spencer, which must fit closely and be stiffly boned. The spencer was of the same material as the skirt, but the waist was sometimes of colored linen, and sometimes of white. Grandmother preferred plain blue linen; Mother wanted white for Sunday; and I wanted the brightest color that the peddler's pack afforded. Over the spencer we wore a kerchief, brought around the neck and to a point at the waist. Here again our tastes differed, for Grandmother preferred figured calico, Mother wanted white, and I agreed with Mother. Grandmother always wore a close-fitting cap of figured calico and covered it with a black hood when she went out; but I wanted to run bareheaded except when it was necessary to wear the hood to meeting. Grandmother also had a large bag or pocket of the figured calico, into which went keys and many of the other things which a busy woman must carry. Many housewives wore pin-cushions and scissors hanging from their waists by ribbons or chains, but Mother refused to do this for fear the babies might be hurt when they clung to her skirts or climbed into her lap.

Mother also gave me more responsibility in the care of the

younger children and began to instruct me in the more important lines of housekeeping. She wanted to make of me as expert a housewife as herself, but I knew that only many years of experience could do that, and had little hope of becoming her equal no matter how old I might grow.

2.

OUR NEW FRIEND, SPANGENBERG

———

LOOKING BACK ON THESE YEARS I KNOW THAT IT WAS ABOUT THIS time that my father's religious views began to crystallize and that he became concerned over the fact that the various denominational groups which had established themselves in Pennsylvania were giving all their strength to debating and struggling with each other, instead of promoting the kingdom of God. I can still hear him call the roll of the sects, and still see his wry smile as he agreed with someone who said that a man with "the Pennsylvania religion" had as good as no religion at all.

Father belonged to the Reformed Church of Falkner's Swamp, but he had an open mind, and it seemed to him that if the men in each sect who really cared could be brought together, some of the differences could be eliminated, and others could be accepted as valid and deserving of respect. The matter went so far that he and a few friends, representing five of the religious groups, organized "The Associated Brethren of Skippack," with the idea of ignoring non-essential differences and strengthening one another in the Christian life. Among the men who were interested in an extension of this association were Christopher Wiegner, of the Skippack Woods, and his friend, George Boehnisch. Mr. Wiegner belonged to the so-called Schwenkfelder, and Mr. Boehnisch to the Unity of Brethren. Mr. Wiegner owned a large farm, and Mr. Boehnisch lived with him, helped on the farm, and did religious work among the Schwenkfelder, although he was not a minister.

One day Mr. Wiegner came to our house, bringing with him

a stranger whom he introduced as Mr. Spangenberg, a Moravian minister, just up from Georgia. I was sitting in the next room sewing, and I listened idly to what was said. As I remember the conversation after many years it was something like this:

After some general remarks my father asked, "Mr. Spangenberg, do you mind telling me why Christopher Wiegner called you a Moravian? I understood that you belong to the same church as Mr. Boehnisch, and he is a member of the Unity of Brethren."

"The two names have different origins," said Mr. Spangenberg, "but they have come to mean the same thing." Father must have looked puzzled for Mr. Spangenberg added, "When descendants of the Ancient Unitas Fratrum, or Unity of Brethren, fled from Moravia to Saxony seeking religious freedom, and founded Herrnhut on the estate of Count Zinzendorf, the neighbors called them 'the Moravian Brethren.' It happened also that the first Brethren who went to Georgia were natives of Moravia, and when they were detained in London waiting for a ship to Savannah the Englishmen called them 'the Moravians.' "

"And are you a Moravian?" asked my father.

"Yes and no," replied Mr. Spangenberg. "I was not born in Moravia, but I belong to the Unity of Brethren, which is the same as the Moravian Church. My parents were Lutheran, and I was first ordained as a Lutheran minister. Why I transferred to the Moravian Church is a long story, but I thank God for His leading in the matter, and I am glad that my service in the Unity of Brethren has brought me to Pennsylvania to meet men like you."

After this visit Mr. Spangenberg was often at our house, for he and my father found that they had much in common, though he had been educated in the universities of Europe and my father's opportunity for study had been limited to a few years before he came to America. Mr. Spangenberg was staying at the Wiegner farm, helping with the work while he made acquaintance with Mr. Wiegner's friends. He said that he had come to Pennsylvania partly to see how the Schwenkfelder were getting along, and partly to see whether there was an opening for a Moravian settlement and for missionary work among the Indians.

When there were guests, the older children were usually allowed to come to the table, although we knew that we must be entirely silent unless someone asked us a question. In this way I came to know Mr. Spangenberg, and was greatly drawn to him by his kindly smile and the pleasant word he always had for me. At that time he was a man of medium height, and had not yet put on the flesh which later gave him a round face and a portly figure. He wore his hair brushed straight back from his high forehead, and it had a natural wave at the ends, where it touched his coat. His suit was brown, with knee breeches, and a coat which he wore buttoned straight up the front; the coat was without collar or lapels, and had but one row of button-holes, and they only of a size to fit the buttons. His plain white linen stock was crossed in front, the ends hidden under the coat. Severely plain as the attire was, it seemed to harmonize with the intelligent directness of his speech.

Everyone within hearing listened eagerly to what he said, but we children were most interested when he talked about his travels, and told us of his experiences in far-away Georgia. There, under his leadership, the first Moravian colony in America had been established through the influence of Count Zinzendorf.

One day Father asked him, "Do you think the Georgia settlement will be a success?"

Mr. Spangenberg hesitated, and then answered, "If you mean our Moravian part of it, I do not know. A second and larger group arrived in Georgia just before I came north, and they will do their best, but some things look unfavorable. There has been much sickness among us, caused, I suppose, by the change in climate and in food. We found it impossible to settle on the large tract granted to Count Zinzendorf; it was too far from Savannah, and the Indians were too dangerous. In Savannah we have good lots, but there are many chances of friction with neighbors who do not understand the Moravian aims; at the same time there is more opportunity to earn money and pay off the sum we had to borrow from the Georgia Trustees for our traveling expenses. Only time can tell how things will work out. I am hopeful, but I am not sure."

It dawned on me one day, when Mr. Spangenberg and Father were discussing their respective voyages to America, that people who crossed the Atlantic had a rather hard time of it, with storms tossing their ships and threatening shipwreck, to say nothing of the monotonous diet on shipboard. They agreed that even when the weather was clear and the wind in the right direction the sailing was rough, and some people were seasick for the entire voyage.

"I am a good sailor," said Mr. Spangenberg, "and I am never seasick, but salt beef and dried prunes four days a week, salt pork and dried peas two days, and salt fish with a little butter on the seventh day, with stale water and a little beer to drink, are apt to disagree with a man, and I was quite ill for a day or two on the way to America." The voyage from England to Georgia had taken his party nine and a half weeks and that was considered a fair trip.

"I believe you came from Georgia to Pennsylvania by boat also," said Father.

"Yes," said Mr. Spangenberg. "It is practically impossible to come by land, for there are long distances where there are no roads and no white settlers. It would be impossible for an ordinary traveler to find food or lodging, and he would be in constant danger from roving bands of Indians."

That introduced the Indians as another topic of conversation. Father told about the Indians in Pennsylvania and Mr. Spangenberg spoke of the Creeks in Georgia and especially of their king, Tomochichi. "In any group you could single him out and say, 'That is a king,' " remarked Mr. Spangenberg. The Indians in the neighborhood of Savannah, he told us, often came to the Moravian house for a meal, and in return brought gifts of fish and game which were most welcome. When he left Savannah the Moravians were planning to build a school for the Indians, with General Oglethorpe bearing the expense for the Trustees, and Mr. John Wesley furthering the project.

I shall never forget the first religious service which Mr. Spangenberg held at our house. He asked my father to call together the children of our household and several of our playmates who happened to be there. Having seated us, Mr. Spangenberg placed himself before us, and talked to us of the love of the Saviour for children, urging us to give our hearts to Him and serve Him all our lives. It impressed me deeply, and I made all sorts of good resolutions. In the years that followed, many of them were forgotten, but his words remained as seed which would some day germinate and grow.

Another Moravian, Bishop David Nitschmann, came to our house one day with Mr. Spangenberg, but I was at the inn and did not see him. Bishop Nitschmann had been the leader of the second group of Moravian colonists of whom Mr. Spangenberg had spoken, and had come from Georgia to Pennsylvania on his way back to Europe. He asked Mr. Spangenberg to visit St. Thomas, in the West Indies, where the Moravians had begun a mission to the slaves about five years earlier. Bishop Nitschmann had started that mission, and regretted that he could not stop there on this trip; so Mr. Spangenberg agreed to go, and was away for several months. Then he returned to Mr. Wiegner's farm and resumed his friendship with my father.

However a conversation began, it always included a discussion of my father's desire for coöperation among the sects and the possibility of a Moravian settlement in Pennsylvania. On the latter point Mr. Spangenberg was slow to commit himself.

"I will write to Count Zinzendorf of your plan for some sort of synod of the Pennsylvania denominations," he told my father. "I know it will greatly appeal to him, and might influence him in favor of a settlement here. Frankly, though, I fear that if the Brethren should try to lead in such a movement the sects would unite against us as newcomers, and unwelcome newcomers at that."

"May I make a suggestion?" asked my mother, who was listening with interest to the discussion. "Send us a woman who has the ability to make friends easily, is skilled in household arts, and is fully informed as to the Moravian plans and aims. As she visited with the women in their homes she could win their liking, and that would influence the men."

"Have you such a woman in your ranks?" asked Father.

"I know of one, Sister Anna Nitschmann," said Mr. Spangenberg, "but it would be hard to spare her from the responsibilities she carries in the church at home. The idea is worth considering though, and I thank you, Mrs. Antes."

In 1737 a messenger came from Georgia, bringing distressing news to Mr. Spangenberg and begging for help. The Moravians were having trouble on account of the war which had broken out between England and Spain, and which threatened to involve English Georgia and Spanish Florida. Men were insisting that the Brethren take up arms, saying in effect, "You must fight, go to jail, or get out," while the Moravians were determined to retain the immunity from personal military service which had been promised to them by the Trustees.

"They want me to hurry to England to straighten out matters with the Trustees," said Mr. Spangenberg, "but I have decided to write to England and go to Georgia myself." So to Philadelphia he went, where he found a companion for the voyage, and they sailed for Savannah. The voyage was unduly prolonged, and a report reached us that the ship was lost. So it was with the greatest relief and joy that we welcomed our friend back later in the year.

"We had almost constant head winds," he explained, "and twice the ship was driven back beyond Cape Hatteras. The captain and crew were evil men, given to cursing and swearing. They were very superstitious, and several times my companion and I were in great danger of being thrown overboard, on the charge that we were sorcerers and the cause of the head winds."

"What utter nonsense!" said my mother, indignantly. "What could possibly give them that idea?"

Mr. Spangenberg laughed. "Oh, superstitions need no foundation, but I suppose this one was based on Jonah and his experience on his way to Tarshish. It is a not uncommon belief among sailors that it is unlucky to have a preacher on board. We tried to persuade the captain that we were not dangerous, and that we were as eager to reach port as he, but there is no telling how it might have turned out if the captain had not discovered that the helmsman was hindering the progress of the ship for some malicious purpose of his own, and that cleared us in the captain's eyes. But it was a trying voyage, for it lasted seventy-seven days, and the firewood gave out so that no cooking could be done. For a month we lived on hardtack, dried cherries soaked in water, and raw fish—dolphins which were caught from time to time."

"I thought you were taking extra food along," said Father.

"So we did, but our supply of butter and sugar was soon exhausted, and dried ham and tongue only increased our thirst. We tried soaking tea leaves in cold water, and we thought that at least a little better than the stale water alone. Then even the water gave out, and we would have suffered greatly if the Lord had not sent rain. We were able to catch enough to permit an allowance of one pint a day apiece. Finally the captain opened a keg of beer which he found in the cargo, and from that he sold us enough to relieve our thirst. For this we were very grateful."

In Savannah, Mr. Spangenberg had found things better than he had expected. The war scare had died down, and he was able to arrange for some of the Moravian colonists to leave. Others were willing to stay until their debt to the Trustees had been met, for it was agreed that this must be cleared before the Georgia attempt was abandoned, although it had become evident that the end was only a matter of time.

"It seems a great pity, in some ways," said Mr. Spangenberg. "A free school for the Indians of Tomochichi's tribe had been established, and our Brother Peter Rose and his wife were doing good work there. But war made the Indians restless and many of them moved away. A number of our group have died, others have returned to Europe, and the rest will leave Georgia as soon as they can do so honorably."

"Where will they go?" asked Mother.

"That I do not know. I told them I intended to recommend the establishing of a settlement in Pennsylvania; so they may decide to come here and join the company which I hope to send over from Europe."

"Then you have decided to plant a Moravian colony here!" exclaimed my father. "That pleases me greatly, for we need men like you in Pennsylvania."

Mr. Spangenberg smiled deprecatingly; then putting his hand into his capacious pocket he drew out a handful of button-molds, such as we cover with cloth and put on men's coats.

"Take these, Mrs. Antes," he said. "I carved them during the voyage, and they may be of service to you."

"Indeed they will," she answered. "I will use them on the next Sunday coat I make for Henry. But you have given me more than I will need for a long time. Why do you not take some of them with you as souvenirs of your adventurous trip?"

So the button-molds traveled with him when he left in October, 1739, to make a full report of all that he had learned in America during his four-year visit, and to advise with the other leaders of the Unity of Brethren concerning the sending of colonists to Pennsylvania.

3.

GROWING PAINS

━━━━━━

IN THE YEARS THAT FOLLOWED THE DEPARTURE OF OUR FRIEND
Spangenberg, things went rather badly for the eldest daughter
of Henry Antes.

Father was busy with his farm and mill, and with public
affairs. Mother was burdened with the care of house and children,
and claimed my help. I must nurse and sew and cook and bake and
wash and iron and clean, as a proper housewife should. But I was
fourteen, as tall as I would ever be, and I craved variety and young
companionship.

"Are you going to Sophy's party?" Lenel would ask.

"No."

"Why not?"

"Father won't let me."

"And why not?"

"Oh, he thinks parties are useless if not wicked."

"That is just too bad! Uncle John says your father is very
religious, but I don't think much of a religion that won't let you
have a good time."

And privately I agreed with her, pitying myself and thinking
that with my father's position, he ought to want his daughter to
be popular, instead of keeping her shut up like a Sister in the
Ephrata Cloisters.

Or Maria would say, "Bring your knitting over this afternoon."

"Can't."

"Why not?"

"Mother is going to the meeting house to help clean it before the preacher comes."

"Then come tomorrow."

"Tomorrow I have to help with the baking."

"If it isn't taking care of those children, it is doing the work in the kitchen! Your father is making money; why can't he hire a maid instead of expecting you to do the work of one without pay?" And again I felt abused and unhappy.

Sometimes I evaded the restrictions imposed upon me and joined the group of less well guarded boys and girls. They never did anything really wrong, but it was bad for me, for it meant disobedience and deceit and made me feel guilty and ashamed. I was torn between their way of looking at life and the way my parents were trying to bring me up, and often I felt lonely and estranged.

Several months after Mr. Spangenberg sailed for Europe, the remnant of the Moravian colony in Georgia arrived in Pennsylvania, led by the Reverend Peter Boehler. They were disappointed not to find Mr. Spangenberg here, and my father and Mr. Wiegner took them in until they could decide what to do.

To me, the most interesting person in the group was David Zeisberger, a slender, quiet, dark-haired young man about nineteen years of age, and I was annoyed when the Zeisbergers went to the Wiegner home instead of coming to ours. The girls reported an interesting story about David. When the second group of Moravians went to Georgia, David was left behind at school. But the master was cruel and unjust; so David and another boy ran away, went to London, and persuaded General Oglethorpe to send them to Savannah. Naturally, David's parents were astounded when he appeared, and he was scolded and called a bad boy, but he won his way to the favor of the colonists and was now quite one of them. His companion in the runaway escapade died of fever in Georgia, while on a missionary tour with Mr. Boehler.

The Georgia Moravians had come north with Mr. George

Whitefield, who had invited them to take passage on his sloop. Before long it was arranged that they should build a house which Mr. Whitefield intended to use as a school for Negroes and which he wanted erected on a tract he bought and named Nazareth.

Winter came on before the house was finished, and at that inopportune time Mr. Whitefield became angry because he could not out-argue Mr. Boehler on some point of doctrine, and peremptorily ordered the Moravians to leave his land and the two log cabins in which they had been living while building his large stone house.

"It is a shame to turn them out into the cold and snow!" declared my father indignantly; and Mr. Nathaniel Irish was so stirred up that he intervened, and succeeded in securing permission for the Moravians to remain where they were through the winter. He further offered to sell them a choice piece of land on the Lehigh River, which he had been commissioned to dispose of by the owner, Mr. Allen, and which he had planned to buy for himself.

In December a company of Moravians arrived from Europe to arrange for the founding of a settlement. The official head of the group was Bishop David Nitschmann, and with him came Miss Anna Nitschmann and her father (who was another David Nitschmann), several other men, and Mrs. Juliana Molther. Miss Anna was twenty-five, and was the woman selected by Mr. Spangenberg as best fitted to make friends among the women of Pennsylvania. Mrs. Molther was only twenty-two, born a countess, the wife of a Moravian minister who meant to come with her but had missed the party in London.

The men immediately gave careful consideration to the offer of Mr. Irish and decided to accept it. My father attended to all the details of the purchase and took title for them until they could decide who should serve as "proprietor" of the new settlement.

Miss Anna and Mrs. Molther followed the plan suggested by Mr. Spangenberg and visited at various farms, helping in the work and making acquaintances. My sister Margaret became greatly attached to Miss Anna, and whenever she heard that Miss Anna was at a neighboring farm spent all the time she could with her. I fancied that this threw part of Margaret's work on me, and I resented it.

My friends were divided in their opinion of Miss Anna, and many were our discussions about her.

"She is so sweet," Margaret would say. "I love to be with her and hear her talk."

"She had better tell you to stay at home and do your share of the work," said Sophy, to whom I had confided my grievance.

"She always says that duty comes first, and I do my work before I go to her, you know I do, Catharina." Margaret's eyes filled with tears and she looked at me so reproachfully that I felt both ashamed and angry.

"Well, her clothes are queer, and I never before saw a grown woman wear pink ribbons in her cap," said Sophy.

"Mother says that it is rude to criticize the dress of another person," said Susel Barunt. "She says that if we went to another country our dresses and caps would look just as odd to the people there, and we would not like them to make fun of us. I know her low-cut spencer is not like ours and she does not wear a kerchief, but what difference does that make?"

"The pink ribbon is certainly pretty and becoming," said Margaret, loyally, "and if the Single Sisters want to wear pink ribbons, I do not see why they should not do so."

"And what in the world is a 'Single Sister'?" asked Sophy scornfully.

"Miss Anna says that is what the Moravians call an unmarried woman," answered Margaret.

"Well, what do they call a married woman?" queried Sophy impishly, to which Susel retorted sharply that if the Moravian women wanted to be Single Sisters and Married Sisters that was their business, not ours.

"Miss Anna is certainly smart," put in Betsy hastily. "My father says she can dispute a point of doctrine as cleverly as any man he ever saw, and my mother will say nothing but good about her since the day she showed us how she could spin. Mother and

I were spinning when she came in, and when she found that Mother had a headache, she made her go and lie down. Then she took Mother's wheel and spent the morning spinning with me. She worked fast and wonderfully well, and she taught me a pretty spinning song that she said she had learned as a girl about my age. At our house we all like Miss Anna, just as Margaret does."

"Does she talk to you about your soul, and do you like that, Miss Betsy?"

"At first it embarrassed me," said Betsy honestly, "but now I like to have her do it. She tells me such interesting things and makes the Bible seem real, not far-away and grown up."

"She will not get a chance to talk religion to me!" I declared with some heat. So I avoided Miss Anna and was careful not to be left alone with her. Then, quite perversely, I persuaded myself that she and Mrs. Molther looked down on me and wished to have nothing to do with me. Thus my inner conflict grew.

The new Moravian village on the Lehigh was begun in February, 1741, with the building of a log house. Father went there often to aid the workmen, but I took little interest in it.

In November Mr. Louis Thuernstein, his daughter Benigna, and several other persons arrived in New York and came to Philadelphia, where they were met by Miss Anna and by my father also. Mr. Thuernstein's coming created quite a stir, though it is hard to see why it was greeted with such a storm of criticism and abuse. Father said he thought it was partly a reflex from the opposition with which he was surrounded in Germany, and Mother recalled Mr. Spangenberg's fear that the sects in Pennsylvania would unite against any newcomer.

Sophy's family was among the critics and I heard much from them. One day I ventured to ask my father, "Is it not strange that a man should come to America under an assumed name?"

"Catharina," said my father sternly, "it grieves me that a daughter of mine should be so ignorant and so unjust. Mr. Thuernstein does not hide the fact that he is better known as Nicholas

"Something Concerning My Journey Through Time"

This first page of Anna Catharina's autobiography contains the names of her four husbands, her own age, and the dates of her four marriages. Original in the Salem Moravian Archives.

Second page of Anna Catharina's Autobiography

A translation of this passage appears on page 2.

Count Nicholas Louis von Zinzendorf as a young man

From an oil painting by A. S. Belle, Paris, 1720. Reproduced from the frontispiece in
Die Welt der Stillen im Lande, *Berlin, 1925.*

Louis, Count Zinzendorf, but when a man has several names and titles he has a perfect right to select the one which he wishes to use on any given occasion. He is so truly a gentleman that he does not wish to embarrass persons in America who are not in a position to entertain the nobility; so he uses one of his less pretentious titles and comes simply as Mr. Louis Thuernstein. He goes even further and requests his associates to call him only 'Brother Louis.' "

"Miss Anna says that he is a great and good man," added Margaret, "and she ought to know, for she lived in their family and helped to take care of Miss Benigna, She says that his wife, the Countess Erdmuth Dorothea, is one of the finest women that ever lived and that the Unity of Brethren owes as much to her self-sacrifice and good business management as to the Count's zeal in the affairs of the church."

"I am much attracted to him," said Father. "He seems to me to be a deeply religious man, and any nobleman who can meet his tenants on terms of brotherly equality and retain their respect and gain their love, who can face all the privations of an Atlantic voyage in order to encourage a handful of his Brethren in the New World, must be a man of unusual character and worthy of our admiration. Now remember, Catharina, this is your father's opinion and you are to pay no attention to the unfounded criticisms of others."

Of course I dared say no more, but what Maria and Sophy had said was not so easily forgotten, and my mind remained divided between the two points of view.

Not long after Mr. Thuernstein and his party reached Pennsylvania, Christmas drew near, and he and some of his attendants passed our house on the way from Philadelphia to the new Moravian house on the Lehigh. Father joined them and spent Christmas there.

When he returned, he told us that he had found Mr. Thuernstein a wonderfully attractive leader of devotional exercises, and had been particularly impressed by the vigils on Christmas Eve. Just before midnight, Mr. Thuernstein suddenly rose, beckoned

the company to follow him, and passed out of the house-door and
into the adjoining stable, singing as he went an old, old hymn, of
which the second stanza began with the lines:

> Not Jerusalem
>   rather Bethlehem,
> Gave us that which
>   maketh life rich.

In the unusual midnight setting of the little frontier settlement, the
words had a strange, new meaning, and the name Bethlehem was at
once given to the new village.

Two days later Mr. Thuernstein approved of Father's suggestion that a call should be issued for a "Conference of Religions" to
be held in January. Father signed the call and presided at the first
meeting; Mr. Thuernstein was elected to preside at the six which
followed before the middle of June. When these "Pennsylvania
Synods" failed of their purpose Father was bitterly disappointed.
Mr. Thuernstein took it more philosophically, and turned his attention to the Indians.

While in America, Mr. Thuernstein and his daughter Benigna
occupied a rented house in Germantown, where Mr. Thuernstein
was doing what he could to serve a struggling Lutheran congregation, then without a pastor. Miss Benigna was only seventeen, a
year older than I, but much more mature, and she gathered some
girls into a school while her father was busy with other matters.
She left the school in other hands, however, when her father began
going out into the forests to visit the Red Men, of whom neither
she nor her father seemed to have any fear, though we Pennsyl-
vanians knew only too well how dangerous and uncertain they
were.

His first trip was in August, 1742, and lasted only a few days.
He had a conference with some of the friendly Indians at a place
called Tulpehocken, and they gave him a belt of wampum. This he
brought home with much pride, took it with him to Europe, and

later gave it to Mr. Spangenberg to bring back to America, where on several occasions it was of real service.

Three days later he set out again, this time taking his daughter Benigna, Miss Anna, and others of their party. This trip took twenty days and reached into New York as far as the Indian town of Shekomeko.

Pleased with the success of these efforts and the contact made with representatives of the Six Nations, he decided on a more arduous journey, planning to go to the Upper Susquehanna River and to the Wyoming Valley. My father tried hard to dissuade him, for the way was rough and dangerous, the Indians wild and treacherous. There was indeed much reason to fear that the party would never return. But Mr. Thuernstein not only insisted on going but again took Miss Benigna and Miss Anna with him. We had been brought up to keep on good terms with the Indians, but to be forever on guard against them, and to me the undertaking seemed utterly foolhardy.

But the party returned safely, perhaps because of an incident told by Mr. Martin Mack. Mr. Thuernstein's tent had been pitched on a sunny eminence and he was inside, seated on the ground, with many papers spread around him. Mr. Mack, outside the tent, suddenly saw two blowing adders gliding toward the tent and sprang to stop them. They were too quick for him and disappeared under the side of the tent, wriggled across Mr. Thuernstein's thigh, and went down a hole. Investigation showed that the tent had been placed over a den of adders, and it was promptly moved to a less dangerous spot. Mr. Mack thought that news of this escape spread among the Indians and that they believed Mr. Thuernstein to be under the special protection of the Great Spirit and feared to molest him. However this may be, the party was unharmed, and Miss Anna actually told Margaret that she enjoyed the trip, even "the camping for forty days under the open sky among poisonous snakes and other wild beasts and wild men!"

I admired the courage of Mr. Thuernstein, but one remark he made hurt me terribly, although it was probably justified. Toward the close of his stay in America he asked my father to return with him to Europe.

"But what would I do with my family?" asked Father.

"Take them with you, all except your eldest daughter. Better find a husband for her and leave her in Pennsylvania," was the reply, and Father said that he would think it over.

But Mother needed no time for thinking it over. She was vastly indignant at the implied criticism of her eldest daughter and declared definitely that she would not go. So the matter was dropped, except for Margaret, who begged to go with Miss Anna. As Mr. Thuernstein had no objection to Margaret, she accompanied the party to England, where in the course of time she married the Reverend Benjamin La Trobe.

Hitherto, as I have said, I had avoided Miss Anna when she came to our house, but under the sting of Mr. Thuernstein's remark I deliberately put myself in her way the next time she came, and when she began to talk to me in a friendly fashion, I answered flippantly, with a toss of the head and a shrug of the shoulders. For a long minute she looked at me sternly. Then she smiled, laid her hand on my arm and said gently, "Never mind, Catharina, some day you too will love the Saviour." She must have thought of the time when she too was a rebellious, impertinent child and of the wonderful experience that came to her. Thank God, her prophecy was fulfilled, but I have always regretted that my childish perversity kept me from knowing her more intimately, for she was one of the great leaders of the Unity of Brethren.

More settlers came to Bethlehem and Mr. Thuernstein helped them to organize. Then, on the last day of 1742, he bade Bethlehem farewell and set out for New York, followed in a day or two by the rest of the company including Sister Margaret. David Zeisberger drove one of the wagons, and it was understood that he also was to go; so we were surprised to see him return. He told us that as he stood by the rail, looking sadly toward the shore, Bishop Nitschmann said to him, "David, do you not want to go?"

"No," he had answered. "I would much rather stay and serve the Lord in America."

"Then go ashore and stay," said the Bishop, and he spoke so kindly that the young man knew it was full permission without reproof; so he hastened to leave the ship and return to Bethlehem.

4.

SINGLE SISTER CATHARINA

————

M R. THUERNSTEIN'S RETURN TO EUROPE DID NOT PUT AN END TO the criticisms which seemed to his friends so viciously unfair, nor did it leave me less unhappy. Indeed I was more restless and miserable than a girl of sixteen should be.

Outwardly things were calm enough, with progress being made in the building of Bethlehem, whither my father continued to go often to aid with his counsel. Members from Bethlehem were frequently at our house, but they seemed to me distant and disapproving, and there was no one in whom I could confide. The days were busy and therefore endurable, but at night bitter tears of resentment dampened my pillow and religious fears disturbed my rest. At intervals Miss Anna's words came back to me, bringing a ray of hope, but that soon vanished and again I wept.

At last we heard that Mr. Spangenberg was returning, but it was reported that he was now a bishop, and that he had married and was bringing a wife with him. What would she be like, I wondered, and would his new dignities make him so far above me that he would not even remember me?

But there was no need to fear, for his smile was as ready as ever, his greeting as kind; and Mrs. Spangenberg was so friendly that almost before I knew it I was pouring out my whole heart to her, mistakes, fears, and all. And how she comforted me! "You must forget the past and look toward the future," she said. "You must trust and not be afraid. You really belong in the Unity of Brethren, and I am sure you would be happy there."

"But the Brethren do not like me; the Sisters do not want me," I faltered, on the verge of tears.

"You have misunderstood the whole situation," she returned gravely. "You have held them at arm's length, not they you. Stop fighting against your better self, and they will meet you more than half way. Am I not right?" she asked, turning to Bishop Spangenberg, who came in just then.

To his questioning look she replied by giving him an outline of our conversation, and he smiled. Then turning to me he asked, "Catharina, do you remember the first service I held at your house when I came up from Georgia?"

I nodded, afraid to trust my voice, and he said gently, "What I said then is still true; the Saviour wants your heart and your life, and I think He has work for you in the Unity of Brethren."

This was indeed balm to my injured feelings, and my unhappiness faded away in the sunshine of their kindness. Another year slipped by while my sore heart healed and I was unconsciously preparing for the next step.

That step came in June, 1745, in my nineteenth year, when my father yielded to Bishop Spangenberg's desire and decided to move with his family to Bethlehem to take charge of the building operations there and in the surrounding outposts. I was very reluctant to make the change, but a vivid dream was given to me and I dared not disregard it. I agreed to go on trial, little realizing that this was the turning point of my life.

For lack of room in Bethlehem the unmarried women were then living in Nazareth, which had been bought by the Moravians not long after the purchase of the Bethlehem tract. Thither I went, at first finding it hard to adjust myself to the simple life, poor almost to poverty and a great contrast to the abundance of my father's farm. But I soon grew accustomed to the meagre furnishings and plain fare, and began to take pleasure in the life of the house. I had heard the Sisters referred to as the Moravian nuns, but there was nothing conventual about the place; rather it was a busy family circle, with plenty to do and much that was pleasant. Work was planned in conferences, in which devotionals, a simple meal, sociability, and a business discussion were combined. Religious services were frequent, but they were short and varied in character, and many beautiful hymns were sung. It seemed to me that the Sisters were always singing. They sang as they churned, they sang as they spun, and one Sister claimed that she never used her three-minute glass when she boiled an egg, for she knew a hymn which took exactly that long to sing!

"Are all Moravians so fond of music?" I asked one day.

"It is an inheritance as well as a present pleasure," was the reply. "John Hus, whose preaching and martyrdom led to the founding of our Church, stressed the value of congregational singing, and the leaders of the Renewed Unity feel the same and make it even more personal. We have hymns from the Early Christian Church and from all the ages since. Many others are being composed today, for Count Zinzendorf has a remarkable gift as a hymn writer, his wife and son have written some beautiful hymns, and others are doing the same. We sing because we like to sing," a sentiment which I echoed willingly, glad of the training I had received as a child.

I admit that it seemed odd to be told never to speak to a young man, for the Single Brethren had a large farm not far from Nazareth at a place called Christian's Spring, and we often saw them on the street. But Sister Elisabeth Engfer, forewoman of the tailoresses, with whom I had become rather intimate, reminded me that life in a town differed from the freedom of the country; and that in the higher classes of society in Europe it was considered improper for young people of the two sexes to associate informally. "As Christians we must observe the best rules, even in our social life," she added, "and it has been found by experience that it is conducive to the religious life of young people to be carefully guarded and directed."

Perhaps because of the distress which the surreptitious enjoyment of social life had caused me, it was not hard for me to see her point and accept it as logical. I conducted myself according to the rules of the house and did it willingly.

I had been baptized and confirmed in my earlier years, but in view of the time of confusion in my spiritual life, I expected a somewhat extended period of probation before I was received into the congregation as a full member. The formal reception came more quickly than I had dared to hope, and when I was admitted to the Communion table my happiness was complete.

There was one custom in Bethlehem and Nazareth which did much to prevent monotony in the rather strenuous life we led. Bishop Spangenberg was an excellent organizer, expecting much from the strong and getting it, considerate of the weak, even insisting on kindness to the animals in the place, so that, as he said, "The cattle might praise God in their own way for gentle treatment." That all might share and share alike, he shifted persons from one position to another as often as feasible. This was the more easily arranged because the congregation, like the Sisters House, was organized on the principle of a large family, where expenses were borne by a common fund and each individual contributed what he or she could in the way of service, in turn receiving support. Bishop Spangenberg had tried this plan in Savannah with great success, and he introduced it at Bethlehem, where wonderful things were accomplished through it.

My own life during this period shows how variety was secured. After holding various minor offices among the Single Sisters, I was made treasurer of the group, though I was not quite twenty-one years old. The next year additional building in Bethlehem released room for the Single Sisters, who moved thither, I of course going with them.

Then Bishop Spangenberg resigned his position as general director of the Moravian work in America, Bishop John Nitschmann having come from Europe to succeed him. Bishop Spangenberg and his wife moved to Philadelphia, taking me with them, and for eight months I labored for the spiritual welfare of the unmarried women of that city who were friendly to the Unity. So far as I know, this custom of pastoral work of an unmarried woman for other women of the same condition in life was unique. Miss Anna had started it in Herrnhut when she was a girl of seventeen, and it proved so helpful that it was introduced into all the congregations of the Brethren. I felt highly honored at being entrusted with the office, never dreaming that I was serving an apprenticeship for which I would be most grateful in later years.

While we were in Philadelphia, an official visitor came to Bethlehem, Bishop John von Watteville, who was accompanied by his wife, the former Benigna von Zinzendorf. It was the Countess Benigna's second visit to America, but again I saw little of her: when she and her husband sailed for Europe, Bishop and Mrs. Spangenberg went with them. I returned to Bethlehem, only to become seriously ill and to spend long weeks in the sick-room of the Sisters House.

My twenty-third year I spent in the nursery at Emmaus. This was an institution which outsiders found it hard to understand, but it filled a real need in the busy life of the Moravians. To an inquirer it was sometimes explained in this way: "On farms when fathers are in the fields all day and the mothers are overburdened and unable to look after their children the little folk often fare but ill, improperly fed, dirty, untrained, an easy prey to every malady of childhood. Our Moravian children are tenderly cared for, clean, well trained, in the series of school-homes which begin with the nursery and continue up into the boarding schools for boys and for girls."

"But that breaks up families!"

"It does interfere with normal family life, and of course it is hard for parents to give up their babies, to see them only at intervals, but our Brethren and Sisters are brave pioneers, missionaries at heart, ready for any personal sacrifice. Knowing that their children are safe, they can give their whole mind to their work, whether the task is in Bethlehem or out among the Indians in the mission stations which we are establishing among the red men."

Not much could be said to this argument, backed as it was by experience.

The following year brought another crisis in my life, for I returned to Bethlehem to find that things were not going well. Under the leadership of Bishop David Nitschmann and of Bishop Spangenberg there had been enthusiasm and coöperation, but under Bishop John Nitschmann both were waning.

"I do not like the man," said my father, "and he is going to ruin Bethlehem."

"What is the matter with him?" asked Mother. "Some of the Sisters think he is wonderful, and others shrug their shoulders and will say nothing."

"Well," said Father, "to begin with, he has brought over a head full of metaphors, which mean a lot to him and to those who know, or think they know, what he means. To others his words sound strange and full of mysticism, verging on folly to say the least, and this will be used against the church which he represents. Moreover, he is perfectly sure that he is right, and that everyone is wrong who does not agree with him. This means that only his followers can work with him, and all others will cease to coöperate, and that spells disaster for Bethlehem and all the work of which it is the center."

"What can we do about it?" asked Mother.

"Not one thing," said Father. "I have tried and failed, and have made up my mind to move back to the farm and get out of it all."

"If only Bishop Spangenberg were here," sighed Mother.

"Pray for his return if you want to save Bethlehem!" And Father began to prepare for his return to his farm with all the haste of irritation and determination combined.

"I hope you will go with us, Catharina," said Mother, forcing the decision which I dreaded to make. In the end I determined to remain in Bethlehem and wait patiently, feeling that the present disturbed conditions surely must be only temporary. In that I was right, for at the end of the year Bishop Spangenberg returned and again took over the leadership of all activities. It was a long time before the comment and criticism aroused by Bishop John Nitschmann among those outside our Church ceased to torment us, but within our own circle peace and united service were soon reëstablished under the sane, wise management of Bishop Spangenberg.

It was about this time that the Brethren began to call Bishop Spangenberg "Brother Joseph," a nickname given to him by Count Zinzendorf.

"The name suits him exactly," said Father. "Like Joseph he is resourceful and kind in the treatment of his Brethren."

"Does he object to a nickname?" asked Mother.

"On the contrary, he likes it. He says that 'the Lord was with Joseph' in Egypt, and I know no man more desirous of the presence of the Lord than our Joseph in Pennsylvania."

"Do you plan to return to Bethlehem since Bishop Spangenberg is back?"

"No. My presence there is no longer necessary, and I wish to remain on the farm." This suited Mother and delighted the younger children, who enjoyed the life in the farmhouse and at the mill.

I remained in the Bethlehem Sisters House, where during the following year I had another attack of illness. I took a severe cold, and it settled in my head, giving me so much trouble that I was confined to the sick-room for three months. When I recovered I went as teacher to the girls' school near Bethlehem.

In the summer of 1752 Bishop Spangenberg asked my father to go with him to North Carolina on a tour of exploration. The Bishop had received letters from the governing board of the Unity of Brethren, then sitting in London, and had been told that the board wished to begin a settlement on land belonging to Earl Granville, located in North Carolina. The Granville land covered a wide territory, and Bishop Spangenberg was instructed to go thither and select a suitable place for the settlement, and he wished the advice of my father as to mill sites and the like.

Father was not well when the letter came, but he recovered in time to join Bishop Spangenberg's party and was away for nearly six months. When he returned I went over from the school to see him, and listened with much interest to the account of his trip. As it took him to the land which was to be my home for the second and longer part of my life it seems worth while to interrupt my own story to repeat his account of his journey.

MY FATHER VISITS NORTH CAROLINA

"YOU WILL REMEMBER," SAID MY FATHER, TURNING TO MOTHER, who had seated herself with her knitting to listen to the full story of the journey, of which she had heard only scattered bits, "you will remember that when Brother Joseph's letter came asking me to accompany him to North Carolina I was suffering from a severe attack of gallstones, and it seemed doubtful whether I could make the trip. You wanted me to send a refusal, but I insisted on waiting to see how quickly I recovered, thinking that if the Lord wanted me to go He would give the needed strength. When the party arrived on August the fifteenth, I felt sure I was able to travel, though you seemed to have some misgivings."

"Misgivings is too mild a word," murmured Mother, but Father only smiled and continued, this time addressing me.

"We made quite a party, Catharina, for besides Brother Joseph and myself there were Timothy Horsefield, Joseph Miller, Herman Lash, and John Merk; and, in addition to the horses we rode, there were others to carry the camp outfit. The men had been carefully selected. Herman Lash, brought up on a farm, was to care for the horses and was especially charged to study the roads, for convenience of access would mean much for the new settlement. John Merk, a saddler by trade, was to keep the harness in order and would inform himself as to the openings for craftsmen. I was to consider the land with respect to farms and mill sites. Joseph Miller, who had studied medicine while on a trip to Europe, was to investigate the probable healthfulness of any suggested location and was also to serve as nurse for the party in case of need—a comfort to me, sick as I had been. Brother Horsefield, a justice of the peace and one of the leading men of Bethlehem, would note important local laws and economic conditions. Brother Joseph would keep the diary, correlate all we found out, and decide all important questions.

"We went first to Philadelphia, hoping to secure some information about North Carolina. There was little to be had, and that little was not encouraging, though of course that did not prevent us from continuing.

"The weather was clear, but hot and dusty. In Delaware the grass was so parched that pasturage was hard to find, and at some places we could buy neither corn nor oats. In Maryland the residents were only reasonably polite; in Virginia, more so, and at one place the tavern host urged us to abandon the idea of North Carolina and select Virginia, saying that toward the west much land could be secured on favorable terms. He could not tell us where this good land lay, and we wondered whether it might be in the part of America claimed by the French, but he could give us no further information. As our instructions definitely said North Carolina, we made no effort to find out, but continued southward, finding the road along the east shore of Chesapeake Bay remarkably good, level, smooth, and free from stones. At Cape Charles we took a boat across to Norfolk.

"The good weather lasted until we reached Edenton, but then we had a week of rain, which raised the streams and swept away a number of bridges. Perhaps the rain had something to do with it, but we were not favorably impressed with Edenton.

" 'It lies low,' said Joseph Miller, 'surrounded by water which has neither ebb nor flow. This was explained to me as caused by the sandbanks which lie between the main land and the sea and hinder the tides. Chills and fever prevail, and it seems to be taken for granted that everyone will have an attack each year.'

" 'Some of the colonists were born here,' reported John Merk, 'but others came from the North, or from England, Scotland, or

Ireland. Most of them seem lazy and improvident, and if all the settlers are like these, there is a great need for craftsmen, but little with which to buy their wares.'

"To a Pennsylvania farmer," continued Father, "the condition of the fields seemed pitiful, for there was little attempt at cultivation. There were no meadows for the winter feeding of cattle, which are turned out to shift for themselves in winter, we were told, and by spring are so poor and thin that it takes them all summer to regain condition for sale. There is practically no local market; so cattle and hogs are driven to Virginia and sold on the hoof, the Virginia butcher getting all the profit."

"Men ought to be ashamed of themselves for being so shiftless," commented Mother, and I added the opinion that they needed some Moravian Brethren to teach them how to farm. "Oh, we did not even consider settling there," said Father. "We could not have found the necessary land, even if the other conditions had been favorable."

When I asked how the officials had treated them, Father said they had been most courteous, especially Mr. Francis Corbin, the agent of Earl Granville, to whom Brother Joseph had taken letters of introduction and who gave to Brother Horsefield much information about the laws of North Carolina.

"We were surprised, though," he added, "to find that the Granville land office had no map of North Carolina, nor even of the Granville property. Mr. Corbin told us that when the Proprietors of North Carolina sold their claim to the Crown, Earl Granville decided to retain his proportionate part, which was laid off for him adjoining Virginia. His land is supposed to be eighty-four miles wide, and to extend from the Atlantic seaboard westward to the edge of the continent, wherever that may be."

That meant that somewhere in this eighty-four-mile strip of indefinite length, the prospecting party must discover and choose the one-hundred-thousand-acre tract which Earl Granville had agreed to sell to the Moravian Church.

ANNA NITSCHMANN.

Sister Anna Nitschmann

From a portrait in the Bethlehem Archives.

The first house in Bethlehem

From a drawing by C. F. Seidel. Original in the Bethlehem Archives.

"I asked Mr. Corbin," said Father, "how we could tell where to find suitable land if there was no map."

" 'That is always the question,' he replied. 'The custom is for a man to select land on which no one is living, camp on it, and then report to this office that he wishes to buy. Men often live on the land for a number of years before they take the trouble to have it surveyed and secure a deed.'

" 'How, then, do you collect the quit rents?' asked Brother Joseph, thinking of all the traveling and trouble this must cause.

" 'There are probably many living on the land of whom we do not even know, and there are many more who never pay anything. But some are honest enough to pay from time to time, especially after they have taken a deed. We lose much, but there is so much land that settlers are more important than the quit rents we lose.'

" 'We know nothing of the roads,' said Herman Lash, 'not even in which direction to start.'

" 'I will send Mr. Churton with you,' said Mr. Corbin. 'He is a surveyor and knows as much as any man about the more settled parts. I suggest that you go out on the Trading Path to the back of the Colony, and there begin to look for the large tract you want.'

" 'We had hoped to secure land on a navigable river,' said Brother Joseph, at which Mr. Churton laughed, assuring him that there were few rivers that were navigable for many miles from the sea, and that the land along them was already occupied.

" 'And if we find nothing on the Trading Path?'

"Mr. Corbin shrugged his shoulders. 'You will have to find your own way, on less known trails or through the forests'—a proposition which seemed so vague that less resolute men would have been tempted to give up the project. Not so Brother Joseph, whom nothing could daunt. So when the rain finally stopped, we set out.

"The Trading Path led us near the Tuscarora Reservation, and we stopped to see this Indian tribe, which was living on about twenty-five thousand acres along the Roanoke River. Someone suggested that the Moravians buy this land from the Indians, who were poor and might welcome the chance to sell and join those of their tribesmen who had moved north to the Five Nations. But although the location was not bad, Brother Joseph doubted whether such a purchase could be arranged. The Indians received us hospitably and gave us a meal of the best they had, corn boiled on the cob. It was not bad," said Father, adding that he had been told in Edenton that Indian corn was the chief grain crop in North Carolina, and that men and beasts alike depended on it for food.

Then he told us to follow the party in imagination for one hundred and fifty-three miles, as they rode along the Trading Path, not finding any suitable land which was not already occupied.

They had been congratulating themselves on having escaped the Edenton chills and fever, but at the home of John Sallis, where they stopped to rest, the disease overtook them. One after another they became ill, only Joseph Miller escaping. He nursed them faithfully, but he had no proper medicines, and this worried him. Finally he decided to use a certain herb growing in the neighborhood, which induced sweating. It had a favorable result on Lash, Merk, and my father, but, as they improved, their nurse was further troubled by the lack of proper food for them in their weakened condition. The worst of it was that Brother Joseph remained so critically ill that they feared he would not recover.

"You may imagine how earnestly we prayed that he would be spared," said Father, "and how we thrilled when Joseph Miller came back from the woods one day and told us that he had received assurance that our prayers were answered."

Brother Joseph himself doubted whether he would recover, and feebly but calmly he gave his companions their orders. "If I am taken, my Brethren, you must go on and finish our task, and the Lord will lead you."

"Could you have persuaded them to do that, Henry?" asked Mother.

"I do not know, but fortunately the responsibility did not fall upon me. After a few days there was a slight improvement in

Brother Joseph's condition; but we thought he must be delirious when he informed us that on the next day we would start again on our journey. 'We cannot possibly go yet,' we argued. 'You could not sit on a horse for an hour.'

" 'Last night the Lord spoke to me,' whispered Brother Joseph, 'and told me that our hope of recovery lies in getting away from this low land and reaching the hills. It will be hard for you, for I am very weak and you will have much trouble with me, but the Lord will give me strength.' "

This determination persisted, and on the next day he insisted on starting. After riding an hour he fainted, just as his companions had feared; but when he revived he positively refused to be taken back to the Sallis home, and they found a small cabin where he and Joseph Miller could spend the night. The next day was not much better, but by lifting him from his horse at short intervals and letting him rest on the ground, they made a few more miles. It seemed a miracle, for after a few days of this he began to improve rapidly, and the rest regained their health, except Brother Horsefield, who had recurring attacks of the fever and grew so much worse that Joseph Miller decided it would not do to take him further. Brother Joseph made arrangements for him at the home of a friendly settler, and Joseph Miller was left to care for him. Had he recovered in time they would have rejoined the party, but by the time he was able to travel it was too late, and they returned to Pennsylvania.

"I saw him recently," said Mother, "and he still looked thin, but he had much to say about Brother Miller's kindness, and the impression it made on the settlers in that neighborhood, who said they hoped more people of that sort would move to North Carolina."

The rest of the party went on and reached the ford of the Catawba River, but not one place had they found for the Moravian settlement. After discussing the matter at length and getting what information they could, they decided to try to cut across to the head waters of the Yadkin River and follow that down stream, hoping for better success. Supplies were bought, and two hunters were employed, who thought they could guide the party across. There were neither roads nor trails; so they made their way through forests, around hills, and along streams, occasionally finding a small tract that looked promising and stopping to take it up, Mr. Churton surveying it for them. This was merely a matter of precaution, in case they found nothing better, for none of them pleased Brother Joseph, who could not imagine the artisans of Bethlehem and Nazareth living safely or making a living on such isolated farms on the frontier.

"It was hard riding," said Father, "for we wound through forests, climbed up and down mountains, and sometimes followed buffalo trails, but one day we found a stream which seemed to come from the direction in which the hunters thought we should go. [Father did not know the name of this stream, but it was later called John's River.] We had no trouble in following it up stream, but at last found ourselves at the end of a narrow valley, with the steepest of mountain sides to right, to left, and in front of us. To go back seemed futile, to proceed almost impossible, but we finally managed it by taking the packs from the backs of the horses. They then succeeded in climbing to the top, though by the time they reached it they were trembling from head to foot. We men scrambled up as best we could, dragging the packs after us, and when we had caught our breath enough to look around, we found ourselves on a ridge with a wonderful panorama of mountain peaks beyond the valley from which we had come. To our right the ridge ended abruptly in steep descents; so we turned left and soon found the head waters of a stream which we hoped might be the Yadkin.

"We had followed it hardly a day when it began to snow and turned bitterly cold. Soon the snow was so deep that our horses could find no forage, and almost as soon our own food supplies ran short. I still have some skill with a gun, but there was nothing to shoot, and starvation stared us in the face. Had it not been for Brother Joseph's courage I think we would have given up."

"I cannot imagine you giving up, Henry," said Mother, affectionately.

"Well, Brother Joseph cheered us on and we were ashamed to complain while he was so brave. Cold and hungry, we followed that stream, which ran now north, now south, now east, now west, until we were utterly confused. The hunters admitted that they were hopelessly lost, and then Brother Joseph took the lead, compass in hand, saying that civilization lay to the east, and that eastward we would go.

"It was a terrible ride, but we followed our leader until we reached another stream, and following that we found three men, the first we had seen since we left the Catawba ford. One of them, Mr. Owen, took us to his cabin, which was too small to give us shelter but we gladly pitched our tent near by. Never in my life have I been so glad to rest, for a few days earlier I had hurt my arm quite badly and had taken cold in it; riding was little short of agony."

"It was too bad Joseph Miller was not with you," said Mother.

"He could not have done much while we were riding," said Father, "and it improved when I could rest and eat and apply hot water, though it still troubles me at times. Added to our fatigue was great discouragement, but as usual Brother Joseph was looking ahead expectantly, and Mr. Owen told him that this stream ran down into the long-sought Yadkin River and he thought we might be able to find the land we wanted in the three forks of Muddy Creek, a tributary of the Yadkin.

"This proved to be the case, and after we had camped there for some days and had looked over the land, Brother Joseph declared: 'The Lord must have saved this for the Brethren, for it seems to be the only good and large piece of land left in Earl Granville's part of North Carolina.' I found mill sites and timber and building stone; Brother Joseph found springs and home sites and meadowland; Herman Lash found what a squatter called 'the King's Highway,' which led to the north, not much of a road, it is true, but an evidence of contact with other settlements.

"And so, Catharina, while you were sharing in the Christmas services at the school, your father was camped in the forests of North Carolina, snow around our tent, but well and happy, under the wings of the Almighty."

That ended the adventurous part of their journey. The surveyor measured and plotted the land they selected and then went back to Edenton. The explorers returned directly to Pennsylvania, and Brother Joseph made arrangements for sailing to England to recommend the purchase. He also planned to suggest that the tract be named "Wachovia," since its hills and valleys and streams reminded him of the estate of that name in South Austria, the earlier home of the Zinzendorf family, still belonging to one branch of that family, which remained there when the grandfather of our Count Zinzendorf became a Protestant during the Reformation and moved into Saxony.

"We will know about the name and all else when Brother Joseph returns from Europe," said my father.

6.

AN INTERLUDE

———

THE NEXT FIVE YEARS WERE A SORT OF INTERLUDE IN MY LIFE. Soon after my visit home, the head tailoress in the Sisters House, Sister Elisabeth Engfer, died, and I was called to Bethlehem to take her place. There the days were full of willing service, but it was unexciting except for the events taking place around us, and these I watched from my quiet haven.

Of our missionaries to the Indians I still found David Zeisberger the most interesting, and listened eagerly to his reports as he came and went. After studying the Mohawk language with a Brother who knew something about it, David went to the Mohawk Valley and made arrangements with the chief to stay and study with him. Ten days later he and several other missionaries were arrested and were imprisoned for seven weeks. The excuse given was that they had come into New York without a pass, but probably it was because of the false reports that were being circulated that the Moravians were in league with the French Indians. A little later he was one of the delegates from Bethlehem to the Iroquois Confederacy, and was formally adopted into the tribe of the Onondagas, clan of the Turtle. In 1750 he was sent to Europe to report on the Indian work; and when he returned two years later he settled in the Indian town of Onondaga, and reports of his work were given in our meetings from time to time.

"I am surprised that Brother David does not marry," said Sister Betsy, one day, and we all looked at Sister Lawatsch, who was visiting us; as the wife of a Moravian minister she was a member of the Board of Elders, and all marriage proposals passed through that Board.

Sister Lawatsch shook her head. "You must not ask me to discuss Board matters," she said with a smile, "but there is no harm in telling you that Brother David does not intend to marry; he says that he would be handicapped in his work if he had a wife," and if this was a disappointment to any Sister present no one admitted it.

Because of my father's part in the North Carolina project, all developments along that line interested me; and when letters came from Brother Spangenberg saying that it had been decided to buy the selected tract, we Single Sisters were as much on the alert to see who would go south as the Single Brethren themselves could possibly be.

Selection was made from among the Single Brethren living on the farm at Christian's Spring, and we heard that the choice was influenced partly by their willingness to go and partly by their aptitude for trades that would make their little settlement self-supporting, for it was well understood that our tract was in the forest on the frontier.

On October 7, 1753, the congregation of Bethlehem gathered in the prayer hall, in a farewell meeting for those who were to leave in the morning for North Carolina. As their names and duties were announced, we looked across to the front benches on the Brothers side of the hall, identifying those we knew or thought we could recognize. There were:

Reverend Bernhard Adam Grube, pastor of the group, who was also to serve as cook and gardener when needful.

Jacob Lash, another ordained man, charged with the duties of treasurer and general supervisor of work.

Hans Martin Kalberlahn, their surgeon. He had not been in America long and I had never seen him, which may have been the reason why I specially noted his height, his light hair and blue eyes, his general air of dependability.

Besides these leaders there were the Brethren Pfeil, Ingebretsen, Feldhausen, Lung, Petersen, Beroth, Merkley—handy men who could serve as shoemaker, mill-wright, carpenter, cooper, sieve-maker, turner, gardener, washer, tailor, wood-cutter, baker, or farmer, could take care of the stock, could, in short, do whatever might need to be done.

Herman Lash, who had been on the prospecting trip, was sent because of the information he had then gathered; and John Lischer was instructed to go, note the road, and return in a few weeks to report, ready to go back as messenger or guide whenever one might be needed.

Bishop Nathaniel Seidel left his important duties in Pennsylvania to accompany the party and see them settled; and at the last minute the Brethren Gottlob Koenigdorfer and Joseph Haberlahn, who had intended to escort them for two or three days, decided to go all the way and return with Brother Seidel.

Very heartfelt were the prayers offered for these pioneers, very earnest the singing of the hymns wishing them a blessing on their journey. I should not be surprised if more than one of the younger Sisters wondered secretly whether in time she might be called to follow to the new settlement. Most of the women of my age were already married, and I had concluded that my call in life was to serve as a Single Sister, leaving matrimony to others; but it might be anticipated that wives would be needed for these pioneers, and that our group of Single Sisters would be expected to supply them.

For the first five days the travelers passed over familiar territory, and, from people they met, we heard quickly of all that happened to them. Their canoe almost upset in Tulpehocken Creek. Doctor Kalberlahn was asked to turn aside and bleed the sick servant of a farmer. We could imagine their pleasant rest of two nights and a day at the Lash home, and could smile and pity them for having to unload their big wagon so that the running gear could be made three inches narrower, to make the wheels track in the ruts on the road. Knowing the hospitality of the Lash home we could figure to ourselves the bountiful supply of bread and meat which Mother Lash prepared for her sons and the others. We heard that their first woodland camp was made on the night of the 12th, and most of the men slept in their blankets around the fire. "But they say," giggled Sister Betsy, "that Brother Koenigdorfer does not like to sleep on the ground; so he has taken a hammock which he suspends between two trees, and the wind rocks him to sleep."

At Harrison's Ferry they forded the Susquehanna River, the water being very low; and there the Lash wagon turned back, bringing the friends who had accompanied them thus far, and our immediate contact with them ceased.

In January the four Brethren who went with the pioneers to North Carolina returned to Bethlehem, and Brother Seidel took occasion at one of the services to tell us more about their journey, and their beginnings in Wachovia.

They had been advised to take the "upper road," as leading more directly to our tract, and this they did, but often had occasion to wonder whether they had done wisely. The roads at that season were very bad, and their wagon was so heavily loaded that on steep hills the men must push to help the horses up, or tie on a small tree as a drag and hold back with all their might in going down grade. Food, forage, and water were problems constantly with them in varying form; rain and snow made the going doubly hard.

When after weeks of laborious travel they had crossed Virginia and reached Dan River they found the water so high that they could not ford it and were delayed for several days. They sent Brother Jacob Lash across in a canoe to look over the land and select a camping place, and he was followed by Brother Seidel and another man, also using a canoe, with their horses swimming alongside. These scouts found a one-room log hut, built by a squatter who had moved when he heard that the land had been bought; so when the Dan could be forded the party reassembled at the home of a Mr. Altem, and on the following day, November 17th, they proceeded to the hut. People at a plantation which they passed gave them two sacks of pumpkins as a welcoming gift, and offered a wagon-load more free of charge. Another neighbor gave two bushels of turnips; so their immediate needs in the vegetable line were supplied.

"We reached the little hut toward evening," said Brother Seidel, "and made immediate preparations for the night, though little could be done except unpack a few necessaries as at a night camp. Our first service was held with rejoicing that our long journey had been accomplished in less than six weeks; and right heartily we sang the stanza composed by Brother Grube for the occasion:

> We hold arrival lovefeast here
> In Carolina land;
> A company of Brethren true,
> A little pilgrim band
> Called by the Lord to be of those
> Who through the whole world go
> To tell of Jesus everywhere,
> And naught but Jesus know.

As accompaniment the wolves howled loudly in the forest near by, a contrast of vast significance."

The next day, Sunday, was spent largely in resting, for the Brethren were travel-weary and the night had been none too comfortable. It was cold, the roof of the hut was full of holes, and the dirt floor a harder bed than the forest had supplied and barely large enough for fourteen of them to lie down while Brother Koenigdorfer swung above them in his hammock. One of the Brethren shot two wild turkeys—a welcome addition to their meals.

The following month was spent busily in making a beginning. A field was ploughed and planted; a clapboard floor was laid in the hut; barrels were made by burning out hollow logs; cornmeal and meat were bought from Mr. Altem, and a little fresh meat was secured by hunting, one or two deer having been shot.

"Brother Feldhausen gave us a fright when he went out one morning and did not return at night; but the following day he reappeared and explained that he had not lost his way but night had overtaken him. Because of rain he could not light a fire and was obliged to keep in motion all night, hearing wolves and panthers all about him, though he was not attacked. It was a warning," said Brother Seidel, "that more care must be used lest the Brethren be in serious danger from the wild beasts."

Ten days after they arrived Brother Kalberlahn had his first patient, a friend of Mr. Altem's, whom he bled and gave medicine, the man promising to pay two bushels of corn. Several of the Brethren explored the adjacent territory and selected the site for a grist mill, and bottom lands for pasturage. Their religious life was not neglected; they arranged a schedule of services patterned after those in Bethlehem, and the ministers in the party took turns in conducting them. Their first lovefeast was held on the day they arrived, as already said, and the Lord's Supper was celebrated for the first time on November 21st.

"They would have been glad to keep us with them over Christmas," said Brother Seidel, "but on account of the season we thought it better not to delay our journey; so the four of us who were coming back to Bethlehem left on December 19th and reached home safely, with these encouraging accounts to give you."

In June, 1754, Brother Grube arrived in Bethlehem, accompanied by Brother Lischer, who had guided Brother Jacob Friis to North Carolina to take the place of Brother Grube, who was now to enter service as a missionary to the Indians. With much natural ability, and trained to studious habits in the University of Jena, Brother Grube mastered the Delaware Indian language, and then was stationed at Gnadenhuetten, where several of our Brethren and a few Sisters were gathering a congregation of Christian Indians.

Naturally, on his arrival in Bethlehem he gave us further information about the progress of affairs at "Bethabara," as the little village had been named. A stable had been built for the stock; and a small house of large split rails had been erected for the accommodation of visitors. A garden had been laid out and fenced, additional land cleared for fields, peach trees brought from Dan River and set out. A few accidents had occurred: Brother Kalberlahn had scalded his foot, and Brother Petersen's head had been wounded by the limb of a falling tree. Several of the Brethren had been ill, though none seriously.

"Brother Kalberlahn's fame as a doctor is spreading," said Brother Grube. "Patients are coming to him from as much as eighty miles away, and he has been called to others at points nearly as far distant. Work is beginning to come to the craftsmen. The men are being faithful to their religious duties and are working energetically and willingly despite plain fare and an occasional actual shortage of food. Travelers soon found the Moravian cabin a convenient and hospitable stopping place, although it was so small that any additional person spending the night caused real inconvenience to the Brethren until the rail guest-house was finished."

Quite at the end of August Brother Jacob Lash appeared in Bethlehem, having come to make a further report, and we listened eagerly to what he had to say concerning the months following the departure of Brother Grube.

"The usual and best food of the Brethren has been milk and mush and whatever can be made from cornmeal. The garden did well, and from May 8th to July 5th we had salad every day for the midday dinner, and often at the evening meal. When the salad came to an end we had cucumbers for three weeks, with three or four meals of sugar peas, beans several times, occasionally cabbage, and squash twice. Meat has been scarce, and we have had only four deer and two small bears—the bears generally are smaller than in Pennsylvania. Hunting has not proved profitable, and we give little time to it.

"We have been trying to build up a herd of cattle, and now have twelve cows, twelve calves, one bull, and one steer. The cattle in North Carolina are generally very wild, for it is usual to feed them little and let them run in the woods, so that the settlers get little good from them. The Brethren have been trying to tame our cattle, at night tying the cows to the feed troughs, and it is gradually coming to pass that at the proper time in the evening the cows come home."

Brother Lash said that the Brethren in Bethabara have some good, helpful, pleasant neighbors, and are well thought of by the other settlers. "People have come more than a hundred miles to get medicine and advice from Brother Kalberlahn, and he has gone far and wide to visit patients. It is often said that Carolina is unhealthy, and this is probably true of the eastern section where the land lies low and the streams are sluggish, but the criticism does not apply to the western portion where our land lies; there the air and the water are fresh. Brother Kalberlahn thinks that much of the sickness in our section is caused by the irregular life of the people, now with an abundance of food and now in want; and among our Brethren the occasional attacks of illness may have been caused by doing work to which they were not accustomed."

Brother Lash had made a trip to the Cape Fear River, on which there is a storehouse one hundred and forty miles from our settlement. From there he went one hundred and forty miles further to Wilmington to look into the opportunities for trade so that he might bring an intelligent report to Bethlehem. He found that Wilmington has a port into which sea-going vessels can sail, and from there goods are taken up the Cape Fear River in large boats to the storehouse already mentioned, where they can be bought at a reasonable price.

"Our Brethren have lived happily together," added Brother Lash, "and their religious services have continued to be helpful. In addition to their regular meetings they have kept in touch with other activities of our church by reading reports from other congregations, including Brother David's diaries from Onondaga and its Indians."

About ten days before Brother Lash returned to North Carolina, Brother Peter Boehler and the surveyor Hoeger set out, accompanied by Herman Lash, who had come north with his brother Jacob. Brother Boehler was commissioned to inspect our tract and measure it, and to inform the Brethren that the name "Wachovia" had been officially given to it. He also visited New Bern; and when he returned to Bethabara he found that Brother Jacob Lash had arrived, bringing eight Single Brethren to live there. Of course we heard more about Wachovia from Brother Boehler when he returned to Pennsylvania, and from Bishop David Nitschmann, who visited Wachovia in the spring of the next year. Thus we were kept informed as to the progress of affairs, and I, for one, always listened with intense interest, seeing clearly in my mind the incidents as they were told to us.

I might add that in the early summer of 1755 six more of the young Moravian men moved from Pennsylvania to North Carolina, followed at intervals during the summer and fall by seventeen more Single Brethren and seven married couples, word having been received that building had progressed far enough to afford shelter for these additional colonists.

I said that during this period my own life was uneventful, but this is not strictly true, for I had the experience that comes to all in turn and lost one of my beloved parents. Father had not been well for some time, indeed not since his return from Carolina, and on July 20th, 1755, he was released from pain and weariness and passed to the reward reserved for those who have served faithfully and well. His remains were interred in the family graveyard on his farm, and the esteem in which he was held was revealed in the large number of people (six hundred) who attended his funeral, conducted by Brother Spangenberg. During my visit home some weeks before the end, he asked me to take my youngest sister, Benigna, to Bethlehem and supervise her training there, and she came to the Boarding School soon after his departure.

Shortly thereafter I had an attack of fever and was so seriously ill that it was believed I would follow my father; but my time had not yet come, and I gradually recovered.

The leaders of Bethlehem, meanwhile, had become much concerned over the Indian situation. Our mission work was progressing, and converts were being added to the groups at several mission stations; but our very success was being used as an argument against us, and the malicious report was spread that we were in league with the French and were enemies of the English—which of course was utterly false and was so proved before the year was out, but at a terrible price.

In November David Zeisberger came to Bethlehem for a few days, and on the morning of the 24th he set out for Gnadenhuetten, taking messages to the Brethren and Sisters stationed on the Mahony, a tributary of the Lehigh River. At five o'clock in the morning of the 25th the assembly bell rang in Bethlehem, and we hastened to the meeting-hall. At one side sat a man with his head buried in his hands—could that be David? Brother Spangenberg stood at the table, his face pale even to the lips. He commenced morning prayers in the usual way, and then told us the story which David had brought, his voice trembling with emotion in spite of his efforts to control it.

On the way to Gnadenhuetten David had caught up with a company of militia, who detained him several hours for questioning, thereby saving his life, though they little knew it. When they permitted him to proceed he rode on up the Lehigh to the mission house where Brother Grube, Brother Mack, and others were living, surrounded by the huts of the Christian Indians. Brother Mack urged him to spend the night, as it was already dusk, but he had messages to deliver and decided to go on to the "House of the Pilgrims" across the Lehigh on the Mahony, where the rest of the missionaries had their lodgings. As he was fording the river Brother Mack, alarmed by the sound of guns, shouted to him to return, but the splashing of the horse's feet in the water prevented him from hearing, and he was greatly surprised when he reached the bank and young Joseph Sturgis came running from the woods, gasped out the words, "Painted Indians," seized his horse's bridle, pulled him around, and hurried him back across the ford, clinging to his stirrup leather. With Brother Mack they found Joachim Senseman and George Partsch, and from the three the story was soon learned.

The missionaries in the "House of the Pilgrims" were sitting at supper when the dogs began to bark. Suspecting that straggling militia were about, Brother Senseman went out to close the schoolhouse, which he remembered had been left open. As he turned back he saw a group rush to the door of the dwelling, and as it opened shots were fired; the fiendish yell which followed showed only too plainly that the attackers were savages. Brother Senseman was unarmed and could do nothing alone; so he made what speed he dared to the river to call for help.

When Martin Nitschmann fell dead at the first shot, George Partsch, who happened to be near a window, automatically slipped through and was half way to the river before he realized what was happening. To return was futile; so he too went on, hoping to bring aid.

Four more of the missionaries fell, before those who remained could climb the ladder-like stairway to the attic and close and barricade the trapdoor. For a quarter of an hour the savages shot through floor and roof and window, their war-whoops mingling with the terrified screaming of the babe that Sister Anders pressed so closely to her breast. Then the savages quieted, and young Sturgis, looking out of the window, saw none on that side of the house, instantly leaped, and escaped to the woods in safety. Looking back he saw someone else jump, a man, and him they tomahawked. Then he saw the fiends bringing armfuls of dead leaves and brush, saw a firebrand passed from pile to pile, and saw the flames spring up. Sick at heart he stole away and reached the river in time to stop Brother David; Senseman and Partsch swam the river fearing that the ford would be guarded. All agreed that there was no possible chance of rescue. So while a warning word was given to the Christian Indians, the mission house was prepared as best it might be for defense, and Brother David set off at full speed to find the militia that he had passed yesterday, and then take the news on to Bethlehem, which he reached at three o'clock in the morning.

As the militia had started at once, there was nothing more that could be done until morning; so Brother Joseph had allowed the

Brethren to rest in peace until the approach of day, though his own heart seemed breaking.

As the tragic story came to an end I looked about me and saw David's dark head bowed in anguish, and the stricken faces and streaming eyes of those who mourned for relatives and friends; and I heard Brother Spangenberg say, with an uncontrollable sob, "Let us pray."

Then minutes passed that seemed like hours, with no sound save weeping. I could not pray, my thoughts were too busy with what must have happened in that attic room—the screaming babe, the men and women facing the inevitable with Christian fortitude, the perilous leaps from the window, the closing of even that doubtful means of escape, the smoke, the flame, silence! It was a picture that haunted my dreams for weeks, and still recurs at intervals. Thank God, the dream does not stop there. Again I am in our meeting hall in Bethlehem, and after the seeming eternity of sorrow Bishop Spangenberg suddenly rises, and in a voice steady, confident, exultant as the voice of a herald bringing glad tidings, he proclaims:

"Blessed are the dead who died in the Lord; they rest from their labors, and their works do follow them, and they live forever with their Saviour and ours! Thanks be to God who giveth us the victory! Keep us, oh Lord, in everlasting fellowship with the Church Triumphant! Amen."

Half an hour later a dozen men were on their way to Gnadenhuetten, David in the lead. Others began to build a stockade around Bethlehem, Brother Joseph believing that we all needed the mental as well as the physical protection.

Arrived at the mission house our party found Sister Partsch there, badly shaken but uninjured. Immediately after Sturgis jumped, she had followed and had reached shelter at almost the same moment; so he had not seen her. She had hidden in the woods until morning, then had made her way to the river, and had been found by a party from the mission house, her husband among them.

Fabricius they found where he fell, shot, tomahawked, and scalped, watched by his faithful dog, the only living thing in the desolate scene. Into one coffin went his body and the charred remains found in the ashes of the "House of the Pilgrims," and they were solemnly interred in the little cemetery near by.

Susanna Nitschmann was one of those who fell in the first onset, and she was counted among the dead, but a year later it was learned that the shot had not killed her, that she had been captured and taken to Wyoming, where some of our friendly Indian women tried to help her. But her brutish captor took her on to Tiago and in his wigwam she suffered unspeakable things until her end came, six months later.

Of the years of Indian war that followed I need not write in detail; indeed I have but a confused memory of it all. Christian Indians gathered into Bethlehem, where the constant alertness of our men and their Indian allies prevented the sudden and unexpected attacks upon which the hostile Indians depended to secure their victims. Bethlehem was a refuge for many frightened settlers, was indeed the frontier post which held the savages from sweeping down on Philadelphia.

While terror swept in waves over the countryside; while government officials sat in safety and delayed action; while men, women and children were murdered, and militia in unprotected stations were overpowered; while Brother David and Brother Mack and Brother Post went hither and yon, risking their lives over and over in order to retain their influence on the friendly Indians and prevent more bloodshed, we women, steadied by Brother Joseph, went quietly on with our daily routine of work and prayer.

From Carolina we heard but seldom. Four visits were made there during the next two years, and more of our young Brethren and a few additional married people moved thither, two couples taking one child each. The journey was dangerous, but when everything was full of danger that did not seem to matter.

7.

MY DOCTOR

━━━━━━━

IN THE SPRING OF 1758 I WAS APPOINTED TO VISIT ALL OUR OUT-
lying stations to speak on religious matters with the unmarried
women and girls in our care. It was fortunate that I had learned
to ride as a girl, for the tour must be made on horseback, which
added to the pleasure of the trip from my standpoint. I never
rode alone, but my escort varied. Sometimes a missionary would
be passing to or from his post; occasionally a farmer and his wife
would be going in my direction; if necessary one of the older
Brethren would be sent expressly to take me to the next place.
There were always homes open to me where I was welcome and
safe.

It was necessary to make the journey in two parts, for in
March the Indians were murdering in the neighborhood of our
more distant stations. So I went to the places that were reasonably
safe, and returned to Bethlehem on the 2nd of May, just in time
for the anniversary and Covenant Day of the Single Sisters, observed annually on May 4th.

In June I went as a delegate to the Synod meeting in Lebanon;
and after the Synod, as the Indians had quieted for the moment,
I was able to complete the task assigned to me.

On June 21st I left our congregation of Heidelberg, accompanied by Brother Casper Schmidt, who was on his way to Bethlehem from his home in Manakasy, Maryland. As we rode we
talked of many things, and he told me that when the Manakasy

congregation was begun he and his family had moved thither, hoping for more security when the Indians were on the warpath.

"Our hopes were only partly realized," he said sadly, "and I would give much to know whether my little daughter is living or dead or worse than dead."

"What happened?" I asked, half reluctantly, for stories of Indian outrages were heard so often that one almost dreaded a new one.

"Christina was nine years old in August, 1755," he said, "and she had gone with me to our farm, eight miles from the school-house in Manakasy, when the French Indians suddenly attacked us. The first that I knew of it was a shot from the woods, and the glimpse of a redskin hiding there. Hastily lifting Christina on a horse I told her to ride at full speed to the school-house, but the horse balked, and before I could get him started the Indians were breaking cover and running toward us. To delay was sure death, to escape meant a chance to save the family in Manakasy; so I had no choice except to leave my child. You can imagine my feelings as I hastened toward the woods on the other side of the clearing, with bullets singing by me, though the aim was bad. I did get word of the attack to Manakasy in time, and the rest of the group there were saved, but oh, Sister Catharina, my child, my child!" and his voice broke as he wiped his eyes.

"You have heard nothing from her?" I asked.

"Nothing. Other whites were taken on the same raid, and we heard that many were tortured when an Indian camp was found ruined. One man who escaped spoke of a white child who laughed at the agony of those into whose bodies resinous splinters had been stuck and lighted, with the day-long torture that brought; but it could not have been my tender-hearted little girl, unless her brain had snapped under the shock. Sometimes I think it would have been easier to stay and die with her."

"But that would have made the loss doubly great for your wife and other children," I said, trying to give comfort where none could be offered that was of any avail.

"Yes," he said, and rode on in a deep silence that I did not try to break.

Perhaps I too was preoccupied and less careful than I should have been, for suddenly my horse shied and I was thrown heavily to the ground. My escort hastily dismounted and came to my assistance, but when I tried to rise I found that my right leg was badly cut and bruised, and my knee appeared to have been strained. There was a farmhouse in sight, and Brother Schmidt insisted on going there for help, but I felt ashamed of my accident and re-membered my father's advice: "If you are thrown, mount again at once, never let a horse think he has the best of you," and I in-sisted that Brother Schmidt help me to the saddle and take me on to Bethlehem. I was probably dazed from the fall and my leg somewhat numb from the injury, or I could not have stood the pain of the next hours. As we journeyed on for more than twenty miles, our discomfort was increased by the coming of a storm with heavy rain. This convinced me of the folly of trying to reach Bethlehem, and I agreed to stop at the inn on the south side of the Lehigh. A chair was brought, and I was carried to a room and helped to bed, where I spent a night that I will never forget. Meanwhile Brother Schmidt sent an urgent message to Bethlehem, asking that the doctor be sent as soon as possible.

Next morning the innkeeper's wife came to my room and told me that the doctor had arrived from Bethlehem, and I asked her to bring him in. Imagine my surprise when instead of Brother Otto, the Bethlehem doctor, I saw a man whom I had never met, but whom I recognized as the blond young doctor I had seen in the group about to start for Wachovia five years before. He explained that Brother Otto was away from home, and that he had been sent to attend to my injury and take me to Beth-lehem in the one-horse chaise which Brother Joseph had provided.

My leg had become very painful, but even so there was a certain pleasure in the short ride, conscious as I was of that in-tangible something which had given my doctor such a far-reaching reputation in North Carolina. Little was said, but he did explain that he had left Bethabara after Easter, had reached Bethlehem during my absence, and expected to remain in Pennsylvania for some months before returning to Wachovia.

When we reached the Sisters House several of the Sisters received me with expressions of sympathy. To my surprise my doctor picked me up as though I were a child and carried me to the sickroom, where the Sisters put me to bed, and he did all that he could to make me more comfortable. Brother Otto was away for ten days; so the ministrations of Brother Kalberlahn continued for that length of time, and I found myself looking forward to his brief visits and to the casual conversations between the doctor and myself, and the Sisters who were nursing me.

I must admit that the arrival in Bethlehem of six Single Brethren from Wachovia had created something of a stir in the Sisters House, for it was generally believed that they had come for the purpose of marrying. Since no Single Sisters had as yet gone to North Carolina, no suitable marriages could be arranged in Bethabara, and there was at least some surmising as to the Sisters who might be selected. "We know one who will be suggested," said our irrepressible Sister Betsy, teasingly. I pretended not to understand her, but the idea was not unpleasant, though I dared not dwell on the possibility, for even if I were the one suggested the suggestion might not be approved by the Elders or by the Lord.

When Brother Otto returned he took charge of my case, and as I improved slowly the days began to seem long and tiresome, and I wanted to be up and about again. Not even to myself would I admit how much I missed the visits of the younger doctor.

Sister Betsy and her bits of news were now my chief diversion. "Sister Anna Rosel called Catharine Binder to her room this morning, and we hear that Catharine has accepted the proposal that she marry Brother Christian Seidel and go with him to Bethabara as pastor's wife."

"She will make a good one," I replied, and spent the rest of the day planning what I could do to help her get ready for the change, for by this time I could use my fingers if not my feet.

"Sister Elisabeth Leinbach is in a quandary," was the next gossip Betsy brought. "She has no particular objection to Michael Ranke, from what she can hear about him, but he is a farmer, and she knows little about the life on a farm and is dubious about undertaking the duties of a farmer's wife." Remembering my own life on my father's farm, and the many times I had missed its activities, I was ready to talk over the matter with Elisabeth when she came to see me about it, and she decided to accept the proposal.

"Something is wrong with Barbara Eirich," said Sister Betsy another day. "Sister Rosel has had a conference with her, but she looks so unhappy it must have worried her."

"She has a perfect right to refuse, if she does not wish to marry," I reminded her, at which Sister Betsy grinned, shaking her head as she replied: "Well, she does not look as though she enjoyed refusing, either."

With this case I had nothing to do, but it developed that at first Barbara refused the proposal to marry Adam Kramer. Then her conscience troubled her lest she might be refusing the leading of the Lord, and after several unhappy days she went to Sister Anna Rosel, who was the head of our Sisters House, and told her that if the matter was still open she would withdraw her refusal and accept the proposal. Having made up her mind that way, she joined the group of those who were preparing happily for their changed condition in life.

It was not our custom to have any considerable delay between betrothal and marriage, and Catharine and Barbara had been wedded before I was able to be out of bed. When I had been sitting up a little for a day or two, Sister Rosel came to see me. At once I sensed her purpose, and my heart beat faster as I wondered whose name I would hear.

"Sister Catharina, I bring you a proposal of marriage from Brother Martin Kalberlahn," she said gravely, and I stifled my emotion and asked steadily: "It has the approval of the Elders and of the Lord?" to which she answered, "Yes, certainly." At that time I had never been present when a marriage proposal was referred to the Lord through the *lot*, but we all knew that such a matter was first considered by the Elders, and if they approved, affirmative and negative *lots* were prepared and the Lord was asked to signify whether it would have His approval if they submitted the question to the Sister whose name was proposed. If the *lot* was negative the matter was dropped; if affirmative the question was taken to the Sister and she was at liberty to accept or reject, for the *lot* decision governed the action of the Elders, not of the men and women who were to wed. We believed that the approval of the Lord, given through the *lot*, guaranteed the wisdom of any move that was being discussed; so with the comforting assurance that I was following Divine leading (as well as my own inclination), I gave my answer as "Yes."

There was a short delay until I was able to walk a little, and then my wedding day arrived. Rather I should say our wedding day, for at that time multiple weddings were not uncommon in Bethlehem, and no less than eight couples were married on that occasion.

It was a silent group of eight Single Sisters that listened to the parting words of Sister Anna Rosel, and then walked with her to the small room adjoining the meeting-hall, where we were met by the eight Single Brethren, their leader, and Brother and Sister Spangenberg. More words of fatherly counsel from Brother Spangenberg, and then we walked into the meeting-hall two by two, I very conscious of the tall young man beside me. Three of the other Brethren were from Wachovia: Herman Lash, who was walking with Barbara Beroth; John Beroth, who was with Elisabeth Neumann; Michael Ranke, who accompanied Elisabeth Leinbach. I had no premonition that one day I would help to celebrate the "wedding jubilee" of two of them, nor did I dream of all that would befall me before that day came. On that 29th day of

July, in the year 1758, I had thought only for the solemn questions, the grave answers, the new life and responsibilities to which we were pledging ourselves.

Eight times those questions were asked and answered, eight times the hands of man and woman were joined, pledging their troth until death should break the bond. Then we withdrew to the small room where we had gathered, and Sister Spangenberg removed from each Sister's cap the pink ribbon, and substituted the light blue ribbon of the married Sister, and from there we went out to face our new life.

It has been said that there could be no romance in a Moravian marriage, but those who say that never rode with my doctor in a one-horse chaise, and never imagined that courtship might follow instead of precede a marriage ceremony.

"Dear Little One," said Martin, "I did not dream that love could come like this to a Moravian Brother, but when I saw you lying all forlorn in that inn room my whole heart went out to you, and I wanted to take you in my arms and carry you home."

"Was that why you carried me into the Sisters House?" I asked.

"Really it was," he answered with a smile, "though if the question had been raised then I would probably have explained that I hoped to make moving less painful for you than it had been when we took you out of the inn."

"The Sisters wondered," I told him, rather shyly.

"And you?"

"Oh, I assured them it was just because you were such a good doctor, that it was merely professional sympathy."

"No, Dear Little One," he said, looking down at me with a smile, "I have felt professional sympathy for many persons, but this was something different."

With my face turned away and my cheeks burning I murmured: "It was new to me too," an inadequate answer, but one with which he seemed quite content.

One day I ventured the question: "Why did you come to

Bethlehem?" more because I wanted to hear his answer than because I needed the information.

"Wife hunting," he replied rather grimly, as if half ashamed of the deliberate action. "I needed a wife to cook my meals, and wash my clothes, and look after my house, and leave me free to look after my patients."

"And how did you expect to find that wife?"

"I expected to say to the Elders: 'Please select a suitable wife for me,' and I expected calmly to accept whatever they offered, trusting that their judgment would be good!"

"You certainly did not expect to marry the head tailoress of the Sisters House!"

"Dear Little One, I could not have expected you, because I did not know."

And I, who had been the eldest of the family, who had been given important office before I was twenty-one, and ever since had been held responsible for the well-being of others, I thrilled each time he used his affectionate diminutive, reserved for my ears alone. To others we were a sedate married couple, quite settled and mature, but in our hearts we knew that we were young and very much in love.

The remainder of the year passed quietly at Bethlehem. The Indians quartered near or camping in the neighborhood finally moved away, to the great relief of everybody, for while the Christian Indians behaved well, many of the others were a menace to the town. Always there was the danger that something might precipitate trouble, as happened when the baptized Indian William Tatemy, while on his way to Easton, was wantonly shot by a white man. He was taken to the home of John Jones, and was cared for by our Doctor Otto, but his father, old Chief Moses Tatemy, threatened vengeance on the whites if he died, and we felt that it was a signal blessing of the Lord that he lived until the conference at Easton was over and the Indians had scattered. The Governor of Pennsylvania was so alarmed by the danger of an uprising that he sent a special message to Brother Otto, urging him to use every means in his power to keep Tatemy alive until the conference ended, though he might have known that Brother Otto would do his best and that only the Lord could lengthen life.

Another incident made us all shiver, though no ill results followed. A Nanticoke chief and some of his followers passed through Bethlehem. Some weeks later part of the company returned, and it was noticed that they had with them a bundle wrapped in a dirty blanket, which they handled with a care amounting almost to reverence. When questioned they explained that their chief had died of smallpox, that they had scraped all the flesh from his bones, and that they were taking the bones back to his native village where they would be buried with the usual ceremonies! At that time no means was known whereby the recurring epidemics of smallpox could be prevented; so time after time the scourge swept a village, white and Indian alike, only those escaping who had already had the disease. You may imagine how relieved Bethlehem was when the Indians and their blanket-wrapped bones departed, and smallpox did not break out. A few people never took smallpox, but I had it as a child, and my sister Benigna died from it in 1760 in the Bethlehem Boarding School.

In November the Indians finally made peace, our Brother Frederick Post having an important part therein, though at great risk to himself. He had gone to Indian headquarters at Kaskasking, bearing proposals from the Government to the chiefs. A letter which he sent back to Bethlehem was captured by the French, who translated it into the Indian language, purposely changing its tenor completely. The chiefs refused to believe that Brother Post had written the letter, but the younger Indians were very angry, and for five days he dared not leave his hut. Finally the chiefs forced the French commandant to produce the original letter; and when they found that the letter sent to them was a base forgery, they made all amends in their power to Brother Post and accepted the proposals which he brought to them. The British forces drove the French from Fort Duquesne about the same time; so at the end of the year the Province could give thanks for peace.

During the fall of 1758 and the spring of 1759 Martin and I had many delightful rides and drives. Brother Otto had a widely extended practice, and was glad for the help that Martin gave him. It was also a fine opportunity for Martin to see the country and the various places where the Moravians were working. My friends and acquaintances made us welcome and were interested in our coming journey to North Carolina, and I was happy in seeing them once more before moving south.

These trips on horseback or in the chaise gave me a chance to draw Martin on to speak about himself and to tell of his childhood and youth in the Old World. "I was born in Drontheim, Norway," he said, "and was educated in a Lutheran school. Medicine and surgery I learned by serving as apprentice to an older doctor; then I took the usual year of travel, paying my way by practicing medicine or performing operations in the cities and villages through which I passed."

"What brought you to the Moravian Church?" I asked.

"I liked several of the Brethren whom I chanced to meet in my travels, and saw more of them while I was in Copenhagen. Finally I decided that I would like to join them; so I went to Herrnhaag, where they were so kind as to accept me and receive me into the Unity of Brethren."

"I think you were kind to them to give them such an excellent doctor, for you could probably have done more for yourself in a worldly way had you stayed in Copenhagen, for instance."

"Possibly," he said with one of his ready smiles, "but I have never regretted my decision, nor that I accepted the call to serve in America. On my way it was interesting to visit Zeist, in Holland, the great city of London, and New York City, and I enjoyed the short stay with the Brethren at Christian's Spring in Pennsylvania before we left for Wachovia."

"Did you feel me looking at you during the service before you left for North Carolina?"

He laughed. "Tall as I am you could hardly help seeing me, but I cannot say honestly that I was conscious of your scrutiny. At the moment my look went no further ahead than the new settlement in North Carolina."

"And you like Wachovia?"

"Indeed I do," he replied enthusiastically, and went on to tell me about the fine start that had been made in Bethabara, and how glad he would be to go back and to show me all that had been done there, and I surprised him with comments which showed him how closely we had kept up with all that happened in Wachovia.

8.

MY DOCTOR GOES HOME

—————

IN THE LATTER PART OF APRIL, 1759, WE SET OUT FOR NORTH Carolina, accompanied by the other five Brethren from Bethabara and their wives. It was not a long journey, only one month, for our big wagon was drawn by six horses and we had others for riding; so we made good time. It was a pleasant experience; the country was new to me, and the budding trees and balmy air made us forget the bad stretches of road. Even the night camps had their charm, though we began to hear of renewed Indian activity. Cherokees who had accompanied General Forbes in the campaign against Fort Duquesne, were returning home along the mountains and were involving themselves in quarrels with the back settlers of Virginia and Carolina. We were taking the lower road by Frederick, Maryland, and Orange Court-house, Virginia; so we were not in great danger and saw no red men.

Some food we took with us, ham and tongue, chocolate, tea and coffee, and of course salt and other seasoning. Johnny-cake, baked at the evening campfire, usually served as bread for the next day also. Mush, made from cornmeal, was often our breakfast. Occasionally we could buy a little meat from a farmer living near the road. More than once we were detained for several hours, or even a day, while oats were threshed at some farm so that we could buy for our horses, but as a general thing we had to be satisfied with corn on the cob for them. It was too early for much pasturage or it would have been easier to care for their feeding, and it surprised me to see them eat the shredded corn-cobs along with the corn.

We had little rain and no snow, which pleased Martin, who had a vivid recollection of his first trip south. "We took the upper road," he said, "which was little more than a trail, and worse than usual because of the deep mud."

"We heard that the trip was a hard one," I told him, "and some said you should have avoided the mountains at that season of the year."

"Perhaps winter came early that time, but we certainly suffered from cold and sleet. One of our worst days was the one on which we neared the crest of the ridge. The trail was so slippery that the horses could not pull the heavily loaded wagon, even with all the help that we men could give. We were forced to unload the wagon, pack the goods on the horses, and lead them to the summit, and after a number of trips we succeeded in pulling the empty wagon to the top. By that time night had come, and in spite of the bitter cold we had to camp there, since we could not see to repack or to drive down."

"It is a wonder you did not all take cold."

"One becomes accustomed to exposure, I suppose, and while we were uncomfortable it did not hurt us."

"Was that your worst experience?"

"The most trying because of the cold, but not the most puzzling. On another occasion the track wound round the side of a steep hill, and it looked as though we could not possibly drive over it. There was grave danger that the wagon would turn over and roll down the hill, spilling its contents all the way to the bottom. We discussed ways and means for quite a while, and finally tied a rope to a stout tree, took the other end across the wagon and tied it to the running-gear and so steadied the wagon that the dangerous turn was passed safely."

Such stories made our present journey seem the more delightful, and I was almost sorry when we reached the ford of Haw River and must send a messenger ahead to give notice of our

August Gottlieb Spangenberg, "Brother Joseph"

From an engraving in the Salem Moravian Archives.

Parts of the Travel Diary of "Brother Joseph," 1752

Original in the Salem Moravian Archives.

approach. Martin volunteered to go; and four days later, as we neared Bethabara, he rode out to meet us, to my great joy. "You will find the village crowded," he told us, "for fresh Indian alarms in this neighborhood have sent an unusual number of refugees to Bethabara and to the mill, and the Brethren have thought it wise to stockade both places for greater safety."

"Where do the refugees come from?" I asked. "I thought the Brethren were almost alone on the frontier."

"There were a few scattered settlers when we arrived in 1753," he answered, "and since then a number of farms have been begun along the Town Fork of Dan River, along the Yadkin River, and between the river and our Muddy Creek. Ours is still the only village, and the farmers feel helpless alone in their scattered houses, and many of them have come to Bethabara for protection."

"Of what nationality are the farmers?"

"Largely German and Swiss, with some English. Many of them went first to Pennsylvania, and came south after a few years in that province. Some lived near one or another of our Moravian preaching places in Pennsylvania; others have learned to know the Brethren only since they have been here."

"Has any religious work been done among them by our Brethren?"

"There has been no opportunity as yet, but this Cherokee war may open a way for us to approach them."

There was no time for further conversation, for Bethabara was in sight, and I looked at it with pardonable curiosity.

The road ran along one side of the stockade; then we turned to the right and entered the gate which had been left on the southeast, Martin pointing out to me the new log house just outside the gate, which had been erected for the doctor and contained his laboratory and several living rooms. "That is new," he said, "and has been built for us," but he could not add more for at that moment the French horns began to play to welcome us to Bethabara, and we rode in to dismount at the Congregation House,

the center of the village life. There, in the evening, the congregation had a lovefeast, during which the members sang for us the
stanza which had been composed for the reception of the first
group of married people, who had reached Bethabara in November, 1755:

> Welcome into Wachovia,
>   Dear Sisters and dear Brothers,
> Our great High Priest has led you here
>   As He has led the others.
> Now rest the weary pilgrim feet
>   That hither bravely brought you;
> The Lord who gave your bodies health
>   Has strength and courage taught you.

The night which followed was our first in our own home,
for in Bethlehem we had occupied temporary lodgings. The
furnishings were few and simple—bed, table, two or three chairs,
all homemade. We had been able to bring but little from Pennsylvania, but with what we had, added to our affection for each
other, we made of it a place of cheer.

Martin devoted the next day to showing me about the village
and visiting with me in the various houses of the place. I found
Bethabara a compact little village, with twelve larger and smaller
houses protected by the stockade, and others near by. The stockade
was built of long, strong stakes, cut from trees of the right size;
it was of irregular shape, taking advantage of the walls of several
houses which formed part of the defense. In addition to the gate
by which we entered, there was a smaller one on the southwest
side, opening on a path which led across a meadow, over a small
stream, and up a steep hillside to the little graveyard on the top.
"God's Acre" they called it, and it also had been stockaded.

The Congregation House was just inside our gate, on the
right-hand side, and as we had seen its meeting hall the preceding
evening and had greeted the members living in its dwelling rooms,
we did not enter, but began our tour at the house across the street.
On the first floor we found Brother and Sister Seidel, just ready

to start out on a tour of their own; so we did not detain them but went up to the second floor, which was occupied by Brother Jacob Rogers, his wife, and wee daughter. "Brother Rogers is the English Minister of Dobbs Parish," said Martin, introducing us, and I remembered that North Carolina was an English Colony in which the Church of England was the state church.

"Do you find many people belonging to the Church of England?" I asked.

"Very few," he replied, "but when the Assembly of North Carolina granted the request of the Brethren and constituted the Moravian land as a separate parish, with the name of Dobbs Parish, our Brethren obligated themselves to provide an English-speaking minister to care for the spiritual needs of English-speaking settlers of whatever denomination living within the parish, and I was called for the purpose."

"We also must elect a vestry and two church wardens," said Martin, "and the liturgy of the Church of England must be read four times a year."

"Is that troublesome?"

"Not in the least. The vestrymen are selected from our membership, and the church wardens serve as almoners, caring for the beggars who come to the village."

"And," added Brother Rogers, "every now and then we have English visitors in the village, who are glad to hear the Church of England service, and it is good for those of our own number who do not understand English and are trying to learn."

While we were talking I had been smiling at little Salome Rogers, and now I held out my arms to her and she came to me willingly. "You know how to win children, do you not?" said Sister Rogers, and I told her of my younger brothers and sisters, and of the nursery in which I had served. "Come and see us often," said Sister Rogers. I accepted the invitation gladly, and we became very good friends.

We did not go into the Brothers House, but I noticed that it was the largest house in the village. Martin said that the Single

Brethren were scattered, some living on the farm, some in the workshops, but most of them in this central house. Their many different handicrafts had served to draw visitors to the place and had attracted favorable notice, besides furnishing the needed supplies for the village.

The shoe-shop was near the path leading to God's Acre, and Martin stopped there and introduced me to Brother Pfeil. "Had any more rat-hunts?" asked Martin, smiling.

Brother Pfeil's eyes twinkled, and as he took his pipe from his mouth he said, "You enjoyed the last one, didn't you?" Then turning to me he asked, "Did Brother Kalberlahn tell you about it?" I shook my head and he told me that the rats had swarmed in, no one knew from where, and had taken possession of his shoe-shop, nibbling the wax and gnawing the leather and driving him nearly distracted. "The doctor will not admit it, but I suspect he invented the idea of the rat-hunt. He certainly planned it, and gathered the men and boys and dogs that day, and saw to it that the men and boys were armed with stout sticks. Then as the carpenters took down the logs of the shop, and the rats ran out, everybody got after them, and had a fine time, chasing and killing them."

"The boys buried thirty of them in an unhallowed grave while the men were laying up the logs again," chuckled Martin; and Brother Pfeil said that since then there had been much less trouble, "though I suppose one never gets entirely rid of rats, even on the frontier," he said.

Across the path from the shoe-shop was the house occupied by Brother Jacob Lash and his wife, whom I had known as Anna Blum in Pennsylvania. They had been married two years, and it was pleasant to see them again. Brother Lash was one of the most important men in the village, being the treasurer, supervisor of work, and in effect an attorney, since it was his duty to familiarize himself with the laws of North Carolina and see that they were observed. His office as justice of the peace made it possible for him to enforce the law. For two years also he had been the official captain of an independent company of men for the protection of Bethabara and the mill. "We claim the exemption from military service granted to us by the English Parliament in 1749," he explained, "but we recognized the necessity of protecting ourselves and our neighbors from the attacks of Indians; so Bethabara asked for authority to act, and the Governor appointed me as captain. We hope never to be obliged to fire a gun, but the right to control the refugees for their own good is a real advantage; and the Indians know that we are ready to protect ourselves and therefore hesitate to attack so strong and well-manned a stockade."

The tavern, I found, was a substantial building outside the stockade, near the site of the cabin which the pioneer Brethren found when they first came to Wachovia. It was on the road leading to the Shallow Ford of the Yadkin River, the best ford in this part of the country, and Martin pointed out to me that this Shallow Ford road ran west from Bethabara; the road to the Hollow ran northwest; the road to the Town Fork ran northeast; and the King's Road to Salisbury ran south; so Bethabara had become easy of access from all directions.

On another day Martin took me to the mill, where we found the same crowded conditions as in Bethabara. Refugees had been permitted to cut down trees in the neighboring forest, and had built eight log cabins in a row, the back walls of the cabins forming one side of the stockade. The other three sides were built of boards, for a saw-mill had been erected for our own convenience, and it was possible to saw the boards, and less trouble than to use palisades. Neighbors seldom took the trouble to haul away boards, but the grist-mill, the only one in a radius of many miles, was used by a great many persons. "They have built a very large bin in Bethabara," said Brother Kapp, the miller, "and I have sent thither a large amount of flour, so that if we are besieged both places can be fed."

A week after we reached Bethabara we were glad to welcome

Brother Spangenberg and his wife, who had not been able to come with us because of a synod called to meet in Lancaster which they needed to attend.

"Oh, Sister Kalberlahn," Sister Spangenberg told me the first time we met, "Christina Schmidt has been found!"

"Christina Schmidt?" I asked, not remembering the story Brother Schmidt had told me, for there had been nothing unusual about it and it had been put out of my mind by the many things that had since happened to me.

"Daughter of Casper Schmidt, of Manakasy, who was riding with you when you were thrown."

Then it came back to me and I asked with interest, "Where and how?"

"Brother and Sister Schmidt came to Lancaster, to the synod, and someone told them that a man living there had recently returned from Philadelphia, bringing with him a girl about twelve or thirteen years old, whom he claimed as his long-lost daughter, though the girl declared that she had never seen him before he appeared in Philadelphia. Their interest aroused by the story, they went to the man's house, saw the girl, and there was immediate recognition on both sides. The man who had her insisted that she was his daughter, that he had been told in a dream that she was the child kidnapped from him by Indians years before, and that the magistrate in Philadelphia had accepted his appeal and had given the child to him. When he absolutely refused to give her up Brother Schmidt took the case to a magistrate in Lancaster, who listened with interest and gave her to Brother Schmidt, saying emphatically 'Flesh and blood will not be denied.'"

"But how did she get to Philadelphia?"

"She says that when her father left her, an Indian seized her, took her on his back, and started to carry her to the forest. She screamed and fought, insisting on being put down, to which he grunted 'Yes, Yes,' but continued to carry her. Then in a childish rage she took a pin from her dress and stuck it into his back with all her force."

"It is a wonder that he did not kill her on the spot!"

"Indeed it is, and her guardian angel must have stayed his hand, for he put her on the ground, searched her for more pins, and threatened her with the tomahawk, but did not hurt her. Forced to go with the Indians, and threatened again with the tomahawk whenever she cried, she learned to restrain her feelings. The scene of torture, which was all too true, was nearly too much for her, and the reported laughter was largely hysterical, under threat of her own death if she did not show merriment at the sufferings of the victims."

"What an awful thing for a child to live through!"

"Somehow she survived, and when they reached the Indian village she was not badly treated. Once she was rescued from the death-hug of a bear; another time she was nearly drowned, but was pulled from the water just in time. She does not know why the three chiefs took her to Philadelphia when they went to the treaty conference, but her release was part of the treaty agreement. A kind Quaker took her to his home, and promised to try to help her find her parents if they were still alive, but the man with the dream interfered, secured possession of her, and took her to Lancaster."

"Wonderful are the ways of the Lord, and I wish all the sad stories we have heard had as happy an ending!"

"That is not quite the whole story," said Sister Spangenberg. "It seems that as far back as she could remember Christina had a desire to live in Bethlehem, and during her captivity the longing to be there increased. Hearing of this, my husband spoke with her and with her parents, who first protested against giving her up again and then consented to follow her wishes. It was a touching and dramatic scene in synod when my husband introduced her to the assembled company, told them her story, and turning to her parents asked them: 'Are you willing to give this child to the Saviour and to the Unity of Brethren?' 'Yes,' they answered, and the shining face of the girl was witness of her delight. Now she has gone home with them for a visit; when that ends, her father will take her to the Sisters House in Bethlehem and place her among the older girls living there under the care of the Sisters."

"How terrible the Indian atrocities are!" I sighed, for the results of the dread of them were on every side of us in over-crowded Bethabara, where it was impossible for the Brethren to continue their placid routine of work and church services, because so many outside needs must be met.

This distressed Brother Spangenberg, who had selected the site for Wachovia, and had directed its development from Bethlehem, but was paying his first visit to the village of Bethabara since its founding. Doubtless this made him the more ready to accept the proposal of Michael Hauser, Sr., one of the mill refugees, who did not wish to return to his farm and asked that the Moravians would begin a second village, not too far from Bethabara, and allow him and his family to settle there. He discussed the matter with the Bethabara Brethren, and several of the men stated that they would be glad to join in the movement to establish a second Moravian village. On June 12th Brother Spangenberg, his wife, and several Brethren, rode to what they called the Black Walnut Bottom, and there they selected a suitable site, about three miles from Bethabara, on the road that led by the mill. Lots were laid off there on the 30th of the month, and the name of Bethania was given to the new village.

As plans developed eight married couples decided to move from Bethabara, and they were joined by eight of the neighbor families, including Michael Hauser, Sr., two of his sons, George and Michael, Jr., and their families. Definite contracts were made with the proposed residents of the new town, and Brother Spangenberg urged them to make Bethania "a village of the Lord, established according to His desire and principles, where nothing of worldly spirit and action should find place." High ideals are a good thing, even if frail human nature does not always measure up to them; and doubtless our bishop's admonition was remembered often, when differences in background and inherited viewpoints threatened the welfare of the village, and was helpful in the finding of satisfactory solutions of its problems. On July 18th Brother and Sister Grabs moved from the old town to the new, into one little house which had been finished, and with them went the seven other Brethren from Bethabara who were to become residents. The men from the mill also began work on their houses; but all the women except Sister Grabs remained where they were until more living quarters were ready.

On July 19th, during dinner, announcement was made of the departure of Sister Rogers, after an illness of eight days. This was the beginning of a great time of sorrow for Bethabara—and for me. A strange kind of fever had broken out amongst us, and most of those living in Bethabara had it in a more or less serious form. My doctor was much worried, for the usual treatment for fever gave little relief, and it nearly broke his heart that his friends should look to him in vain.

"Oh Martin, don't worry so," I begged. "You are doing your best, and no one could do more."

"Dear Little One," he answered, "my best is not enough; they suffer and I cannot give them ease; they pass away and I can do nothing to hold them back."

"And if that be the Lord's will, Martin, can you not submit?"

"Dear Little One, you are wiser than I, come, let us pray to the Saviour for His help and comfort," but beginning with those petitions he soon was uttering such fervent appeals for help for himself in his great task, such an agonizing prayer that where he failed the Lord would aid, that I burst into tears.

"There, there, Dear Little One," and turning he took me in his arms. "Continue to stand by me and we will trust and not be afraid." And of this faith we were to have greater need than we knew, and he stood the test much better than I.

Of those who left us Sister Rogers was the first, but not the last. I had helped to nurse her and she had asked me to take her baby girl. So when the end came her little Salome was placed in my care, where she remained until she was six years old and could be sent to the school for little girls in Bethlehem.

Next came Catharine Seidel, and it seemed almost impossible that, only a few short weeks before, she had traveled south with us, filled with high hopes of service in her new home. Her husband was submissive, but missed her sadly, and it was only a few days later that he returned from a visit to Bethania, oppressed by the feeling of utter weariness which we were learning to recognize as the first symptom of the disease. He did not seem very ill at first, but when hope was expressed for his recovery he shook his head, saying, "No; life was lonely without my Catharine and I asked my Lord to take me to Himself, and He has heard and answered." And so it was, and his remains were borne up the steep path to the little God's Acre on the hill.

And then my Martin! Perhaps because of his unremitting efforts for others he was seriously ill from the first. He saw what was coming and sent for Brother Jacob Lash, made his will, and advised that Brother Jacob Bonn be taken again as community doctor. Brother Bonn had served during Martin's absence, returning to Pennsylvania shortly before we came; then he had conducted Brother Spangenberg hither and so had been able to help Martin during the epidemic and could continue the work without interruption.

For me the following days were full of anguish, and yet they were precious days. His burden of responsibility lifted, Martin's every thought was for me, and he bade me think beyond the present and try to realize what heaven would mean when we were reunited there.

"Our time together has been short, Dear Little One, but it has been a happy time. Let us forget that we must separate, and think only of the eternity which lies ahead, where there shall be no more pain nor any crying, for the Lord Almighty will have wiped away all tears and will have conquered all disease and death itself."

"Oh Martin, I love you so; I cannot give you up!"

"Not even when it means that I need suffer no longer?" for

his pain was intense, as it always was in the earlier stages of the fever.

"Oh my dearest, yes, if it is best for you."

"Then stay by me and hold my hand, hold it tight." And when fever mounted, when the terrible red splotches broke out on his body, when delirium came, he still felt my presence, and was quieted as I held his hand in mine, spoke gently to him, or sang some of our best loved hymns. Then he became unconscious of pain or weariness; but we were still hand in hand when the call came that took him to the eternal home where none shall ever say, "I am sick."

Others followed him up that steep hill and were laid to rest beside him, but I was stunned and rebellious and nothing seemed to matter much. Why was so beloved and able and much needed a man taken? Why must Bethabara lose pastor and doctor and so many others? Why must there be such pain and suffering in the world? Why was I brought this long distance only to be left desolate? Why could I not have stayed in the quiet Sisters House in Bethlehem? Why was I left untouched when so many others were ill? Why? Why? Why?

Brother Spangenberg tried to comfort me, but in vain. I asked him to take me back to Bethlehem, and when he said me nay I felt that my last friend had failed me. "The Lord has brought you here, my child, and He has work still for you to do; wait patiently for the revelation of His will." So said the bishop, but I did not want more work, I did not want to wait, and his advice fell on closed ears.

No light pierced my gloom until one day when the Lord sent a friend to show me a poem which had been written by our surveyor, Christian Reuter, as he was recovering from a serious attack of the dread fever. The lines set forth a dream he had had, in which two angels stood beside his bed, but passed him by because he was not yet ripe for the heavenly harvest; and a second dream in which he saw the Lord looking down upon sorely tried Bethabara, and heard Him say:

"This hundred-thousand-acre field
Now truly consecrate shall be,
Therefore the angel reapers come
And bear the first fruits home to me."

So that was what *God's Acre* meant! Not a place of burial, not even a measure of land consecrated to God, but a field in which the bodies of believers were laid awaiting the glories of the resurrection! I knew that, of course, but I had never realized what it could mean to one whose best beloved lay there. How sweet it was to think of my Martin, one of the pioneers in this hundred-thousand-acre field that we call Wachovia, now one of the first-fruits standing in that glorious presence, his labors accepted, his soul ripe for the harvest. Humbly I accepted the comfort which the Saviour gave me, and the last lines of Brother Reuter's poem became my prayer:

"Lord Jesus Christ, Thou art so true,
Thou art so merciful to all,
I pray for grace Thy will to do,
To trust Thy love whate'er befall."

9.

WIDOWHOOD

WIDOWHOOD IS A TIME OF LONELINESS, NO MATTER HOW BUSY the hands or how full of employment the hours. This was doubly true in my case, for the care of little Salome prevented my sharing in the activities of the other women, and my known skill with the needle naturally resulted in my taking over as much as possible of the community sewing, leaving the other women free for other tasks.

Of course I moved at once into a room inside the stockade, Brother Bonn going to the laboratory, for Martin's advice was followed and Brother Bonn was kept in Bethabara as community doctor.

Salome was a good baby, and I was able to take her with me to morning prayers, where the New Testament text of the day was considered, and to the short service at noon when the Old Testament text was the theme of the address, but usually I must miss the song service in the evening, and the short reading of Unity news which preceded it, because she grew too sleepy. Our simple breakfast of bread and tea and mush I prepared in our room, but our noonday dinner, cooked in the community kitchen, we shared with the rest of the inhabitants of the village.

Sometimes Sister Lick left her little Magdalena with me for some hours, or Sister Anna Lash would bring her little Christian, and I encouraged this, for the children amused each other and watching them took my thoughts away from myself. But there were many long hours when my needle flew and my thoughts were far away, sometimes with the relatives and friends in Pennsylvania, but much more often with my Martin in his new heavenly home. What would a doctor find to do, I wondered, in a land where none were sick? Something fine and worthy surely, for Martin would never be happy unless he was useful, and we have the assurance that "His servants shall serve Him" in that heavenly country. The fever which took Martin from me persisted until late in the fall, though with decreasing violence, and we heard that it was prevalent in many parts of North Carolina and Virginia.

The Indian alarms waxed and waned, and refugees came and went.

"Henry Benner is here again," said Sister Lash one morning.

"Who is Henry Benner?" I asked, for in truth I had paid little attention to the refugees, my thoughts largely centered on myself.

"Jacob says that he lives north of us, near the Town Fork of Dan River. He was most kind to the first Brethren when they arrived, and they are glad to return his courtesies by giving him shelter, but he is a timid man and comes in at the first alarm, however unfounded it may be. Jacob says that he has been here a dozen times at least, and that he will keep on coming as long as the Indians trouble us."

"Have they ever attacked him?" I asked, not particularly interested, but I was unusually lonesome that morning and eager to hold Sister Lash for further converse.

"He had one bad fright," she replied, "though Jacob is not sure whether it was caused by Indians or by roaming white miscreants."

"Were you here at the time?"

"It was in 1755, before any of the Sisters had come south. Mr. Benner and one of his neighbors stopped at Bethabara toward evening, returning after a two-day search for strayed horses. They went on to his farm, but about four o'clock in the morning the Brethren were aroused by the sound of terrible crying. Hurrying out they found Mr. Benner almost frantic with fright and grief, but he managed to tell them that when he reached home he found his wife and children gone, the house wide open, and everything in disorder. He searched and called, but receiving no answer he knew nothing to do but come here. The Brethren comforted him as best they could. By Jacob's order a gun was fired twice as a warning to lurking savages that our men were awake and on the alert; then the trumpet was blown at intervals in case anyone who needed shelter was within hearing. Just about dawn there was a call from the forest and some of the Brethren hurried thither. To their joy and relief they found that it was Mrs. Benner with her four children. They called Mr. Benner, and the husband and wife fell into each other's arms, weeping for joy."

"One can well understand that," said I, "but what had happened?"

"Mrs. Benner said that during the evening the dogs became restless, and when she went to the door she saw several men in the shadows at the edge of the woods. She could not tell whether they were white or red, but shutting the door she hurriedly picked up the baby and pushed the other children before her out of the back door and into the woods on that side of the house. Looking back she saw four men rush into her house, and she hastened to run deeper into the forest. She had never been to Bethabara, but she knew the general direction; so giving the baby to her oldest child she picked up the next youngest and they made their way hither as best they might, hoping and yet fearing, looking around them at every step. When they heard the trumpet they knew they were saved, and hurried toward the village, shouting to attract attention."

"No wonder they are nervous," said I, and we agreed that the red man was enough to shake the courage of the bravest.

Late in the fall, danger from the Indians increased again, and the Governor called out the militia to march against the Cherokees. Brother Lash, as captain of the independent company formed to protect our stockade, felt that our Brethren and the refugees with us were exempt, and others went further and thought that all the militia in the frontier counties of Rowan and Anson should be allowed to remain at home. General relief was felt, therefore, when the Government accepted this position as correct and sent to Bethabara a supply of powder and shot, which fortunately the Brethren were not forced to use.

One precaution taken by Brother Spangenberg was of definite advantage. When he was in Georgia he several times went out with the forest rangers. They always rode rapidly and explained that Indians could not hit a man on a galloping horse. When Bethania was founded three miles from Bethabara, there was of course much passing between the two villages. On one occasion Brother Spangenberg went with some of the men, who were plainly nervous, word having come that morning that Indians had been seen in the neighborhood. "Brethren, you do not know how to ride, let me show you," he said gaily, urging his horse into a gallop, which he maintained for the entire distance. Thereafter that was the custom whenever there was an Indian alarm, and when the war finally ended, and Indians passed again in friendly fashion, they admitted that time and again they had planned to take prisoners between the old town and the new but "the Dutchers had big fat horses and rode like the devil!"

Four events of October of that year remain in my memory. Early in the month Brother John Ettwein and his wife arrived from Bethlehem, he to take the place of Brother Seidel as pastor of Bethabara. He served Bethania also as occasion demanded, though Brother David Bischoff had moved to the latter village soon after New Year to look after the work and give such pastoral care as was possible for a layman.

The day following Brother Ettwein's arrival, a little child died at our mill, where the family were living as refugees. As our Bethabara God's Acre was intended for the interment of our members only, a parish graveyard was laid out on the hill above the mill, and Brother Rogers held the funeral of the child there. Later in the month Brother Rogers left us, planning to go to Bethlehem and

The Reverend Bernhard Adam Grube, first
pastor at Bethabara

From a portrait in the Bethlehem Archives.

ESSAY

OF A

Delaware-Indian and *English*

SPELLING-BOOK,

FOR THE

USE OF THE SCHOOLS

OF THE

CHRISTIAN INDIANS

on *Muskingum River.*

By DAVID ZEISBERGER,

MISSIONARY among the *Western Indians.*

❦

PHILADELPHIA,

Printed by HENRY MILLER. 1775.

Title-page of Zeisberger's Delaware-Indian and English
Spelling-Book

Copy in the Salem Moravian Archives.

then to England, leaving his little Salome in my care, as her mother had desired.

A welcome visitor was Mr. William Churton, who had not seen Brother Spangenberg and Brother Herman Lash since their adventurous trip across the state in the search for land for our Moravian settlement. When he learned that I was the daughter of Henry Antes he made special request that he might meet me, and told me much about my father's part in the search and what he had meant to the other members of the expedition.

The next year, 1760, was a year of fierce Indian war, the worst Wachovia had known. On the 10th of February whites were killed by the Cherokees in North Carolina; on the 19th refugees arrived telling of great alarm on the Yadkin; and two days later letters to Brother Jacob Lash reported that the country about Salisbury was much disturbed and a large party of Indians was believed to be headed this way. The stockade at the mill was at once repaired, and a watch was set there and in Bethabara. Preparations were made for the defense of Bethania should the foe attack there, and I have never known why that village escaped, except that it was shielded by the hand of the Almighty.

One afternoon early in March a Sister came into my room, rather pale of face, exclaiming, "Word has come that last week the Indians tried to lure the soldiers outside of Fort Dobbs, and when they would not come out, the Indians attacked the Fort and there was a great fight. Oh, Sister Kalberlahn, what shall we do if they attack us here?" I began to answer her, when suddenly the words on my tongue were arrested and I pointed silently through my window toward the east where a beautiful rainbow showed a complete arch, spanning the sky above our village, a divine promise of protection that even frightened women could not doubt.

A few days later one of our neighbors had a miraculous escape. Happening to look from my window toward the stockade gate I saw a group of men moving about in a way that denoted excitement. I could not leave the children, but presently I saw one man lead a horse through the gate, probably taking him to the stable, and a few minutes later half a dozen of the men seemed to be carrying someone out through the same gate—to the doctor's laboratory, I surmised. It was a real relief when Sister Lash hurried into my room exclaiming, "Did you see what was happening?"

"I could see little," I said, "do tell me, was one of the Brethren hurt?"

"Not one of our Brethren, but a man whose name I did not hear. Several of our Brethren were coming toward the stockade when they heard the sound of a galloping horse. At first they thought it riderless, but presently discovered that there was a man on its back, leaning far forward in the saddle and clutching the horse's mane. As it neared the stockade the horse slowed to a walk, and they let it enter the gate and caught the man just as he fainted and began to fall from the saddle. Imagine their horror when they found that his body had been pierced by an arrow! It was hard to move him without increasing the laceration, and he was bleeding from another arrow wound also. Someone ran for Brother Bonn, who took advantage of the victim's unconscious state and cut the head from the arrow and pulled the shaft out of his body.

"Why had it not killed him?" I asked.

"Not even the doctor could answer that question, but he was still living and beginning to revive when they carried him to the laboratory."

"Do, please, Sister Lash, find out what happened and come and tell me," I begged, but it was not until the next day that we heard the rest of the story.

On the morrow Brother Jacob Lash visited the wounded man, and as he was stronger Brother Bonn allowed some questions.

"Do you feel able to tell us what happened to you?"

"I'll try," he answered feebly. "William Fish and his son and I set out for the Fish farm to get provisions for the families gathered on the Yadkin River. Some miles up the river we met a party of Indians and before we could escape they fired at us, first with guns and then with arrows. William Fish and his son were killed, and I was hit twice. I succeeded in putting a rough bandage on my arm, but could do nothing with the arrow which had driven through my body. Why I did not fall from my horse I do not know, but I suppose fear of the scalping knife gave me strength and I rode to the Yadkin, my horse swimming the river bravely. The Indians did not try to follow me across, but on the other side the forest was full of Indians. They did not see me, and turning back to the river my horse brought me over the water again. By that time it was dark and raining and I was suffering dreadfully and lost all sense of direction. We must have wandered for hours until we found a road into which my horse turned. I scarcely knew what was happening but did realize that I was growing very weak and urged the horse into a gallop. Finally I saw the stockade in the distance, and the thought of rescue sapped my last particle of strength. Of what happened then I know only what this good friend tells me," and he looked gratefully at Brother Bonn.

"Well, you are safe now, and I think you will recover if you will lie very still and rest," said the doctor, and with another look of gratitude the man shut his eyes and fell into a gentle sleep.

"And is it really possible for him to recover?"

"Jacob says that the doctor thinks there is a good chance," said Sister Lash, and results showed that the doctor was right.

Next day the fifty persons who had gathered at the Yadkin came to the stockade for protection; and on the day following a company of militia passed, going to find the bodies of William Fish and his son in order to bury them. They found the Indians out in force, and so had to content themselves with visiting the families who had thought to hold their ground and bringing them to our stockade. Then a message came from the Town Fork, where another group was surrounded, and the militia hurried there, only to find that two men had been killed and the rest had escaped.

The next night Indians were seen in Bethania. The watchman shot at them and they ran; then a strong wind rose and on it came "a sound as of the howling of a hundred wolves," as Brother Grabs described it. The Indians had two camps in our neighborhood, one about six miles from Bethania, and the other, a smaller one, only half that distance. When a light snow fell, the Brethren in Bethania could see the smoke from their campfires as dark lines against the white.

From the mill stockade, parties of some size went out safely to secure food from the farms belonging to the refugees, but there were fatalities when one or two went out alone. So far as we knew everybody who possibly could had left the neighborhood, and our stockades were the only protection for the frontier.

We learned later that two things had contributed to the safety of Bethabara. Some of the Cherokees, excusing themselves for their failure to capture our stockade, told their comrades: "The Dutchi are a dreadful people, very large and very smart; we have seen into their fort." Others explained that over and over they had crept close to Bethabara, but always they had heard a large bell ring or a horn blow, and knowing themselves discovered had waited for another opportunity to attack. "This was providential," said Brother Ettwein, "for there is no doubt that the horn was the trumpet which the night-watchman blows each hour on his rounds, and that the bell was ringing for our early morning prayers, but so does the Lord protect His Brethren."

Things had quieted in April when Brother and Sister Spangenberg returned to Pennsylvania after a stay in Bethabara of nearly ten months. Brother Spangenberg had escaped the fever, but Sister Spangenberg had had a rather severe attack from which she recovered slowly. Before they left, the Bishop organized the congregation of Bethania. Ten houses had been erected there, and the eight Bethabara families had moved thither, with two families from the mill and more to follow. How I felt on the day when I saw Brother and Sister Spangenberg leave may be better imagined than described. I bade them goodbye with a smile, but my pillow that night was wet with homesick tears and heartsick tears, as I faced the lonely years ahead. Nor were mine the only tears shed at their departure, in view of the risk they ran, but "Fear not, my Brethren," said Brother Spangenberg, "the Lord will give His angels charge concerning us to keep us in our way," and in due time we heard that they had made the journey safely.

That spring and summer crops were planted under guard and were harvested in like manner, but the refugees were thankful for the food that was raised. Some families went to their farms, only to come back to us in the late summer when there were further Indian alarms. During the fall the red men were again in our neighborhood, but the necessary precautions had been learned by sad experience and not so many lives were lost.

In October the Brethren in America were saddened by news of the departure of Count Zinzendorf in May, at his home in Herrnhut, Saxony, at the early age of sixty years. I had long since overcome the childish resentment I had felt toward Mr. Thuernstein, as I had known him in Pennsylvania, and had come to see him as my father did, as a great and good man, who had spent his entire life in the service of the Lord Jesus Christ and of the Unity of Brethren. His son-in-law, Bishop John von Watteville, wrote the official notification, speaking of his leadership and his devoted service; telling also of his last illness. He had taken a severe cold which settled in his chest causing him much discomfort, but at the last "the great oppression lifted and he closed his eyes and passed as a prince of God." A large concourse of people, Brethren, friends, and acquaintances, followed his remains up the hill to God's Acre, where he was laid to rest beside his Countess.

The Countess Erdmuth Dorothea had gone home several years earlier, and he had missed her so sorely that his health began to fail. After the year of mourning which custom allows, his friends began to urge him to marry again, for his own sake and for the sake of the church. As a Count of the Empire he might have chosen where he would, but he never had cared for worldly advancement and now less than ever. So his choice for a second wife fell on Sister Anna Nitschmann, the "Miss Anna" of my girlhood. She was his inferior in rank, for she did not belong to the nobility, but for many years she had been his trusted associate in the affairs of the Unity of Brethren and he refused to consider any other suggestion. So they were wedded in the presence of the leaders of the Unity, and spent several peaceful and useful years together. She was ill at the time of his departure, and it had seemed doubtful which of them would be the first to go; indeed, the next letters that came told us that she had followed him into eternity in a few days. She was interred beside him, and with the same honors which had been shown to him, for not only had she been his wife, but she had held high office in the Unity in her own right.

Life is a queer mixture, especially in a small frontier village where one never knows what a day will bring forth. One morning when my thoughts were full of Mr. Thuernstein and Miss Anna and my Pennsylvania girlhood, Sister Lick came in with her little Magdalena and the question, "Did you ever hear of pigeons which travel in huge flocks, thousands and thousands of birds?"

"Never. What do you mean?"

"It is reported that men going from here to their homes on the South Fork of Muddy Creek found a place where so many pigeons were roosting that they killed twelve hundred with sticks."

"Don't you mean twelve?"

"No. It must have been twelve hundred, for they took many home with them and yet sent several hundred to the kitchen here."

"I hope they will serve them at dinner today; I would like to see how they taste," said I.

"Please let me have one, Mother," said Magdalena; and "Me, Me, too!" chimed in wee Salome.

They proved a welcome addition to our rather monotonous fare, and the next week some of the Brethren went to the roosting place on Peter's Creek and killed eighteen hundred. As many as we liked were cooked at once, and the rest were cleaned and salted for use later in the winter.

Their number seemed undiminished by this slaughter, and many were the raids made upon them by our Brethren and the neighbors. In the morning they took wing and departed for parts unknown, but at night they returned to roost, crowding so closely that their weight broke large branches and tore down some of the trees. They were easy to kill at night, for they seemed dazed by the light of a torch and could be knocked down with a stick. When everybody had gathered as many as could possibly be used they were left more alone, and they stayed for about two months, finally moving on when the ground became covered with a deep snow.

I might add that at Christmas all our houses were decorated with pine and cedar from the forests, and in the Congregation House the Sisters arranged a "Bethlehem," with little cardboard houses which some of them made, and especially a tiny cave-stable, with a manger and the Holy Family. A star hung above the stable, and on a moss hill near by, small sheep rested quietly. My little Salome loved the Infant and the sheep, and the refugee children from the mill stockade looked at the scene with eyes of wonder. Apparently they had never heard the blessed story, which was not surprising. Christian once remarked that "the Easter sun rises first upon the Moravian settlement at Tranquebar, in the East Indies, and comes last to the Moravian settlement in Wachovia, both in heathen lands." At the moment it startled me, but the fact was pitifully true. Only our Moravian center was provided with ministers and a place of worship. The other settlers were of Lutheran, Reformed, and Church of England stock, but were without pastoral care of any kind, and their children were growing up in ignorance as complete as though this were indeed a heathen land. Our hearts went out to them, but as yet not much could be done for their relief, though later much fraternal service was rendered to them. At this Christmas time their spiritual poverty seemed doubly tragic, and Brother Ettwein gladly told the "heathen" children what the decorations meant, and explained why we older people rejoiced like children in the coming of the Christ Child. The children were so poorly clad that it would have moved a stone to pity, but cold and poverty were forgotten in amazement, and in enjoyment of the piece of cake given to each of them.

The year 1761 made little difference in my life. The Cherokee war continued, and additional cabins were built at the mill to give the refugees more room. Poor Henry Benner's house was pillaged again, but as he and his family were here for the fourteenth time they were not in danger. South Carolina sent troops across her border against the Indians as did Virginia also, and militia from North Carolina and a few Tuscarora Indians joined the Virginians. The report of hundreds of little homes destroyed and of acres and acres of cornfields ruined almost made one feel sorry for the red men, savage as they are, and merciless as they have been. I sometimes wonder whether different treatment in the beginning might have kept them friendly to the whites instead of making them our enemies.

During this year Brother August Schubert arrived as community doctor and our Brother Bonn returned to Bethlehem for four years. Then he came back to us.

There were several deaths among our married people. The calling of Sister Krause left a little boy and girl motherless, and Sister Ettwein came to tell me that the Elders had decided to establish a nursery.

"You have had experience in Pennsylvania, and have practically carried on a nursery here during the past years. Do you approve of extending the work a little, keeping the children at night as well as through the day?"

"What is the plan?" I asked.

"That you shall continue with the three little girls, Salome, Magdalena, and Christine Krause, and that you shall be assisted by Sister Biefel; that Sister Lick and I shall take the little boys." (Sister Biefel and Sister Lick had both become widows.)

"Yes, I approve, and the help will make it possible for me to begin to teach the little girls their letters and a few other things. I have tried already, but could not do much because of my sewing." And so it was arranged.

LIFE BEGINS ANEW

———

LITTLE FACES TO WASH, LITTLE NAILS TO TRIM, LITTLE HANDS THAT must be shown how to use the knitting needles and the pen; little lips and tongues that must be taught the alphabet and helped to utter the morning and the evening prayer; little minds into which ideals of obedience, industry, and courtesy must be instilled; little souls that must be filled with the sweetest and simplest of the Bible stories; little stitches, countless little stitches, that must be set into the seams of coats and dresses. Days filled with little things, to which one grew as accustomed as to the activities of a Single Sister in Pennsylvania. Little things, but needed, useful things, bringing healthy fatigue and a gentle, restful slumber which usually came as I repeated to myself the hymns we had sung in the song service which preceded bedtime, for with the new arrangement establishing the nursery, I was often able to attend the evening service.

By 1762 the Indians had left our neighborhood, the refugees had returned to their farms or had moved to the new houses in Bethania, and blessed peace descended upon Bethabara, able at last to live as the Brethren wished to live. Yet there were a few sad consequences of the stay of the refugees among us, and it gave the Elders grave concern.

"My Brethren," said Brother Ettwein earnestly, at the close of one of our Unity Days, during which several short meetings had been given to the reading of reports from various congregations of our church in distant lands, "My dear Brethren, I feel moved this evening to draw your attention to our own life here. Few settlements of which I know have been founded as ours was, with a definite intent and with the most definite of ideals. At the center of these ideals is our community life. I do not mean the common house-keeping which has been in force here in Bethabara, for as you well know that was established to meet the needs of the frontier and will be given up as soon as circumstances permit. I speak rather of the spirit which has made the common housekeeping possible in spite of certain hardships which it entails in the surrender of individual preferences; I speak of brotherly kindness and mutual aid, of the service of all for the good of all. Our congregation towns, such as Bethabara, are dedicated to this ideal, and the attainment of this ideal is possible only if each resident in the town, man or woman, is resolved to live for the Lord Jesus Christ, to serve according to His will, and therein to be quietly happy. If any among us does not desire this, has a mind set on another goal, he has no place in our congregation and must be content to seek his happiness elsewhere, and in a different way."

"Brother Ettwein is right," said Sister Rosina Kuhnast, as we left the meeting-hall. "The last years have brought so many refu-gees here, have so often interfered with our services, that we have grown careless in our religious life, and need to return to our earlier simplicity and devotion."

"Jacob is worried," said Sister Lash. "He fears that one and another of the Brethren have gone astray and will not be able to remain here."

"He and Brother Kuhnast and Brother Ettwein will do all in their power to reclaim them and save them for the Saviour and the congregation," said I.

"You are right," said Sister Ettwein. "John spoke from his heart this evening, for he feels his responsibilities deeply and yearns over each member of his flock. Oh Sisters, unite your prayers with ours that none of us may renounce the high calling which brought us hither."

Alas, our prayers failed in one instance, and in midsummer

Henry Field left with many tears, having forfeited his right to remain among us by sin which could not be overlooked. So many people were beginning to observe us that we dared not dishonor our Lord by seeming to condone wrong doing, and our leaders also felt constrained to remove a bad example from among us.

In general, however, Brother Ettwein's admonitions had a good effect. Industry prevailed, work was lightened by willing coöperation, and the changing seasons prevented monotony, each bringing its appointed labor, with seed-time blessed in the harvest. A few outside workmen were employed when work pressed in the fields, or for the threshing of the grain, but as much as possible was done by the Brethren themselves, our few Sisters lending a helping hand now and then, especially with the flax.

"What will be done with the cabins no longer needed for refugees?" I one day asked Sister Kuhnast, whose husband was becoming a leader in the life of the village. "Why are more houses being built when we already have this extra space?"

"Some of the cabins will be taken for the handicrafts that need more room, but plans go further than that. I understand there is a feeling that the time has come when the Single Brethren who have built Bethabara should be helped to establish homes of their own."

This was correct, and after conferences, thorough consideration, and discussion, word was sent to Bethlehem asking for the sending of several Single Sisters to become wives of our Single Brethren. This might seem strange to others, but not to us. The leader of the Single Brethren in Pennsylvania had known intimately the colonists who had come to North Carolina; the leader of the Single Sisters was just as intimately acquainted with the young women; the leaders of both groups were members of the Board of Elders in Bethlehem and could discuss the nature and characteristics of each man and select for him a suitable helpmeet. The Brethren in North Carolina agreed to leave the selection to the leaders in Bethlehem, and the Sisters would be consulted and their consent gained before they started south. There was every prospect for happiness in the marriages so arranged, and I have known of no case in which this method failed, during the years when circumstances made it necessary.

Of course it took several months for the important letter to find its way to Bethlehem and for an answer to come, for this was before the days of a regular post, and we must either send a special messenger or entrust our letters to the care of passing travelers, who usually, though not always, conveyed them honestly and safely. Meanwhile things went on as usual in our village, disturbed only a few times by the evil deeds of outsiders.

On one occasion several men came to our tavern and tried to pass counterfeit money. Unfortunately Brother Lash was not at home; so there was no one with authority to arrest them when they became unruly and threatened "to return with sixty men and tear things up."

"They will do nothing of the kind," said Brother Lash, when he returned. In his capacity of justice of the peace he notified the county clerk and sent advertisements to various places warning people to be on the lookout not to accept their false paper. "Counterfeiting is a very serious offense," he told us, "and the law punishes it very severely; so I think we have heard the last of that company."

"I wish Jacob did not have to leave home again," said his wife a few days later; "it makes me nervous to have him away. Scamps seem to note his going and take that chance to come and annoy us."

"Where is he going this time?"

"To Virginia. You know the Brethren have been looking for days to find those horses they thought had strayed away. Now Jacob has heard that they have been seen in Virginia and he must go and reclaim them."

"Can he prove that they belong to Bethabara?"

"Yes, surely. Have you forgotten that all our horses and cattle are branded with the Bethabara mark, which is registered at the court-house in Salisbury?"

"I hope he will find them in the hands of an honest man who

will not refuse to give them up when he learns that they were stolen." Fortunately this was the case, and although they had to travel one hundred and twenty miles, Brother Lash and the companion he took with him had no great trouble in proving ownership; the man who surrendered them demanded only that they would prosecute the thief, which they did at the next General Court in Rowan County.

In an attempt to increase our trade, wagons were sent to Petersburg, Virginia, and to Charleston, South Carolina.

From the beginning of Bethabara our craftsmen had furnished the most necessary articles, shoes, flour, pottery, buckskin breeches, and the like, but such things as salt, glass for window-panes, sugar, coffee, and spices must be brought from outside. Apart from the very occasional shipments from Bethlehem we had been dependent on what could be secured from Springhill, a storehouse which had been built on the Cape Fear River, to which flat-bottomed boats brought some supplies from the harbor at Brunswick. To Springhill (later known as Cross Creek and then Fayetteville) our wagons took flour, and brought back salt and whatever else could be found there. I remember one occasion on which the return load included rose-bushes, rosemary, Chickasaw plums, and a kind of pine with very long leaves, all of which were set out in the village garden.

During the Cherokee war we had a visit from Colonel Henry Laurens, a wine merchant, from Charleston, South Carolina, who made himself very pleasant and suggested that when he had returned from the expedition against the Indians he would be glad to execute any commissions which the Brethren might care to send to him in Charleston. Many deer-skins were being brought to Bethabara to be bartered for goods at our store; so it was decided to take advantage of the offer of Colonel Laurens and send deer-skins to Charleston, to be exchanged for molasses, wine, hardware, glass, and anything else which would be an addition to the stock in our store. The trade thus begun with Charleston continued for many years; the wagon sent to Petersburg did not fare so well, and there was little further contact with that place until much later.

Jacob Steiner and John Rank took the first wagons to Charleston, and brought back a pleasant letter from Colonel Laurens, and with it a small keg of almonds and raisins which he had sent as a gift to our children. My small Salome was wild with delight over this unexpected present, the other children also, and we elders were not far behind in our appreciation of his kindness.

It was in the latter part of May, 1762, that Brother Henry Herbst suddenly arrived in Bethabara bringing word that Brother Graff and his party had reached Wilmington. "We came in a sloop chartered in Philadelphia," he reported, "and the voyage was long and trying. They are resting a few days to give me time to reach Bethabara; then they will take boats on the Cape Fear to Springhill, and ask that you will send the wagons to meet them there."

"Who is in the party?"

"Brother Graff and his wife, Brother Gammern and his wife, Brother Philip Transou, his wife and three children, one widow, and four Single Sisters."

"No more?"

"Well, I was with them, but I am here now."

"Henry," said Brother Ettwein, looking at him keenly, "you are hiding something. Who else is with them?"

Brother Herbst laughed, "Honestly, Brother Ettwein, there is no one else. I admit that Brother Graff is bringing something as a surprise to the congregation, but he told me not to tell of it."

"Then we ask no more questions," said Brother Ettwein, gravely. "A messenger should be very careful to follow instructions, and no one should seek to make him false to his trust."

That put an end to questions but not to surmises, and for the time that it took our two wagons to go to Springhill and return with the company there was much guessing as to what the "surprise" might be, the suggestions ranging all the way from a bag of coffee to a box of looking-glasses. Brother Herbst laughed and looked mysterious and thoroughly enjoyed the excitement, which he made no effort to allay, giving no information except an occasional shake of the head, and that but seldom.

And when they did arrive it proved that the "surprise" was worth the suspense, for Brother Graff had brought a small pipe organ, the first in western North Carolina. Great was the joy in Bethabara as he set it up in the meeting-hall, tested it, and found that it had not suffered during the seven weeks of travel by sea and over land. Everybody agreed that it was better than anything we had imagined, and though it had but one register Brother Graff's use of it was a great addition to our services and a source of much enjoyment to those of us who loved music, and most of us did.

Brother and Sister Graff came to take over the pastoral care of the married people in our two Moravian congregations, and Brother Gammern had been sent to relieve Brother Jacob Lash of part of his responsibilities, which had grown too heavy for one man to carry. Philip Transou and his family decided to settle in Bethania, and went there as soon as proper arrangements could be made. The five Sisters who came as prospective brides probably attracted the most attention, and within a day or two Brother Ettwein made an important announcement.

"Tomorrow afternoon," he said, "Sister Ettwein and I will open our home to the five Sisters and to the five Single Brethren who have asked for wives. This will give them a chance to become acquainted with each other. Then no definite plans will be made for two weeks, and during that time they are requested to consider every phase of the matter, and see whether any changes should be made." Only one alteration was needed, it developed, and that not personal. Brother Hans Petersen's house was not ready, and his marriage was postponed until November; meanwhile his future wife, Sister Elisabeth Palmer, helped with the little girls in the nursery.

That I would have any part in the proposed marriages had not occurred to me, and it was without any premonition that I welcomed Sister Ettwein to my room one afternoon. Her words filled me with astonishment. "Sister Catharina" (why did she call me that instead of Sister Kalberlahn? I wondered), "I have a message for you. I come to bring you a proposal of marriage from Brother

Reuter. This has been approved, and we hope you will consent. There are many reasons why it is wise for a widow to re-marry here, for we have no arrangements for a Widows House, and you are too young to spend the rest of your life sewing and taking care of the nursery."

I had been feeling middle-aged and in a measure set aside from active life, and for a moment could think of nothing to say except, "But there are others."

"Yes, there are two others in the same circumstances, and we are making like proposals to them; at least I am to do so as soon as I leave your room."

"But oh, my doctor!" That I did not say aloud, but Sister Ettwein must have read my thought in my face, for rising to go she took my hand, saying kindly, "Think it over, Sister Catharina, and remember that Brother Kalberlahn always thought of others. I think he would advise you to do what is best for you and for the congregation; I feel sure he would rather have you wedded to Brother Reuter than continuing through life alone. Companionship with a good man is worth while, even if it lacks the romance which I think you once had."

It was a hard night to which she left me. Restlessly I tossed from side to side, reliving the past, loving it, reluctant to give it up, half dreading and half wishing to begin life anew. Finally I fell into uneasy slumber, and suddenly Martin stood beside me, the old light shining in his eyes, the old smile on his lips, as he looked down upon me. "Dear Little One," he said, "rest content. Take the hand of this good man and journey on with him. It is ordained that in the world men and women should marry and be given in marriage, and in this heavenly country there is no jealousy. We know and we understand."

Was it a dream or was Martin sent to bring healing to my troubled soul as four years earlier he had brought healing to my injured body? I do not know, and it does not matter. I awoke refreshed and content, ready for the next step in life.

On Sunday, June the 27th, we had a lovefeast, that "meal in

common" which in its essence so much resembles the Agape of the early Christians. This was a very special lovefeast, however, for at its close there was the formal betrothal of seven couples, Brother Reuter and I among them, a record which has never since been equaled in Wachovia.

During the three weeks which intervened before our wedding, life went on with little reference to us. Brother Gammern was busy settling the matter of the leases in Bethania, where most of the residents took leases for the lifetime of themselves and their children, each to pay a yearly rent for town lot, garden, and farm land.

It was reported that Governor Dobbs was on his way to visit Bethabara, and the Brethren Gammern and Lash rode to meet him. They returned to report that they had found him most friendly, that they had discussed the necessary matters with him, and that as he was old and the heat intense he would not come further.

Some alarm was caused by an apparently credible report that the Cherokees were about to take the war path again, but nothing came of it, to our great relief.

The 18th of July was the day appointed for our wedding. On that Sunday morning Brother Ettwein went to Bethania, where he preached, held a meeting for the children, and then performed the marriage ceremony for Peter Hauser and Margaret Elisabeth Spoenhauer, who had learned to know each other while refugees at our mill.

In Bethabara Brother Graff led the church liturgy and preached on the Gospel for the day, and it gave me a thrill, as it always did, to remember that our assignment of the Gospel lessons had been arranged in the days of the early Christian Church, and that their use by us was a living link between our church and that of the first centuries after Christ.

Then came the afternoon, and two by two we entered the meeting-hall and were given front seats, the entire congregation of Bethabara and practically all of Bethania assembled on the benches behind us.

It was a strange repetition of the scene in Bethlehem four years earlier, though two of the sixteen of today had already taken their vows. Then my companion had been my doctor, blond, tall and strong. Today I sat beside the surveyor of Wachovia, a man but little taller than myself, dark-haired and slightly built. The similarity and the differences seemed to emphasize the fact that I was beginning life anew, and with half a sigh I turned my thoughts from myself to listen to what was going on around us.

The playing of Brother Graff on the organ was sweet and solemn, and in the same strain was his address on the text selected for the day. He also led the marriage liturgy which was sung without accompaniment. Four of the couples were united by him, and then Brother Ettwein took his place in front of the Communion table and we stood before him.

"I now ask thee, my Brother Christian, wilt thou have our Sister Catharina, here present, to thy wedded wife . . .?"

"Yes."

"In like manner I now ask thee, my Sister Catharina . . .?"

"Yes." And we knelt as the blessing was pronounced.

Twice more the questions were asked and answered; and then we left the meeting-hall and turned into the small room adjoining, where Sister Graff and Sister Ettwein joined us. When I became a Single Sister in Bethlehem I donned the white linen cap with pink ribbons at which we girls had laughed when Miss Anna wore them, but which seemed quite natural in the Sisters House. When I married Martin my pink ribbon was exchanged for the light blue ribbon of the Married Sister. When Martin went home Sister Spangenberg tied in the white ribbon of widowhood, tears streaming down her cheeks. Now, with a smile, Sister Ettwein replaced the white ribbon with a fresh ribbon of blue, and as I turned to rejoin Christian he whispered, "My wife!"

There was no time for more, for we must needs return to the meeting-hall, where a lovefeast had been arranged in honor of the newly wed and as our official welcome into the group of Married People; the married people of the two towns and a few Single Brethren were the guests.

Christian was a shy man, who found it hard to open his heart to anyone, and his first self-revelation came by chance, when I happened to say that I had hesitated to move to Bethlehem with my family, but had been led to go by a dream.

"I, too, have dreamed," he said, and I replied, "Yes, I know," remembering the poem which had brought comfort to me after the home-going of my doctor. He looked surprised, and I hastened to explain that one of the Sisters had shown me the poem he wrote during the fever epidemic, and that I had liked it; then I coaxed him to tell me of the dream he had in mind, which was evidently another. It was hard to get him started, but he finally yielded, flushing a little as though embarrassed, and explained that after he reached Pennsylvania he heard so much talk of conditions in North Carolina that he felt that he could not possibly go thither. He feared the red men; he feared the thunder-storms and the sharp lightning; he feared the snakes lurking in the tall grass; he feared that on that distant frontier he would lose touch with God. "I was a great coward, my wife," he said sadly, "and in my fear I decided to remain in Pennsylvania, or even return to Germany where I was sure of work in my profession."

"But you did come!"

"It was my dream that brought me," and again he hesitated. I waited, and with a look in his eyes that suddenly made me feel that I was entering with him into a holy place he finally continued: "All day I had been afraid, afraid to go and afraid not to go. At last I fell asleep and dreamed that I stood on Calvary. The agony that I endured woke me, and unable to keep still I arose, dressed, and went out to pace the streets for an hour. Finally I went back to bed, and fell asleep, but only to dream again. This time the Saviour spoke to me, and I heard Him say: 'Christian, why do you fear? You can remain here if you wish, and you will not lose your religion thereby; but I have no one else to send to North Carolina, and without you the Brethren there will be sorely distressed. Will you not go for My sake? Surely I will go with you.' 'Yes, my Lord, I will go,' I whispered back, and the vision vanished. The next thing I knew the sun was streaming through my window and a new day had begun. I still feared, but to myself I said, 'What my Brethren can dare, that can I, with the arm of the Almighty to sustain me.' To the Bethlehem Brethren I said simply, 'Tell me when you wish me to start; I will be ready at any time.' They never knew of my hesitation, nor of the reason for my decision; no one has ever known save you, my wife." And I knew that in giving me this confidence he had sealed his marriage vows forever.

"A coward, Christian?" I murmured, putting my arm around him, for as his recital ended he had buried his face in his hands. "You are no coward. It is braver to go forward in spite of fear than never to feel afraid. No man in Wachovia has shown as much courage as you when in spite of such feelings you have tramped the hills and valleys of Wachovia from end to end, making the maps which you know the Brethren need. You are brave, Christian, and I am proud of you and proud to be your wife," and his hand found mine and drew my arm closer around him, and I laid my head on his shoulder in silence.

Christian loved the out-of-doors and so did I, and as long as summer lasted we took many a late afternoon stroll up the path toward God's Acre, sitting for a while on one or another of the rude benches which the Brethren had built along the way, for the path was steep. There we talked of many things, and once I asked him to tell me of his childhood. His face clouded as he said slowly, "It was not a happy childhood and I wish I could forget it."

"What was the matter?" I asked, thinking that if he told me it might make forgetting easier.

"My father was a fanatic on the subject of religion and also a dreamer of dreams, and the combination was hard on his family. When he dreamed that the comfortable living he was making for us by his practice as a doctor was as a huge sack of gold around his neck which kept him from passing through a narrow defile that led to eternal life, he abandoned home and friends and, taking us with him, began to roam around, earning a little now and then but not enough to support us. Often we were hungry, always we were homeless and forlorn."

"And did he feel no pity for you?"

"Not enough to make him settle down again. When my mother begged him to consider her and the children, he would tell her sternly not to mistrust the Lord; and remarkable things occurred just often enough to strengthen his conviction that we would be cared for."

"Remarkable things?"

"Yes, such as this. We were almost starving, and even his self-confidence was shaken. Gathering us about him he offered a most fervent prayer for help, and even as he prayed there was a knock at the door. Opening it, he found the servant of a wealthy lady of the village, reputed to be most miserly, and yet she had sent a basket full of food to the utter strangers at her gate, a supply that lasted us for days."

"How had she heard of you?"

"We never knew. My father said that the Lord had told her, even as He told the ravens to feed Elijah."

"Why did the Lord not tell your father to make a home for his family?"

"I often wondered, but if He did my father never heeded."

"He must have been a hard man."

"Hard he was, and especially to me, for I was a luckless lad, with bones which broke easily, and I was often in trouble. Whenever I broke a bone he set it skillfully enough, but he scolded all the while, until I was ready to bear almost any pain rather than ask him for help. Indeed at the end I went for months with a foot bleeding from injuries received when a horse stepped on it, and did not tell him because I dreaded his tongue more than the really severe pain."

"You say 'at the end'—how did you finally escape?"

"I ran away and went to an older brother who had found

work on a large estate. The owner made a place for me among the apprentices of a surveyor, thinking that if I proved useful he could employ me."

"So in the end your father's harshness drove you into your life-work."

"I suppose one might say that, though I had not thought of it. Thank you, my wife, you have given me new light on the leading of the Lord. It was a rough road, but it did have an end that was worth while, since it brought me here to serve the Brethren."

And his service to the Brethren was many-sided. In addition to his work as a surveyor he helped with the keeping of the accounts, taught arithmetic to the boys, and before long took charge of the store, in which I was able to help him. We were also appointed to the group of those who served in the meeting-hall, seating the members and the visitors, serving the buns and the tea in the lovefeast, seeing that all was done decently and in order. He of course, was on the side occupied by the Brethren and I on the side of the Sisters, but we could plan together, and together we shared in the special lovefeast for the sacristans, which was held in November for the first time.

We also had opportunity to meet the distinguished visitors who began to come to Bethabara, some drawn by curiosity, some by our well-kept tavern, our store, our handicrafts, and the chance for trade. Early in October a botanist from Philadelphia came to the village, and Christian greatly enjoyed showing him around. He was interested in our medical garden, and even more in our wild flowers and shrubs. Christian had been watching the flowers ever since he came to Carolina, and could tell him of those which bloomed in the spring and show him where they grew, and the botanist listened intently, examining every little plant which Christian pointed out to him.

"This slope below your God's Acre is a veritable treasure-house," he exclaimed. "I wish I could spend a year here and list each flower as it budded during the spring and summer! Mr. Reuter, can you not do that? It would be a valuable contribution to the science of botany, and to you has been given the opportunity which is denied to me."

Christian modestly expressed a doubt whether he was qualified for such work, but our visitor was so certain and so insistent that Christian tentatively agreed. During the two years which followed he noted and recorded many things, finally producing a list of the plants and shrubs grown in our gardens, and also of the wild flowers, bushes, and trees, the birds, wild beasts, and snakes that were found in our territory. Brother Graff learned what he was doing and constantly encouraged him, finally asking him to deposit the list in the church archives ready for the return of this botanist or a visit from any other.

Of course I was interested in what he did, but the part of the list which most appealed to me was that which showed the vegetables and grains that Bethabara was then using: beans, cabbage, celery, cucumbers, field peas and garden peas, rhubarb, turnips, garlic, head lettuce, cress, pumpkins, Irish potatoes, sweet potatoes, leeks, horse-radish, water-melons, mush-melons, parsnips, radishes, mustard, Spanish pepper, chives, spinach, asparagus, salsify, onions, hops, grapes, currants, flax and hemp, eight kinds of grain, cotton, tobacco, and gourds—what a contrast to the cornmeal mush and stewed pumpkin of the first Moravian settlers here! Of course luxuries like chocolate and coffee must still be brought from seaboard cities, but by 1762 Wachovia had become self-supporting in the essential foods, with many things that were not absolutely necessary to life but added much to its comfort and pleasure.

I also remember 1762 as the year in which the lighted wax tapers were first used in our lovefeast on Christmas Eve. I think it must have been Sister Gertrude Graff who suggested them, for she came from the neighborhood of Marienborn, in Wetteravia, where Brother John von Watteville had introduced the tapers at a Christmas Eve service for the children fifteen years earlier. At least she knew at once where to find the account of that service in a file of church newspapers which she and Brother Graff brought with them when they came to Wachovia. It quoted the address which Brother von Watteville then made to the children, in which he "spoke of the inexpressible blessedness which came through the birth of Christ," spoke also of the "flame of love" which burned in the heart of Christ, leading Him to give himself for the redemption of the world, which should kindle an answering flame in the heart of every child who heard the story. He told them that each child was about to receive a lighted wax taper, tied with a small red ribbon, to remind them all of what he had just explained to them; and the account in the old church paper even gave the verse he sang for them:

> "Oh little Jesus, Thee I love!
>   Kindle a pure and holy flame
> Within the heart of every child
>   Like that which from Thine own heart came."

The analogy was over the head of my small Salome, but her eyes danced as she held the lighted wax taper, and I think she comprehended something of the blessed Christmas story as Brother Graff told it in simple language to the little ones in their service at six o'clock in the evening. At eight o'clock there was a lovefeast for the older members of the congregation, with Christmas hymns sung in German and in English. In a later meeting the story of the birth of Christ was read from a harmony of the Gospels, and the service closed with the hymn *Te Logos*.

II.

WE PLAN

JUST WHEN THE BRETHREN BEGAN TO DISCUSS THE BUILDING OF
our central town I do not know. Perhaps the ending of the
Indian war brought up the question, or perhaps Brother Gammern
had been instructed to introduce it, for he had come as attorney for
the Unity and was empowered to look after the landed interests.

Opinions expressed by the men naturally found their echoes
among the women, and we discussed them at length.

"It does seem too bad to make a change," said Sister Kuhnast.
"Christopher thinks of all the labor that has been expended on our
fields and on our houses, and of all the expense that must be met if
we start over again at a new place."

"Christian says that in the center of our tract the ground is
hilly, with few natural meadows and not much timber of the right
sort for the building of log houses," said I.

"On the other hand," said Sister Lash, "there is the undeniable
fact that we have much fever in Bethabara, which Brother Schubert
thinks comes from the frequent flooding of the meadows, and if a
town were placed on a hill that might prevent the recurring attacks."

"What does Brother Jacob think?"

"He regrets the expense of moving, but thinks it may be possible to continue the farms here, leaving Bethabara a village as was
first intended, while the handicrafts might be moved to the new
town, making that the center of the trades and the seat of the governing boards. He reminds me that the Wachovia land actually be-
longs to the Unity as a whole, and that the decision rests with the

central board in Herrnhut, which must consider the interests of the shareholders of the land company through which the purchase was made possible as well as the convenience of the settlers here."

"But travelers are in the habit of coming to the Bethabara tavern and store."

"Jacob sees no reason for worrying about that. The tavern and store here might be continued as long as they are needed, and until people turn naturally to the new town as a larger place and better for trade."

"Does Brother Reuter think it will be possible to find a place in the middle of the tract where a town could be built?"

"Oh yes, he says it can be done, but the manner of laying out the streets must be governed by the character of the land."

"Well certainly there is no special arrangement of streets in Bethabara," said Sister Graff. "The houses appear to have been built rather at haphazard around the open space in the center of the village, and none of them for permanence. I was struck by that as soon as I saw them."

"Coming as you did from an old country like Wetteravia you would notice that more than I, who was born in the country in Pennsylvania," said I. "Can you tell us, Sister Graff, what our Brethren are going to do about all this?"

"Michael says that they have decided to write to the Central Elders and leave the matter to their decision, and that action here will be in accord with what they say."

"Then we may as well forget it for a year or two; it takes so long for letters to cross the ocean and return." And we let it go at that.

Of all the newcomers to our community I was most attracted to Sister Graff. She had a sweet face and a pleasant voice, and had seen a good deal of the life in our European congregations. She had also been a member of the Zinzendorf household, and her presence there was in keeping with the unique character of its head, always on the lookout for promising young people to win for the Lord.

She was born in a small village near the castle of Marienborn, she told me, where she lived uneventfully until she was about seventeen years of age.

"One day," she said, "I was sent to a neighboring village for a coffer and was returning, carrying it on my head as the villagers do. Following a path behind the Marienborn inn, I saw a man, dressed in a plain brown suit, walking with his head bent as though in deep meditation. I had no idea who he was, but from his appearance assumed that he was a pastor of some village church. He greeted me pleasantly, asked where I lived, and drew me into conversation with courteous questions about my life and family. Noting my burden he went with me almost to our village, helping me over several ditches and narrow foot-bridges.

"When my home was in sight he stopped, and in saying goodbye asked if I knew who he was? I did not, and when he said that he was Count Zinzendorf I was so astounded that I could not say one word, but stood rooted to the ground and speechless. Smiling he turned away; then I hurried home, but when I told what had happened no one believed me. A few days later our pastor reported that the Count had made inquiries about me; then we heard that he had left home and was sailing for the West Indies.

"Some weeks passed, and the incident had been almost forgotten, when my mother received a message from Countess Zinzendorf, bidding her come to the castle. There she was told that the Count had suggested that I be taken into service, and was asked whether she would be willing. Of course it was a great opportunity for me and my mother gladly gave her permission, and so I went. There were many other persons in the household, some older, some younger, and I soon became accustomed to my duties, which included the care of little Elisabeth, daughter of the Countess. When the Count returned he said he was glad to see me there, and for the rest of his life he counted me among his 'adopted children,' no meaningless term, for he gave us the care and training and spiritual instruction due from a father, and in return we gave him affection and reverence."

"I suppose you were a Lutheran before you went to the castle?"

"Yes, but it was not long before I asked permission to join the Unity, and was accepted. My parents were displeased, for they had not thought of that possibility when they gave me permission to enter the service of the Countess, but I was old enough to decide for myself and remained firm. To make the situation easier for me I was sent for a while to another Moravian congregation, but later I was often at Marienborn. In the course of time I married Michael Graff and served with him in various congregations until we were called to America."

"You must have met many of the leaders of our church."

"Practically all of them, I think. Many of them were trained while serving in the household of the Count and Countess; and all of them visited there from time to time."

"When did you come to Pennsylvania? I remember meeting you there, but quite casually."

"We came in 1751, but you were in the Sisters House, while we had oversight of the nurseries; and when you went to the nursery we were stationed at Nazareth. I heard of you from time to time, and wanted to see more of you, but circumstances always prevented. Now we may be the friends I have always felt we should be." A sentiment which I echoed heartily.

Partly through my friendship with Sister Graff and more through my husband, I now became an active and interested member of the Bethabara community. After my years of seclusion it was delightful to gather with the women in the little house by the creek, where as we washed the clothes our tongues flew fast in the exchange of ideas or items which happened to be foremost at the moment.

"Did you watch the eclipse of the sun yesterday?"

"Yes, indeed, and it gave me a queer, creepy feeling to see things grow dark in the daytime."

"Christian says that in olden days an eclipse frightened people terribly, for they did not understand its cause."

"Did he explain it to you?"

"Yes," and then I repeated his words as best I could, rather proud of my well-informed husband.

On another day we were alarmed when Sister Lash said, "Jacob has received a report that the Indians are out again on New River, and that refugees are coming to Bethabara. The Brethren are to have a conference immediately to decide whether to rebuild our stockade or to erect a guard-house at the end of the village."

"I hear that Brother Gammern favors the guard-house here, and a strengthening of the stockade at the mill."

"Remembering our experiences in 1759 I believe that would be the wiser, for the fever was more fatal than the red men," so one of the Sisters who had lived through that fearful time. I said nothing, but thought of Martin and shuddered.

"Let us pray that the Indians do not come again," said another —and they did not come.

One day I created quite a sensation by bringing in a handful of four- and five-leaved clovers, and one with seven leaves. "Where did I find them? Oh little Salome and I walked out to the end of the big meadow and chanced upon a large patch of clover with many of these unusual leaves. Yes, we left plenty for the rest of you to pick"; and when work was over there was a general exodus to the big meadow and many leaves were gathered, though no one found another stem with seven leaves.

As intimate converse turned wash-day into almost a pleasure, so did the pulling and retting of the flax have its happy side as we worked together in the fields, singing sometimes, and thinking of the shirts and towels and other necessary things which our flax would make when it had been broken and swingled and hackled and spun and woven. The Brethren did the heavy work of breaking and hackling, and some of the weaving, but the rest of it fell to us.

Even the sewing to which I still gave many hours had lost its monotony. When from my window I saw the snow lie thick upon the ground I was no longer homesick for Pennsylvania but I thought of the winter grain, safe beneath its white blanket, preparing to feed us through another year. True, it would be impossible to go to the meeting-hall that night; the bell did not ring, which meant that because of the weather there would be no service, but Christian sat on the other side of the table, busy with his maps and plats, stopping now and then to tell me of this or the other visitor who had come to the tavern. "Those rowdy long hunters are here again," he might say; or "We have distinguished visitors tonight, the Chief Justice of North Carolina and some of the lawyers have come in and are glad enough to reach here. They say we have the best tavern for many miles around." Then tax-paying time would come and I would hear: "Colonel Frohock has arrived to collect the taxes. Our Brethren make it a matter of conscience to pay promptly; so we are in favor with the officials, who have trouble enough in other places."

One evening when I was knitting and incidentally watching Christian draw one of his neat maps I asked him how he learned to draw. With the reminiscent look which I had learned to know he answered: "What talent I have is God-given. The first surveyor to whom I was apprenticed died before I had learned much. The second was under the influence of one of the boys, his nephew, who did not like it that I had been sent there and had determined to injure me. One day, probably at his suggestion, the master brought me a sheet covered with figures and ordered me to go to my room and draw the plat and be quick about it. You may imagine my consternation, for I had not the slightest idea how to proceed. Then I thought of my father's prayers and the remarkable answers given to him; so I fell on my knees and begged the Lord for help. When I seated myself and re-read the figures I suddenly saw what they meant, drafted them, and took the plat to the master, who was so much surprised and pleased that he gave me a little present, and thereafter saw that I was carefully taught."

"What did the unkind boy do?" I asked.

"He was much annoyed, but there was nothing he could do then. Later he imposed on me rather often, forcing me to draw his maps and claiming the credit for them, but it was easier to submit than to fight, and after all each one I drew gave me that much more practice."

"So in the course of time you became a trained surveyor."

"Yes, I was what they call a royal surveyor, and might have made something of a name for myself as well as a good living had I continued in my profession there, but I felt called to the Unity of Brethren, and after many experiences with them in Europe I came to America and to Wachovia."

"In Europe you would have been one of many; here you are the master surveyor, and your work will stand through the years as your own work for your own people."

"You are right, and I do not think back with longing, only with interest, glad of the training for service here."

I think it was my husband who discovered that the great pile of rock which forms the top of the Pilot Mountain furnished good whet-stone, and occasionally a group of our Brethren took a few days off to go thither. No one seemed to know where this strange, solitary peak got its name, but a pilot it was, visible for many miles around. I was a bit ashamed of my childish imagination, and I never told it, but it always looked to me as if some huge giant had taken a huge bite out of the top of the mountain, leaving the end for a second bite which he never took. It was this uneaten end which the men liked to climb, and they said the view from the top was wonderful. I should have liked to see it, but my husband thought the climb too difficult for any woman; so we Sisters stayed at home.

After so many years my memories are not all in sequence, and a summer cyclone, a winter snow, flax, snakes, and Indian alarms are all mixed up, but I do remember that 1764 was an important year to us, for several reasons.

Arthur Dobbs, the governor of North Carolina, being old and stricken in years, resigned, and Governor William Tryon arrived to take his place, though he did not assume office until the next year. In the fall our Brethren Marshall and Gammern went to the eastern part of the state to bid farewell to the one and welcome the other. It was the last time they saw Governor Dobbs, who died soon after, but of Governor Tryon we heard and saw much in the years that followed.

Brother Frederic William Marshall had been appointed the preceding year to have charge of the general affairs of Wachovia as representative of the Unity of Brethren, and in October he had come to Bethabara on a visit, accompanied by Brother Jacob Ernst, who returned with him to Bethlehem but soon came back to become a permanent resident of Wachovia.

Before Brother Marshall left Bethlehem, where he was then living, word had reached us that we were to proceed with the building of the long-projected central town, and my husband had been studying the various parts of our tract, preparing to suggest various sites for the consideration of the officials. With the arrival of Brother Marshall in October the selection of the town site became the chief object of interest. Time after time a group of the Brethren went out to look at a possible site which had been examined by Christian. He suggested a number of places, even some which he could not recommend and which they decided not to consider because of the lack of water, lack of good building timber, or distance from the center of the Wachovia tract. Others failed of acceptance for reasons which were scarcely understood, and sometimes Christian grew discouraged.

"I do wish we could find the right place," he said one evening, seating himself wearily before the fire. "We look and discard and look again until I scarcely know what to do next. I thought we surely had found something that would do, but today the Elders have presented the matter to the Lord and not one of the suggested sites was approved."

The use of the *lot* was our method of ascertaining the will of the Lord in any important matter, and in spite of his lament my husband would never have been content with a site which did not draw the affirmative; so after a night's rest he was ready for further search, which continued for the closing weeks of that year and the first month of the next.

It was the evening of February 14, 1765, when Christian came

AUG. GOTTLIEB SPANGENBERG

Episcopus Fratrum

Bishop August Gottlieb Spangenberg

Frontispiece in the Leben August Gottlieb Spangenbergs, *printed in Barby in 1794. Copy in the Salem Moravian Archives.*

Zeisberger Preaching to the Indians

From a painting in the Bethlehem Archives.

"A View of Bethlehem in Pennsylvania"

From an engraving published in 1757. Original in the Salem Moravian Archives.

in with a radiant face, exclaiming, "Wife, Wife, the Lord has given us the site for our central town!" I asked where it was, and he took out his map and showed me. "See, this is the central portion of Wachovia, where we were told to select a suitable site. This is the Wach, a creek which, as you see, runs into Muddy Creek. From the Wach a ridge runs northward to higher ground, and about one third of the way up there are good springs and a little branch which I have never found dry, not even in summer. This place should be high enough above the Wach to avoid trouble by floods in time of heavy rain, and I hope we shall also be free of the fever which has beset us in Bethabara. The land is not very fertile, but will probably suffice for gardens, and at any rate the town must depend on neighboring farms, for most of us are craftsmen, not farmers. There is little good building timber, but in one of the natural meadows near the Wach, Potter Aust has found clay which he is sure he can use in making pottery, and which can also be used for making brick and tile. That means the building of houses much more substantial than those of Bethabara."

"What about the town plan?" I asked, for Christian had told me of the plan, drawn abroad, which provided for a central Square, with the main houses of the congregation grouped around it, and the streets radiating from it like spokes of a wheel.

"That plan will not do at all," he said. "The ridge is much too narrow, but Brother Marshall promises to consider the matter and send a more suitable plan from Bethlehem."

"When the town is built will we move there?" I asked.

"Certainly. It is planned that all the officials, all the craftsmen, shall move, leaving in Bethabara a branch of the store, the tavern, enough of the Brethren and Sisters to carry on the farm, and doubtless a pastor to hold the services and minister to the religious needs of the group."

"Then Christian—,"

"Yes, my wife, what is it?" for he saw that I hesitated.

"I was thinking that I should like a home of our own, just for the two of us," for little Salome had been sent to Bethlehem the preceding year that she might attend school there as her father had desired. (It was hard to give up the child, whom I loved as my own, and would have been harder still had I known that ere many years passed smallpox would take her life.) "When the plan for the town has been adopted could you not reserve a lot for us and build a small house on it, a house that would be truly our own? I have not minded the common housekeeping here, and realize that it was a wonderful help when the settlement was young, but I think that as we grow older we would enjoy our own home, one which we owned and in which we could do as we pleased so long as we did not disturb the neighbors."

"There speaks the daughter of the successful pioneer, Henry Antes," he laughed; then fearing that I might feel rebuked he added, "My thought has been much the same as yours, for time must change many things for us, and just as soon as I have the proposed plan, you shall select your lot and I will build your house; so be planning what you want."

"Just a small, simple house, Christian, but yours and mine," and many a time during the next years my thoughts ran forward to the little home that was to be my own.

The site for the central town having been selected Brother Marshall returned to Bethlehem, and life in Wachovia resumed its accustomed way. Hunters brought in hundreds of pounds of deerskins, of which Bethabara used what it needed and shipped the rest to Charleston to barter for store goods. Visitors came and went, among them my three brothers Friedrich, William, and Henry Antes, who drove down from Pennsylvania in a chaise to see their sister and the settlement in which she lived. They liked my husband and stayed to share in his birthday breakfast before returning to the north. More than six years had passed since I had seen them, and it may well be imagined how eager I was to hear all the details concerning family and friends, though their laughing suggestion that I go home with them was as merrily refused.

A report drifted in that England wanted more money from her colonies and proposed to get it by requiring that all legal papers be written on stamped paper, which her agents would sell at a price. Christian looked grave. "England is making a mistake," he said. "The settlers in North Carolina are not meek subjects; they are an independent lot, and they will resent such a tax imposed by legislative bodies in which they are not represented." And resent it they did, and so energetically that England had to give up that plan and seek another way to raise revenue from her distant colonies.

Then Brother Marshall's letter arrived, bringing the town plan prepared by him. When Christian showed it to me I saw that it was really three alternative plans laid one upon another so that the relative advantages of each might be studied on the ground. The one Christian liked best, which was selected, called for a main street beginning at the ford through the Wach and running north on the ridge; there was a parallel street to the east and another to the west, and several cross streets. The open Square was to occupy a space between the main street, the east street, and two cross streets. The first family houses were to be built on the west side of the main street, facing the block north of the Square. Christian smiled when my finger sought the southwest corner of an intersection of the main street and a cross street three blocks further south; then he chuckled.

"The pioneer daughter does not want close neighbors! Very well, my wife, I will try to get that corner for you." And get it he did, for Christian usually achieved what he set out to do.

12

THE CENTRAL TOWN BEGINS

―――――――

THE NIGHT BETWEEN THE FIFTH AND SIXTH OF JANUARY, 1766, was the coldest that I can remember. Everything that could freeze froze, even to the drugs dissolved in spirits which burst their bottles on the shelves of the apothecary shop.

"Surely, Christian," I said, my teeth chattering in spite of the good fire which Christian had built up in the living room before he let me throw off the quilts in our ice-cold bedroom, "surely the Brethren will not try to go today to the new town site to begin building."

"Yes, wife, we probably will go," he answered placidly. "Midwinter is the best time to cut timber for building, and logs cut then outlast those cut later in the year. Besides exercise will keep us warm, and the temperature will probably rise in the course of the day."

"Is it necessary for you to go with them?"

"Certainly, since I must show them the place which I have selected for the building of the first log house. It is on the west side of the ridge, between what will be a back street and the branch which will supply the water we need; the spot must be cleared of brush, for it has no trees, but there are good trees for logs in the immediate neighborhood, and it is not far from the site selected for the town itself."

"But you will come back tonight?"

"I doubt it. The Brethren plan to take a tent and camp in the woods, and I will stay with them and come back with the wagon.

Don't worry, Wife, I will be all right," and he patted my shoulder in a reassuring little way he had when he saw that I was troubled.

And go they did, some from Bethabara and some from Bethania, the men walking and the wagon taking their tools, the tent, bedding, and cooking utensils, together with tile for covering the house. The ground was hard as stone, and the wagon jerked and bounced, so that much of the tile was broken before they reached the end of the new road which had been cleared, for six miles is a long way over such a road in such weather.

When they finally reached their destination the horses were unharnessed, the men gathered around the tree which Christian had selected, and singing as they worked they felled it for one of the sills of the new house.

The leaders of our Unity have always taken pleasure in linking the spiritual idea with the temporal action. When the immigrants from Moravia gathered in Saxony in 1722 to fell the first tree for the new town which was to be Herrnhut, Christian David swung his axe and recited the third verse of the eighty-fourth Psalm. Even so the Brethren of Wachovia saw nothing inappropriate in the singing of a hymn as they swung their axes, for they were beginning to build a city dedicated to the service of God and their fellow men, a place in which they hoped to establish homes and live honest, industrious, useful lives which should praise their Saviour and Creator. That some would fall short of this high ideal was to be expected, but their intent was true and their aim commendable, and that day their hearts were as warm as their hands were cold.

So the trees fell and the logs were cut and roughly squared, and were laid up to form the walls. At a proper height, cross logs were laid to support an attic floor, giving additional room for the Brethren who were to build the town.

When they could be spared the men from Bethania went home, and Christian, Brother Ettwein, and Brother Lash returned to Bethabara. "There was one accident," Christian told me. "Brother Triebel, our master carpenter, fell from the wall when a log slipped as it was being raised. Fortunately he was not hurt, and he insists on staying with the rest until the work is finished as far as it can be at this time, for with so many of the tile broken the roof must wait."

"How long will it be before they finish the house?" I asked.

"I rather think they will wait until the Brethren who are coming from Europe reach here."

"It should not take long to finish it now."

"No, but much more timber must be cut before we can build the houses on the main street, and the additional men are needed."

"Is there no danger that evil men may go there and tear down the half finished house?"

Christian laughed. "You will be amused, my wife, to hear what has just been planned. Our hogs are doing much damage by rooting in the turnip field, and one of the younger Brethren is to drive them to the new town site and camp there for a few days, taking care of them so that they may not stray off in the woods. That will relieve the difficulty here, and serve also to protect the new house."

Two days later the entire village was laughing and the young swineherd was looking much embarrassed. "The first thing I knew, the hogs headed for home, and I could do nothing with them! I guess they were hungry, with only the acorns for food, and decided to come back to the turnips."

"Never mind," said Brother Lash kindly. "We have dug the turnips, and they are welcome to what little they can find in the fields now. I do not believe anyone will molest our little log house, and the Brethren from Europe should be here before long."

About the end of the month we heard that they had reached Charleston and were on the way hither, and as arrival usually followed such advance notice almost immediately, Brother Ettwein and Brother Lash and one or two others rode toward the South Fork of Muddy Creek to meet them. It was late when they reached the home of Christian Frey, where they found the travelers already asleep, tired from their long journey; so the Bethabara Brethren waited until morning to give them greeting.

Their arrival in Bethabara added two more to the various nationalities of our Wachovia settlement, for John Birkhead was an Englishman and Jens Schmidt and Nils Petersen were Danes.

"Gertrude," I said to Sister Graff, "do you remember when my father and Count Zinzendorf tried unsuccessfully to organize a union among the sects of Pennsylvania?"

"Yes, the Count spoke of it on his return, and regretted that the effort had failed."

"You and I are probably the only two in Bethabara who remember, but I have been thinking that our settlement here has practically accomplished in a small way what they could not do in 1741 in Pennsylvania. We come from at least five different religious stocks—Moravian, Lutheran, Reformed, Salzburger, Catholic—and who ever thinks or talks about it? We represent I do not know how many different European states, England, the Palatinate, Denmark, Switzerland, Moravia, Saxony, Alsace, Württemberg, the Black Forest, and so on, and yet it would be somewhat difficult, I suspect, properly to assign each man and woman to the place of his or her birth."

"I did not know that there was one from Moravia."

"One of the Single Brethren was born there. And to my list we must add those of us who were born in the colonies of Pennsylvania, New York, and South Carolina."

"What about Virginia?"

"None of our present members was born there—but wait, that colony is represented, for one of the Negroes who have been hired was born in Virginia, and another in Guinea."

"What a mixture we are!"

"And yet we are one church family, a Unity of Brethren and Sisters, living in one community, with a common purpose, practically unmindful of our various origins."

"Who came from Alsace?"

"Adam Spach, our good neighbor on the south line of Wachovia. Christian has met him often; he is one with us in spirit, and hopes that a Moravian congregation can ultimately be organized in their settlement."

"Perhaps so, but at present we shall have our hands full with building our new town. Do not repeat this, Catharina, but Michael tells me that in the letters brought by the new Brethren we have the name for the new town, and it will be announced to the congregation tomorrow. You might as well know now—it is to be *Salem*, meaning 'peace.' Michael says that Count Zinzendorf suggested this name before he passed away, often longing for peace for himself and for the church he loved."

"I have never found this a world of peace, but of wars and rumors of war, but perhaps he thought more of the 'peace which passeth understanding.' "

"May God give us that, whatever the world may do!" a prayer for which we were to have more need than we then knew.

A heavy snow delayed things for a week, but on February 19th eight of the Brethren set out for Salem, to make a real beginning with building. Four of them were of those who had recently arrived, and four others were from Bethabara; two wagons took brick for the chimney, tile for the roof, and other necessary things. The road had been somewhat improved, so that this time not many tile were broken, and the roof was successfully covered. Brother Melchior Rasp, our master mason, built the chimney and daubed the walls and it was not long before they could feel at home and be comfortable. Brother Petersen, though a layman, was charged with the conduct of their morning and evening devotions, but for other church services they were to return to Bethabara for the present.

On the following day Christian went to Salem, and with the help of Brother Lash and two of the boys he ran a straight line along the crest of the ridge, this to be the main street of Salem. Cross streets he placed at proper intervals; and a back street on either side of the main street. One of the blocks so outlined was to be the open Square of the town, but decision as to which it was to be was deferred until the streets were cleared so that a better view of the situation could be gained. The block chosen some months later was what Christian called No. 2, and it was decided to place the first houses on the west side of the main street, facing the block north of the Square. Two years later it was decided to move the Square one block further south, gaining a better fall of water from springs higher on the ridge, and Christian good-naturedly teased "the pioneer daughter who was not to be as far from her neighbors as she planned," but the change was really to my advantage since it put my lot diagonally across from the lower corner of the Square, where in the course of time one of the standards of the water system was placed.

My lot—how long it seemed until I could say my *house!* Christian went and came, staking off one house site after another until there were six in the first group, but I must wait and wait, and building went slowly for the work at Bethabara must go on as usual.

"When will my turn come?" I fretted, as restless as the little girl at the knee of Grandmother Antes, and patiently as she he answered: "All in good time, my wife. We must first build houses enough so that when moving begins as many may go as are needed to start the new town."

The month of April was unlucky so far as accidents were concerned, just at the time that Brother Bonn was absent on a trip to Bethlehem. On the fifth one of the little girls came running to the wash-house calling excitedly, "Sister Reuter, come quickly; Sister Ettwein has fallen in her garden and has broken her leg!" Several of us hurried to her assistance and bandaged her leg as best we could; Brother Lash dispatched a boy on horseback to Salisbury to call Dr. Noonham for her. The doctor came the next day, and we were gratified when he removed the bandages and replaced them, telling us that we had done exactly the right thing, and that he thought the bone would knit nicely.

Nine days later Brother Rasp had a peculiar and more dangerous accident. He was walking from Bethabara to Salem, smoking as he tramped along, when suddenly he stumbled over a root and pitched forward, driving the end of his pipe-stem against the back of his throat, which was severely lacerated. The wound became very sore, the throat swelled, and the rising finally broke both outside and inside. His suffering was severe and his mental torment almost as great. "It is just too bad that I was so awkward," he lamented. "It is dreadful to have to lie by when I am needed for building."

"Don't worry about that," said Brother Lash, trying to comfort him. "You have taught the Brethren how to build the stone foundations, and they are doing their best to follow your instructions exactly. Rest as quietly as you can, now, and we hope you will be well again in time to build the chimneys." His painful illness lasted for seven weeks, but he did recover in time to build the chimneys for the houses in the new town, to our great relief, for at times it had looked as though we might have to give him up.

In May an astounding letter came to Sister Gammern—no less than an offer of marriage from Mr. de Brahm, Surveyor General of His Majesty's Southern District of the United States, resident in St. Augustine, Florida. Sister Gammern had been a widow for about six months, her husband having been called away the preceding November in the midst of a useful and successful life. He had brought our commerce into a flourishing condition, and was taken sick with a chill and fever the day after he returned from a trip to Charleston. Many neighbors had gathered for his funeral, and had said much about how they had respected and loved him. "A real father to the poor, and a benefactor to the entire neighborhood," they called him.

"It is preposterous, Sister Reuter," said Sister Gammern, indignantly. "It is only half a year since Abraham left me, and besides I would never even consider marrying an utter stranger and going with him to a distant colony, outside the Unity."

"Do you known how he heard of you?" for Mr. de Brahm had never been to Wachovia.

"From what Brother Graff could find out, one of the lawyers from Salisbury was in Florida and told Mr. de Brahm about my husband, praising him highly, and speaking of the general regret at his departure, adding that 'his widow must be a person of quality.' That is little on which to base a marriage offer."

"It is a compliment to Brother Gammern and to you, but of course you will not accept. How are you going to reply?"

"Brother Graff has kindly consented to send a courteous answer, thanking him for his good intentions but saying positively that I will not marry him." This was done and no more was heard from him.

The foundation stone of the first house on the main street of Salem was laid on the sixth of June, with some ceremony. Stone that could be broken into pieces of convenient size had been found near by, and beginning with this house all foundations were made of stone laid in clay, for lime was so scarce and hard to get that the Brethren depended on the strength of thick walls built with clay, and not on mortar. It was to be a frame house, of the type suggested by Brother Marshall when the town site was selected. He and Christian and Brother Rasp and Brother Triebel were holding a building conference, and Brother Marshall said, "I think for the houses on the main street you had better build frame houses until you can start a brick-yard."

"How can we build frame houses?" asked Triebel, the practical. "We have no saw-mill in Salem, and to haul all the lumber from Bethabara will be troublesome and expensive."

"I mean the sort of frame house that is used in parts of Pennsylvania," said Brother Marshall. "Where good wood is scarce, as it is here, the trunks of the trees are used for the large timbers and the smaller pieces serve well for the laths. See—" and taking up his pencil he drew a small design. "Here are the heavy uprights, squared, with grooves on opposite sides. These heavy timbers, the height of the wall, are set two or three feet apart. Then small pieces of wood, of the correct length to extend from one groove into another, are used as laths, which need not be uniform or finished, only relatively of the same size. These laths are chipped at each end to fit into the grooves; then each is wrapped in a mixture of straw and clay to form a cylinder of the proper diameter, and each cylinder in turn is slipped into the grooves and pressed down. If the work is well done the result is a solid wall, the thickness of the uprights and as warm as a wall of brick."

"Are such walls permanent?"

"They should be protected by extra wide eaves, and for a two-story house there should be a narrow roof set between the first and second story."

"What about the house roof?"

"It can be made in the same way, but must be covered with clapboards, tile, or shingles; and the inside walls can be made with smaller cylinders, of the straw-clay mixture, to keep them from being too thick. What do you think, Brother Rasp?" for Brother Melchior had been saying nothing as he studied the little sketch thoughtfully.

"I think it can be done," he said. "Give me a stone foundation, and on it we can build such a wall as this, and if or when the clay shows signs of washing out we can cover the outside with clapboards or with good lime plaster."

"It will certainly solve the timber problem," said Christian, when he told me of the conversation, "and I had wondered what we would do for suitable logs for houses."

"And log houses would not look well on the main street of a town," I added, at which Christian laughed, though I saw that he felt the same, as the artist in him naturally would.

So the first houses were built of framing and straw and clay, on a foundation wall of rough stone; and the ceremonial foundation stone was laid at the very bottom of the wall.

Soon it became apparent that more water would be needed than the little branch afforded, and well-master Rothe was summoned; by his divining rod the northwest corner of Block No. 2 was selected as the place where water could be most easily obtained. The men had to dig ten feet deeper than his estimate, but finally found water and walled up the well.

By mid-summer the first house was nearly finished, and a party of Sisters, including myself, went to Salem in a wagon with the Brethren Ettwein and Graff. It was our first visit to the new town, and we were greatly interested in all we saw. Sister Graff walked with me to the corner lot which was to be mine, and I tried to visualize the little house that one day would stand on it, "if the Brethren ever get to it," I thought impatiently. Gertrude spoke encouragingly, however; so it was with a light heart that I joined in the little lovefeast held in the partly finished room in the first house, and with a forward look I sang with the rest:

> Now thank we all our God
> With hearts and hands and voices.

During the fall Brother Richard Utley came to take the place of Brother Rogers as English minister of Dobbs Parish, and with him came his wife, Sister Anna Maria Krause, three other Single Sisters, and twelve girls, twelve or thirteen years old.

"The girls look well," I told Sister Krause, who was their supervisor. "They appear to have stood the long journey without undue fatigue."

"And that in spite of the fact that they have walked most of the way," she replied. "They heard that the two groups of boys who preceded them walked, and they were ambitious to do the same, taking turns resting in the wagon when I insisted."

"This completes the age groups in our congregation," said Sister Graff. "I have missed girlish faces, and am glad to have them with us."

"Have the boys been happy here?" asked Sister Krause.

"They have given no trouble, though some of them seem to like the life here better than others. One of the boys appears to be homesick. He says little about it, and may throw it off, but he should have become accustomed to the new home by this time. The older and stronger boys are being used in Salem, and the others are working in the shops in Bethabara."

Before the year ended the first house on the main street in Salem was finished, and Brother Pretzel set up his loom in one room, Charles Holder began to make saddles in the second room, and the gun-stock maker, Valentine Beck, moved into the third room. Brother Utley was stationed in Salem as temporary pastor, living with the Brethren in the log house, while Sister Utley remained in Bethabara.

During the summer, brick-making had begun in the meadow; so the later houses in the first group were somewhat differently made, a variation on the method proposed by Brother Marshall. Brother Rasp suggested that brick which were only half burned be used inside the walls, in place of the clay-straw combination, to save the trouble of re-burning. The imperfect brick were laid up with clay, in the spaces between the frame uprights, clapboards being used on the outside, with a thin layer of plaster to finish the wall on the inside.

"I like the looks of the fourth house better than the first," I told Christian, after another visit to Salem, to which he replied, "Then we will build your house that way."

13.

NEW LEADERS

————

IN SEPTEMBER, 1767, SALEM HAD HER FIRST DISTINGUISHED VISI-
tors, none other than the Governor of the Colony of North
Carolina and his Lady. In May, Governor Tryon had seen Brother
Lash in Salisbury and had told him that he expected to visit Bethabara in the fall and bring his sister Anne with him; but when the
visit was actually made he brought his wife instead of his sister.
With them came the Governor's suite, including the Reverend
Mr. Mickeljohn, a rector of the Church of England; Colonel Frohock, whom we knew from tax days; and Colonel Fanning, who
was soon to become one of the most hated men in North Carolina,
if one might believe the Regulators.

When an express messenger arrived with a letter from Colonel
Fanning to Brother Lash, in which we were informed that the
Governor would reach Bethabara the next afternoon, a committee
was quickly appointed and met to plan the accommodation and
entertainment of the guests. Sister Lash, Sister Graff, Sister Anna
Maria Krause, and I were asked to look after the comfort of Lady
Tryon; and various Brethren were selected to act as hosts for the
Governor and his suite, assist the cook, and plan the program for
the visit. Brother Grabs and his wife, Brother Transou and his
wife, Brother Bachhof and his wife, were asked to serve as a committee in Bethania, and make suitable arrangements for receiving
the Governor there; Brother Utley, Brother Birkhead, and several
others were selected to show the Governor what was being done

in the new town. All willingly agreed to do anything in their power, which was a help, for the undertaking was not an easy one with the limited resources at our disposal.

Next morning the Brethren Lash and Bonn rode out to meet the Governor and escort him to Bethabara, the party reaching there about one o'clock in the afternoon. They were welcomed with music of trumpets and French horns, and the Governor and his Lady were conducted to the lodging which had been prepared for them in the tailor's house. Half an hour later dinner was served to the entire company in the largest room in the Brothers House, and the meal was accompanied by music, which pleased them very much. After dinner the gentlemen walked about, inspecting our stable, brewery, and so on, but it began to rain, and this brought them back to their rooms.

Meanwhile Lady Tryon conversed pleasantly and familiarly with us. We had heard that she was distant and haughty, but if there was that side to her character we saw nothing of it. Both she and the Governor showed an interest in our arrangements and mode of life, and she was so gracious that it was easy to tell her all she wished to know. Brother Graff lent them a copy of the printed record of the proceedings in the British Parliament when the Unity of Brethren was given official recognition as "an ancient protestant episcopal church," and next morning we learned that they sat up late reading it. When Brother Lash heard this he presented to them a copy of the History of Moravian Missions in Greenland, translated into English, which also pleased them.

"Your Mr. Ettwein told me a good deal about your settlement when he called on me as he was going to Pennsylvania last year," said the Governor. "He explained the purpose of your common housekeeping during these pioneer years, and I can see how advantageous it has been. He said that you did not intend to make it permanent."

"No, Your Excellency," said Brother Graff. "It is to be given up as soon as our new town is ready, and the church boards, the craftsmen, and professional men can move there."

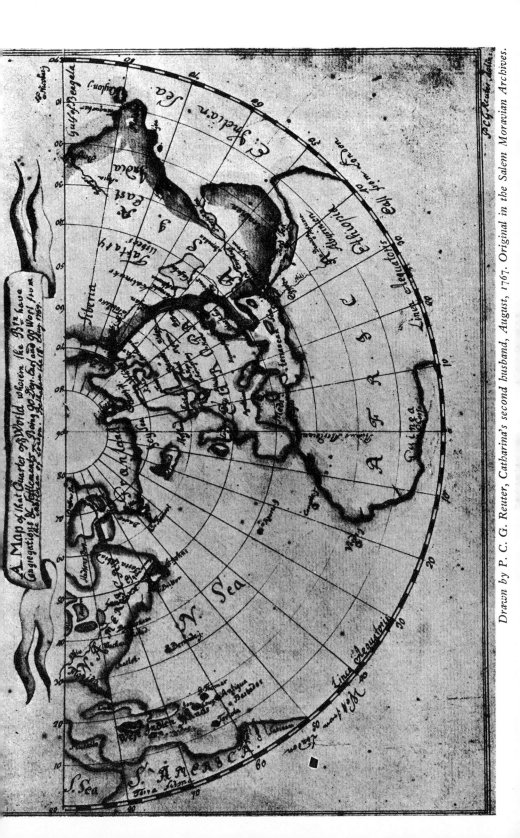

A Map of that Quarter of the World whereon the Brn. have Congregations & Settlements. From 90 Deg. East and 90 West from the Meridian of London. Published the 18th Aug. 1769.

Drawn by P. C. G. Reuter, Catharina's second husband, August, 1767. Original in the Salem Moravian Archives.

Bishop John Michael Graff

From a portrait in the Bethlehem Archives.

"Will it not be difficult to change from the one method to the other?" asked the Governor.

"We hope not. We have not merged our personal funds, only our labor, and for the Brethren who are not able to start an individual business we hope to work out a plan by which they can keep their tools on credit, paying for them in installments. . . . Would Your Excellency care to ride to the new town? The Brethren there would feel honored if allowed to show you what they are doing."

The idea appealed to the Governor and also to his Lady, the latter asking that two or three of us accompany her. Sister Krause excused herself, saying that she had charge of the young girls of the village and that it would be better for her to stay with them, but the rest of us were glad to go. We rode across the big meadow and took the road to Salem; then after inspecting the building there, we returned to Bethabara in time for the noonday meal.

The afternoon was given by the gentlemen to inspecting the pottery and the mill. At the latter place Lady Tryon, Sister Lash, and I rejoined them, and we rode to Bethania, where light refreshments were served to them in the Congregation House. Of course all the children were in the street to see the distinguished company, and Lady Tryon and the Governor were impressed by their number and their good behaviour. "They are dear!" exclaimed the Lady, and the Governor added, "This village should have a bright future, with so many young people to draw from."

Brother Utley held the evening service, speaking in English, and the Governor and his entire party attended. The next day being Sunday, the English rector preached, and baptized several children of neighbors who had come in expressly for that purpose.

In the afternoon Lady Tryon went alone into our meeting-hall, found a tune book, and began to play. At the familiar sound Betsy Colver whispered to Sister Krause, who nodded, and turning to the eager girls she said "Go in quietly and begin to sing the hymn she is playing. If she seems to like it you may stay with her a little while; but watch her carefully, Betsy, and if you see the slightest sign that it annoys her bring the girls out."

Instead of being annoyed, the Lady liked it, and drew the girls into conversation. Learning that Brother Graff was our organist as well as minister she asked that he be brought; then the Governor joined them and a whole hour was spent most pleasantly with music. When the Governor left, Lady Tryon went with the girls to their room, and later brought them back to sing for her again. As our music seemed to give them so much pleasure, our musicians played softly before their house at bedtime.

Next morning Brother Lash took the Governor into every nook and corner of Bethabara and answered his numerous and searching questions. After dinner the company departed, Brother Lash going with them to Salisbury, where as a justice he must sit in the court of pleas and quarter sessions.

Our guests were so courteous in their thanks and so generous in their appreciation of what we had done for them that we felt well repaid for our efforts, and it made us loath to believe all the charges later made against them, which seemed out of harmony with what we had seen of them.

Even as Governor Tryon represented a new era in the Colony of North Carolina, so a new period in the history of Wachovia began in February, 1768, when Frederic William Marshall and his wife Elisabeth, Traugott Bagge and his wife Rachel, and five Single Sisters arrived in Bethabara, for the Brethren Marshall and Bagge were destined to be our able leaders for many years.

Brother Bagge was thirty-eight years old and had been born in Gothenburg, Sweden, in 1729. He was the fourteenth and youngest child of Lorenz and Anna Bagge, and had been educated in the town schools, showing special ability in mathematics. His father was a successful merchant, and trained the lad in his own profession for which he showed much aptitude. After some years of business and of travel he joined the Unity of Brethren in Zeist, Holland, and four years later was called to the service of the

Moravian Church in England. While in England he had a narrow escape from death under unusual circumstances.

"I was going home from a business trip," he told us, "and thinking to make a short cut I took a path across a field. Darkness came on, and when I came to a fence crossing the path I foolishly climbed it. Suddenly my feet slipped out from under me and I fell into deeper darkness, bruising myself badly on the chest. Half fainting I groped about, discovered a wall of earth behind me and an empty void in front, and realized that I must have fallen into one of the abandoned mines which were not uncommon in the neighborhood. How far I had fallen I could not tell, and I was afraid to move for fear of going still deeper. My discomfort was increased when I put my hand on something which moved, what, I knew not, but I suspected it might be a snake.

"The night seemed endless. Time and again I almost lost consciousness but I strove with all my might to avoid fainting lest I fall into a bottomless pit.

"At long last morning dawned, and I found myself on a narrow ledge a number of feet below the surface. Several slender sticks lay within reach and I managed to tie them together with strips from my handkerchief, but they did not reach the top. Then I shouted, but no one answered. Calling at intervals, as loudly as my failing strength permitted, I was finally heard by men crossing the field, and with much difficulty they succeeded in raising me, though I received additional injuries as they dragged me up along the wall."

"It must have taken you a long time to recover from such an experience!"

"Indeed it did. The doctor said that my breast-bone was broken, and I was bruised and cut in many places; but finally I did recover, married, and accepted the call to Wachovia, to take charge of the Bethabara store and of the store in Salem when that is ready."

"What sort of a trip did you have?"

"The captain said it was about as usual. We were on the sea for three months and ten days, coming from England to Charleston; and including the time spent in making arrangements it took us three weeks more to come to Wachovia."

"Tell us something about Brother Marshall," I begged, for it seemed a bit out of order to ask for personal details from Brother Marshall himself when he had come to be the representative of the Unity in North Carolina and therefore our chief executive in business affairs as well as general pastor for the entire settlement.

"He is about nine years older than I, and was born near Dresden, in Saxony. His father, George Rudolph von Marschall, was an army officer and planned that his four sons should follow him into a military life. It is interesting to hear Brother Marshall tell of his life as a boy and the training they received at home, sleeping on hard beds, with windows open even in winter, eating plain food, and in every way hardening themselves for the life of soldiers."

"What a wonderful preparation for his life in the church! No wonder he seems never to mind discomfort or privation!"

"Yes, and he was still further prepared by another, a rather odd, family custom. There were no daughters in the home, and the four sons in turn, a week at a time, were entrusted with the family purse and were taught to buy the necessary supplies, carefully staying within the sum allotted for the purpose. In that way he learned the value and the use of money, and laid the foundation for the administrative ability which has raised him to the rank of a senior civilis of the Unity."

"I had not known that he was a senior civilis," I said, with a sudden longing for my father, who had felt highly honored when that rank was conferred upon him by the Moravians in Pennsylvania, in recognition of his valuable service in financial matters, in real estate transactions, and in dealing with the officials of the Colony.

"He has held all ranks in turn, akoluthe, deacon, and presbyter, and were it not for his outstanding ability in administrative work he would doubtless have been a bishop, for he is a man of keen spiritual insight, an excellent pastor, and a fine preacher. He was educated at the University of Leipzig, and after he joined the Unity he held many positions of trust, being closely associated with Count Zinzendorf and with the Count's son, Christian Renatus."

"It must have been rather hard for his father to have such a promising son turn from the army to the church."

"Perhaps it was, but he was very kind about it, and gave his permission for the change when Brother Marshall was eighteen years old; and he had the pleasure of knowing that his son's talents were recognized and appreciated in his chosen field."

"I notice that our Brother Marshall spells his name without a *c*, and omits the *von*," said Christian.

"He has lived a good deal in England and likes the English language and uses the English spelling of his name by preference. He was naturalized in Pennsylvania some years ago, and he emphasizes the fact that he is an American citizen, which is of value in his office as Administrator of the American estates of the Unity," said Brother Bagge.

"What do you know about Sister Marshall?"

"She was Hedwig Elisabeth von Schweinitz, a daughter of George Abraham von Schweinitz. She was a deaconess when he married her, and has always been active in the work of the church."

"That means companionship for you, Gertrude," I said, for Sister Graff was also a deaconess, and did much to assist her husband by personal work among the women and girls, and by carrying the bread and cup to be distributed to the Sisters during the celebration of the Lord's Supper.

"If you are a deaconess," I asked her once, "why do you never preach or preside at the Communion?"

"Saint Paul said that women should be silent in the church," she said with a smile; then more seriously she added, "When we were being instructed in church history we were told that in the Ancient Unity of Brethren the deacons were assistants to the priests, but not authorized to administer the Sacraments. That has been changed in the Renewed Unity of Brethren, and our deacons today exercise all ministerial functions, but our deaconesses still hold the position as in ancient days when they and the deacons had similar duties toward their respective sexes."

"Most of the wives of our ministers have been received as akoluthes," I said.

"That is a dedication for lay service of the church in business or in religious matters. A deaconess has really been ordained, though her field of service is restricted. It will be pleasant to have Sister Marshall share the responsibility with me," said Sister Graff.

Indeed all the newcomers were a happy addition to our circle, and I hardly know how we could have managed without them during the years that followed.

In Bethabara there was real sorrow when Brother Lash was called back to Pennsylvania, for he had been one of the original settlers, had spent sixteen years in Wachovia, and had been an outstanding leader during the pioneer days. After a short stay in Bethlehem he was placed in charge of the farm at Nazareth. There he served for a number of years, and met his end while on a business trip to New Jersey. As he passed a farmhouse a dog ran out and frightened his horse, which shied and threw him against the blunt end of a limb of a tree, injuring him internally. Word was sent at once to Nazareth, and his wife and sister reached him in time to say goodbye. The funeral was held at Nazareth, and the hour for the service was set at a time when the distressed farmer who owned the dog could attend, and so express his grief over the accident.

Of Brother Lash's end we of course had no premonition when he was called north by the Elders of Bethlehem, who followed Brother Spangenberg's method of changing officials from time to time. With the other Sisters I regretted the parting with Sister Lash and her family, and in later days it was good to see three of her sons return to Wachovia and take their share in the upbuilding of the settlement, especially Bethania, where the little Christian who came to me so often in the time of the Indian war became one of the leaders.

With Brother Lash and his family went also the homesick boy of whom I had spoken to Sister Krause. Perhaps the restlessness of the Regulators affected the boys, for early in that period two of them ran away from Bethabara and were found by Brother Herbst at a farm where they had undertaken to work. They were brought back and were punished by losing their free time and being suspended from certain church services; two other boys who were implicated were warned to behave. Unfortunately, two of the four remained sulky and insolent, and finally one of them in sheer defiance of authority shot a gun into a keg of oil. That was going entirely too far, and the two insubordinates were tried before Justice Lash and convicted. A whipping was ordered and duly administered by Brother Ernst in the presence of the Justice. That brought all four to their senses, and they offered their apologies and were reinstated, but this one boy remained so homesick that Brother Lash decided that the kindest thing to do was to take him back to his parents. The interesting sequel to the story is that when this lad grew to manhood he returned to Wachovia, bought a farm, and became a leader in one of our country congregations. By such devious routes does the Lord lead men to service!

14.

THE REGULATORS

———

Of COURSE AN ECLIPSE COULD NOT POSSIBLY INFLUENCE HUMAN action, but it was an odd coincidence that the year which saw the beginning of trouble with the Regulators commenced with an eclipse of the sun, and had an eclipse of the moon in mid-summer. We know that an eclipse is merely a physical phenomenon which can be foretold with some degree of accuracy, but the superstitious regarded it as a portent of evil, and in 1768 the old dragon of war did lift its evil head again and try to swallow our country.

Toward the end of May some of the settlers on the Yadkin River met at the home of Isaac Free and signed a protest against the taxes due the colony.

"Many of them do not know what they want; it is a contrivance of certain rebellious heads," said Brother Graff.

"Who are the leaders?" asked one of the other Brethren.

"I do not know exactly," answered Brother Graff. "The movement seems to have begun further east, perhaps in Orange County. For some time there has been a feeling of dissatisfaction in certain sections, and men have claimed that the taxes are too high and the officials are charging exorbitant fees."

"We have had no trouble with the officials."

"Perhaps," said Brother Graff, "that may be accounted for in two ways. Brother Lash kept us well informed as to the laws and the acts of assembly, and the officials knew that, and dared not try illegal charges. Then, so far we have enjoyed the favor of the Governor, who has acknowledged that our settlement is an asset to the Colony."

"Do you know whether there is any foundation for the charges made elsewhere?" asked Brother Marshall.

"Probably there is," replied Brother Graff. "A man by the name of Herman Husband, a Quaker by connection, has been doing much talking, and has published several pamphlets setting out the alleged wrongs and stirring up the people to protest."

"A Quaker should stand for peace, not war."

"Oh, he insists that the people ought to secure redress by legal and peaceful means, but he is inflaming the minds of men and I fear is lighting a fire that will spread beyond his control."

"Will any of our Brethren be drawn in?" asked Brother Bagge.

"I hope not. No one likes to pay taxes, but there is no other way in which the expenses of government can be met. So far as I know we have been treated fairly and according to law, and our Brethren should appreciate that all the more if the same does not apply in other counties."

"Brother Graff," said Brother Marshall, "I think we had better discuss this in the next congregation council and warn our Brethren to be on their guard."

This was wise advice, but it did not exempt us from trouble. Governor Tryon ordered two wagon-loads of zwieback from our bakery, and this was sent in September. John Shore and Lewis Leinbach drove the horses, and just as they were starting they were given the written address of a merchant in New Bern, but were told that they would probably be stopped in Hillsborough as the Governor was likely to want the zwieback delivered there for the use of the militia.

They had hardly left town when a rumor spread from the Yadkin and from the Hollow: "The Moravians are sending arms and ammunition to Governor Tryon, and the Regulators are going to stop their wagons on the road!" So ran the report which reached us by way of Bethania, and, false as the accusation was, it alarmed us for the safety of our Brethren.

The same day Mr. Martin Armstrong came from Salisbury and told us that the Governor had left there the preceding day with six hundred armed soldiers, whom he had summoned for the protection of the court of Hillsborough. "That explains the hint he gave us that although the order called for delivery at New Bern the wagons might be stopped in Hillsborough," said Brother Bagge.

A week later the wagons returned. "We saw nothing of the Regulators," John Shore reported, "but in Hillsborough we were stopped with blows by some of Governor Tryon's men, who seized our wagons and emptied them."

"Perhaps Colonel Fanning thought he was doing us a favor by a show of violence, and by saying that he was seizing the zwieback *for His Majesty's service,*" said Brother Bagge.

"Well, they need not have been so rough about it," said John Shore, rubbing his shoulder reminiscently, and we all felt that it was unfair to abuse men who were carrying out the directions of the Governor himself, though we were glad enough that no actual damage had been done, and that the wagons had been allowed to return safely.

After a few more days we heard that General Court had been held without disturbance, and that the Governor was giving serious consideration to the complaints of the Regulators; but still later we heard from Mr. John Armstrong, who had been in Hillsborough with the militia, that court had adjourned without taking any steps to right the wrongs. "That means that the trouble will continue," said Christian. This was unfortunately only too true, for during the next year discontent continued to grow, breaking out here and there into actual violence.

When Mr. John Armstrong passed through Bethabara again he had further news for us. He had been to Anson County and was concerned over what had happened there. "They whipped the sheriff when he tried to collect the taxes," he said. "Now there will be more trouble."

"What will the Governor do?" asked Brother Bagge.

"Just now he is in Virginia, at a conference of Governors,"

said Mr. Armstrong, "but we think that he will call out the militia to deal with the Regulators."

"Will the militia serve against their neighbors?"

"Some of us will. I for one, and my brother Martin, and I think we can control a number of our men. Then the Governor can bring troops from farther east, for that part of the Colony seems not to have followed Herman Husband."

"Do you think the Regulators have any justification for the way they are acting?"

Mr. Armstrong hesitated. "Frankly, I fear some of them have been unjustly treated but they are taking the wrong way to end it. Breaking the law gains nothing, and whipping a sheriff merely angers the Government and makes it less ready to listen to charges of wrong-doing on the part of officials. Personally, I am ready to back any steps which the Governor may take to suppress what is virtually a rebellion, and many others feel the same."

This point of view was intensified the next fall. For more than a year matters had drifted along, getting more tense, both sides becoming more exasperated, and in September the Regulators broke up the court at Salisbury, committing many excesses. "It was a shameful riot," we were told. "They whipped Colonel Fanning and the lawyer Alexander Martin severely, and many others nearly as badly; they tore down Colonel Fanning's house, broke many windows in other houses, drove merchants and others out of town, and for two days acted like madmen."

At this time we had no personal acquaintance with Mr. Alexander Martin, who later became our very good friend, but his experience threatened to become that of several of our Brethren, in spite of our efforts to be friendly with everyone, and it seemed that any pretext served as an excuse for them.

"You and George Holder are in danger," Mr. McNally told Brother Bagge, "and so am I."

"With what are we charged?" asked Brother Bagge calmly, for he was not a man who was frightened easily.

"You sent bread to the Governor last year, to Salisbury."

"That is not exactly correct, but if it were, may a merchant not sell to a Governor without asking the permission of the Regulators? I have done nothing illegal, nor anything against a single one of them. What has George Holder done?"

"Nothing, probably, but they charge that he tried to drive to his farm some hogs belonging to a Regulator."

"Knowing George Holder I feel sure that is not true. What is their charge against you?"

"I am a justice of the peace, and they are opposed to anyone who tries to maintain law and order."

"Do they have no responsible leaders?"

"None that I know around here. The wrongs charged by Husband in his pamphlet were committed in the Hillsborough section, and some of the leaders there may be substantial citizens, but it looks to me as though the matter were largely in the hands of irresponsible men, such as those who rioted at Salisbury and now threaten us."

Mr. McNally had come to Bethabara because of the district muster of militia which had been ordered for October. Mr. Temple Kole, adjutant for the regiment, had selected a small field on the footpath to Bethania for the muster ground, and several Brethren came from Salem and Bethania to help in the store and tavern. Mr. Martin Armstrong's company camped in the meadow; Anthony Hampton's company camped by the Grassy Fork. Major Lindsay told us that many of the militia had fever and could not come, and he promised to do all in his power to prevent disorder. The peddler Hughes reported that a large number of Regulators planned to be here, which boded no good for the village.

The Moravian Church has always prized its daily texts, first prepared by Count Zinzendorf in 1732, and arranged each year thereafter with a new set of texts. It is remarkable how often those texts apply with special force to the day for which they were selected, and the dreaded day of muster was no exception. "Let us now fear the Lord our God, that giveth rain," read the text, and the Lord gave rain which continued until ten o'clock and changed the plans of many. Henry Herrman and his company, mostly Regulators, did not arrive until in the afternoon, when the other companies had finished their drill. Captain Herrman, who admitted that he was "becoming more and more of a Regulator," did his best to excite his men, exercising them in the town and having them fire their guns. They remained in town after the other companies left, but gave less trouble than had been expected. Two of them told Brother Blum good-naturedly that they had been so well served in the tavern that they had no excuse for being unpleasant.

Several of the officers who lived at a distance remained in the tavern overnight. Henry Herrman and his associates kept up a disturbance, and neither Justice McNally nor the officers could control them; but toward morning most of them left suddenly, as though alarmed. Captain Herrman stayed until four in the afternoon, having his drum beaten constantly, but no more Regulators arrived, though we heard that a party who were not called to muster had planned to come and join the others. Adjutant Kole and Major Lindsay stayed for a second night, as they feared to meet the Regulators on the road; Colonel Frohock did not come at all.

Reports of their activities elsewhere continued to drift in. One of the Bethania Brethren, returning with his wagon from Charleston, said that fifteen Regulators had joined him and the other teamsters at their camp-fire, and admitted that they had been to Salisbury.

"We meant to break up the court again," they said, "but the Governor got ahead of us and had soldiers there to protect his pet lawyers. They fought us, and we were too few to overcome them this time, but we will most certainly go again, and next time we will show them what is what!"

Another of their annoying actions was to drive a herd of one hundred and fifty hogs into Wachovia without permission.

"They were ruining my turnips and pumpkins," said Martin Walk, "and I asked one of the men to have the swine removed, but he replied with insults and a threat to take the matter to a meeting of the Regulators."

"You look more amused than injured," said Christian, to whom he was telling his story.

"Well, it really was funny the way it turned out. Bears attacked the hogs, killing some and injuring others, and the rest ran for home. The owners are helpless, for it will do them no good to complain of bears to a Regulator meeting. All they can do is to take the injured hogs home as soon as they can stand the trip, and meanwhile the bears have been chased away, and that benefits all of us."

But it took more than bears to overawe the Regulators, and we continued to hear all manner of accounts of their doings. Henry Benner, our perpetual refugee from the Indians some years before, hurried in one evening.

"Please let me spend the night here," he pleaded, and of course his request was granted.

"What is the matter?" he was asked.

"The Regulators say they are coming to whip me," he groaned, "and they say they are going to whip Mr. Bagge and Mr. Meyer also."

"Don't worry," said Brother Bagge, "they threatened that last fall, but nothing came of it."

"But they have tried to carry out their threat against Mr. McNally. A party went to his house to *regulate* him, and would have done it, too, but he was ready for them. After listening to their accusations he raised a loaded pistol and threatened to shoot the first man who came near him, whereupon the whole party left in a hurry."

"Bullies are generally cowards," said Brother Bagge, "and there are so many of us here that I think we are in no danger. You are welcome to stay with us until you feel safe, but I am inclined to think that a show of courage like Mr. McNally's is the best protection."

So life in Bethabara went on as usual, but trouble continued elsewhere. In March the General Court should have met in Salisbury, but neither the chief judge nor the King's attorney dared attend. About seven hundred Regulators gathered on this side of the Yadkin and stopped all who would have passed on their way to court; then they went to Salisbury and forced a number of lawyers to give bond that they would return excess fees they had taken. Joseph Harris, a Regulator, returning from Salisbury, brought notice to the Brethren Marshall, Bonn, and Bagge that a party of Regulators were coming to Bethabara to see about a piece of land on which George Lash and his brother lived. They claimed that it had been taken from a man named Steward by Brother Jacob Lash, and they intended to demand satisfaction or restitution. A few days later they arrived to make their unfounded claim.

"We have been attacked by wolves of more than one kind," said Brother Bonn in talking about the affair afterwards, "and the one seemed almost a prophecy of the other."

"You mean—?"

"Do you not remember that wolves came into the lane behind the shed, and the baying of the dogs brought people to drive them away before they could break into the sheepfold? Do you not remember the large wolf caught in a trap near the brewery? They were trapped or driven away and did us no harm, and the Regulators met the same fate."

"How was it managed?"

"By calmness and courtesy," said Brother Bagge. "They sent a message that we should come to the tavern, to which Brother Marshall sent back word that if they wanted to see him they should come to his room. That took them down a little to begin with. Then they told us a long story about Brother Jacob Lash and how he had taken their land, which was of course untrue. Brother Marshall, however, did not argue with them, only pointed out politely that they should have brought up the matter earlier, since it seemed to have happened thirteen years ago and Brother Lash had remained here until recently. He explained that it would require the personal presence of Brother Lash for settlement, and if they wished they could send him a legal summons to North Carolina, but for this they showed no inclination.

"Then Edward Hughes, their spokesman, tried to claim that he had paid certain moneys to Mr. Corbin for the land on which Bethabara stands, saying shamefully untrue things about Brother Spangenberg, but when Brother Marshall asked for proof he had none to offer."

"In short," concluded Brother Bonn, "their trumped-up complaints were only groundless babbling, and when their unfounded pretensions were referred to the persons concerned there was nothing they could do but leave."

"Probably they thought that the terrifying name of Regulator would induce us to give them something, whether due or not, but they found themselves mistaken," said Brother Bagge.

Another attempt against us was made several weeks later, when Joseph Harris and several others went to our mill and accused Brother Kapp of having taken double toll on grain brought by one man, and of having returned too little meal from corn sent to the mill by another man.

"But," said Brother Kapp, "how could I have taken double toll when the owner was standing by, and he not object? And as for the meal, the man sent corn to the mill by his children, and I saw them feed some of the meal to their horse, and I hear they sold part of the corn in Bethabara to buy sugar."

Had Brother Kapp been alone he would have been in danger, but several additional Brethren were kept on guard at the mill in those days; so again the Regulators departed with nothing gained.

But still the shadow grew larger and larger and more threatening. The Governor began to assemble an army to meet the army which the Regulators were gathering, and it was reported from the Yadkin that the Regulators had resolved to meet the Governor with force if he tried to suppress them. Groups attached to both parties passed through our village, and some were friendly and some threatened us.

Reports varied greatly. We heard that General Waddell had gathered five or six thousand men; we heard that General Waddell had signed an agreement with the Regulators, and that the latter were going home. We heard that Mr. Gideon Wright and his men had reached the Governor; we heard that a message had been sent to the Yadkin calling out the Regulators to march against the Governor and his troops at Hillsborough where he had captured some of their leaders. Some of the Regulators told us they were going because their neighbors forced them. Others declared that when they had defeated the Governor they would return and destroy Bethabara.

Then we heard that on the Alamance there had been a hot skirmish between the Governor's troops and the Regulators, and again it was difficult to distinguish between fact and fiction. Many had been killed on both sides—a few had been killed and more wounded—so ran the contradictions. In general it appeared that the Governor's cannon had created consternation in the ranks of the Regulators. Some had run, after one round; others had stood a second; none had waited for a third except those who could not go. It was charged that the Governor had set fire to the woods, and that wounded men had died in the flames. It was stated that the Governor had offered pardon to all who would come in and surrender, and take an oath to be loyal, to pay back taxes, and to give up their arms, and many were hurrying to take the oath. The leaders of the Regulators had taken to their heels and their mob after them, said some. There had been a battle with General Waddell's troops, said others. The Regulators dared not trust one another, for some had sued for pardon and some had not, so still others declared.

Just before the battle of Alamance a young Regulator had been captured and was sentenced to be hanged. When the rope was about his neck the Governor twice offered him pardon, and he refused. The Governor turned aside, weeping. "Crazy young rebel," said some; "Brave young enthusiast," said others. "The Governor was cruel," said some. "The Governor could have done

nothing else," said others. "It was inhuman obstinacy on the part
of the Governor to hang the young fellow," said some; "It was
unnatural obstinacy to die rather than submit to lawful authority,"
said others.

Brother Marshall warned us not to be drawn into this or any
other controversy. "Our statutes pledge us to loyalty to those in
authority," he said, "but we dare not condemn those whose consciences have not been so instructed."

"How many of the Regulators whom we have seen have been
led by their consciences?" asked Brother Bagge.

"Few, I fear. I think that with most it has been a rebellion
against any authority, a desire for personal gain, or a restless
following of unwise leaders; but if a man is so sure of the right-
eousness of his cause that he is willing to die for it he deserves our
respect, if not our approval."

It was well for Bethabara that the Governor knew we were
loyal to the existing government, for enemies tried to turn him
against us. Whether they raised a doubt in his mind and he wanted
to see for himself what our attitude was, or whether he remembered his former visit with so much pleasure that he wanted to
repeat it, we never knew, but after hearing that he was about
to take his troops to Salisbury we were suddenly notified that
the army would spend the birthday of King George III in our
village.

This time there was no pleasant Lady Tryon to be entertained; so we Sisters kept out of sight as much as possible. But
the Brethren were more than busy, for the village was full of
soldiers, and guards must be stationed at the tavern, the bakery,
and kitchens. The soldiers complained much of hunger, and soon
there was not a bit of bread left in the bakery nor in any house.
Our friends on the South Fork brought flour to be baked into
more bread, and six oxen to be slaughtered for meat, and Bethania
sent bread and ham; so finally their great hunger was satisfied.

The Regulators aroused our sympathy, rudely as they had
threatened us. Prisoners were brought in bound two by two, some
of them men from our neighborhood. "Please help me," begged

one, whimpering like a child. "Please, Mr. Marshall, say a good word for me?" implored another. "You know I did not mean any harm. Don't let them hang me," so another, shuddering. Brother Marshall felt that as this was a military matter he could not interfere, but watched his chance, and when the opportunity offered he was able to lighten the lot of some whom he knew to be not bad men, only misled. Other Regulators came in to take the oath of loyalty, which was allowed to all except the ringleaders.

On Thursday, June 6th, the royal birthday was celebrated. The troops were exercised for two hours, repeating the maneuvers they had used in the battle with the Regulators; and they saluted with guns and cannon until everything trembled. Four of our Brethren presented to the Governor an address which had been prepared, to which he made suitable reply. He had not asked our Brethren for the oath demanded of others; so Brother Marshall thought it would be expedient to take this method of expressing our loyalty, since he had trusted us in spite of the evil accusations made against us and had issued a sharp order to the army that the slightest insolence or damage done the village would be severely punished.

For two or three more days our self-invited guests remained; then they left with many expressions of thanks for the service which had been given them.

"This bill is too small," said the secretary to whom Brother Bagge handed it.

"We have not charged for what was furnished for the personal use of Governor Tryon," replied Brother Bagge.

"Neither have you charged for breakage and the loss of small articles which have accidentally disappeared," said the gentleman, smiling. "We will just add another item to cover general expense." And so the actual loss to the village fund was reduced to a reasonable amount.

There were still a few groups of Regulators in different places, but as news of the defeat at the Alamance and the submission of the main body spread, these smaller companies melted, and the attempted "regulation" came to an end.

15.

"BETHABARA"

———

THE REGULATORS WEIGHED UPON OUR MINDS AND STRAINED OUR
nerves, but had little effect upon our life except that more
men must be appointed to stand guard at times instead of going
on with their usual work. "Christian," I said one day, "I feel as
though my brain were divided into three equal parts, one worrying
over the danger to the Brethren, one attending to my home duties,
and one filled with desire for that little house I am to have some
day."

"I would advise," said my husband with mock gravity, "that
you re-divide your brain, allow just a small piece for two of those
items, and leave most of it for current affairs that at the moment
are the more important for you and me, my supper, for example";
—he was just back from one of his numerous trips to Salem, and
felt more like eating than theorizing.

Seeing his need for rest I changed the subject and began telling him about my day. "We had white cabbage for dinner. The
heavy snow in January must have been good for the ground; the
cook reported that one of the cabbage heads weighed eleven
pounds."

"I knew the field looked well," he replied. "Any other news?"

"One of the wagons is back from Cross Creek, and brought
salt to the store. The merchant in Cross Creek gave a bushel of
salt for a bushel of wheat."

We no longer had the store on our hands, as Christian was
more needed for his proper work as a surveyor, and besides he

was teaching arithmetic to the boys, with afternoon classes for the little fellows and evening classes for the older boys who were employed during the day. Our experience in the store, however, had made us both keenly alive to the problems of our commerce, and especially the barter value of what Bethabara made or raised. It was good to know that the business was now in the capable hands of Brother Bagge.

Closely associated with the community store, though not a part of it, was what we sometimes called the congregation store, which was not a store at all, but the channel through which articles of dress and all else needed by the residents were supplied during the time of common housekeeping. Each group in the congregation had a representative on the committee, and to this representative requests were made to be passed on to the committee, which had frequent meetings. As seamstress I asked for cloth, pins, buttons, needles; the cook estimated the amount of tea, coffee, sugar, and so on, needed in the kitchen; the shoe-maker wanted shoe-buckles; and the other craftsmen stated their needs for their work. From these requests a list was prepared for the merchant in charge of our community store, and he tried to get the things for us from Charleston, or even from Pennsylvania if a wagon was going thither. Through the same channel went requisitions for flax, cotton, and wool, to be prepared for spinning, weaving, bleaching, coloring, knitting, to make shirts and underwear, aprons and stockings, straw-sacks, bed-covers, etc., chiefly woman's work.

In a family of more than one hundred and thirty persons there were daily calls for things which a private person could hardly get without causing confusion, and while Brother Utley remained in Bethabara he attended to that. "The calls are numerous and varied," he said. "One man wants to make a chest or box and needs a plank and some nails; another wants a pane of glass for a window, a rope, some brick, etc. We try to keep enough on hand to supply such things, and it takes more than I would have imagined." Some nails were made by our nailsmith, others were ordered by the dozen. We made no glass; so all of that had to be brought by wagon from one of the cities where we traded. So long as she was in Wachovia Sister Gammern attended to much of the work as head of the committee, and when she went to Bethlehem to enter the Widows House, Sister Marshall took her place.

The coming of Sister Graff to Bethabara had one definite effect on my own job as seamstress, for she brought with her a new type of Sunday dress, much more elaborate than the very simple growns we were in the habit of wearing.

"It is very pretty," I told her, "and all the Sisters want to copy it. They like the long, full skirt, the white waist with three-quarter length sleeves, and the low-necked bodice with its elbow sleeves and its lacing of cord to match the cap ribbons."

"I have no objection to being copied," she answered gaily. "Many of the Sisters in Bethlehem are wearing dresses like this for their best. Brother Valentine Haidt said the dress was 'artistic' and painted the portraits of several of us so arrayed, and of course that made it fashionable."

"We have been warned not to follow the fashion and to be simple in our attire," I said.

"It could hardly be forbidden when Sister Benigna von Watteville wore a dress of this type," she said. "It is not a 'new' fashion, and therefore does not come under the ban."

"Why didn't you bring your portrait with you?" I asked.

"It would have taken too much room, for it was a life-size portrait. Brother Haidt made one of Michael also, and we left them in the church archives in Bethlehem."

"Are all the Bethlehem dresses gray, like yours?"

"There is no rule as to color, so it be not gaudy, but I think the colored lacing looks best on gray, and I like using a somewhat darker shade of gray for the bodice than the gray of the skirt."

There was no portrait painter in Wachovia in those days, but as women will, we followed the lead of Sister Graff, and before very long all of the Sisters who could afford a new dress appeared in copies, though Sister Marshall declined to issue the material for them from the congregation store, since they were not necessary items of apparel. Christian bought what I needed at the community store and I made it, so it was not very expensive and quite within our means. The seams required pressing, and I was grateful to the potter when he placed an improvement in the wash-house the Sisters used—an iron plate set over a stove built of brick, which gave us a much better method of heating our irons than standing them before the fire on the hearth.

In addition to helping with the congregation store, Brother Utley made a number of preaching trips, an extension of his office as English minister of Dobbs Parish. Brother Ettwein had done a little of this, inspired by the dearth of ministers in our part of the English Colonies, and Brother Utley expanded the service, to the great satisfaction of persons of various denominations who came to hear him preach and to beg him to baptize their babies. He went south beyond the Wachovia line; he went west across the Yadkin; he went north to the Town Fork and over into Virginia; everywhere he was made welcome and asked to come again. In our church register a new page was started, headed "Baptisms of Children of Friends and Neighbors," and in the course of years the pages under this heading became numerous and interesting. It was not an attempt to win members for the Moravian Church, but a purely fraternal service to members of the church universal, the only requirement being that the parents give evidence of a living faith in Christ, and an honest intention to bring up their children in the fear and admonition of the Lord.

Another day I had more news for Christian when he returned from Salem. "The long expected trombones have come," I told him happily, for they had been ordered from Europe many months before. Our little organ was still our joy, and we had a few trumpets and French horns, and even the first trumpet which had been made from a hollow limb by an ingenious Brother soon after Bethabara was founded. But there is something about the music of a trombone which has always appealed to me; I loved their solemn strains in Pennsylvania and had missed them here. Nor was it long before they were used, for George Schmid's little son Friedrich died, and the trombones announced the departure and accompanied the singing at the funeral.

"Gertrude," I asked Sister Graff, "who arranged the announcement tunes for home-goings?" I had long since learned not to use the word "death" in connection with the departure of one of our members, that term being reserved for cases of outsiders of whose spiritual condition the Brethren knew little or too much.

She looked surprised, but answered promptly. "Brother Christian Gregor and Count Zinzendorf."

"What made them think of it?"

"I do not know who suggested it but it was a natural outgrowth of the Choir System. You know Sister Anna Nitschmann began that by organizing the young girls of Herrnhut for the strengthening of their religious life, and the congregation recognized the value of such a grouping of age, sex, and condition, and organized the various Choirs which we have today." I nodded, for that I did know. I had been Single Sister, Married Sister, and Widow, and had learned the worth of having eternal truths presented as they were applicable to each group, and had enjoyed the intimate fellowship within each Choir.

"Each tune is selected with a definite purpose in mind," she continued, "and each has its own stanza, for words mean more than music to some hearts. The first is the actual announcement of the home-going. The second denotes the Choir to which the departed belonged. The third is a prayer for those left behind. So today when I heard the announcement I heard first:

> A pilgrim us preceding,
> Departs unto his home.

"Then for the little boy I heard:

> The Lord to his fold little children inviteth:

and then I joined silently in the prayer of the third stanza:

Lord, when I am departing,
Then part thou not from me.

It is a beautiful custom, Catharina," and again I nodded, for my heart was full.

About fifteen months after the home-going of little Friedrich Schmid, Sister Schmid bore another little son, who was baptized on the day of his birth by Brother Graff, and received the name Johannes. Christian and I stood sponsor at the baptism; but two years later the Lord called little Johannes also into His fold in heaven.

On the other hand, Sister Bagge and her little daughter, Elisabeth, had a wonderful escape when the Lord sent His angels to preserve them for further service here on earth. The baby was but a few days old when a candle overturned, setting fire to the curtains around the bed where mother and infant lay, but the flame was quickly extinguished and no harm was done, except to shaken nerves.

Remembering my own fall from a horse in Pennsylvania, I was interested one day when Christian came home and told me of the experience of Andreas Volk and his wife. "They were riding double," he said, "when the saddle-girth broke and they both fell off, but instead of going in the same direction he went one way and she the other."

"I hope they were not badly hurt," I exclaimed, full of sympathy.

"They were not hurt at all, I understand, though I scarcely see how they escaped," he said, and we thought that angels must have been near to soften the fall.

About the time that Brother Lash went north the Negro Sam was bought for service in Bethabara. He had been hired from his master, and had been working there for some time, and now he asked the Brethren to buy him, saying that he wished to remain among the Moravians. His request was granted, and in due time he received adult baptism and became a full member of the congregation.

Our Brethren never owned many Negroes, thinking that except in certain cases it was better to hire them from their masters; then if they proved undesirable it was easy to send them back. I have never heard the Negroes referred to as "slaves" by the Brethren. In general they were treated more as children, of whom respect and obedience and diligence were required. When they were trustworthy and upright they were allowed their share of the religious opportunities of the congregation, and might depend on kindly treatment; if they misbehaved they were disposed of as quickly as possible.

Our leaders thought it better for our community if we did most of the work ourselves, instead of depending upon bought or hired help. During harvest it was usually necessary to secure aid from outside, but I remember one year when there was smallpox in the Province and the report spread that there were cases in Bethabara, and no one was willing to come near us. The report was false, but that did not help the situation; so the Sisters went into the field, and while the men cut the rye they took the wheat, swinging the sickle, binding and stacking the sheaves, as competently as the Brethren, to the surprise of the latter.

The boys generally helped the Brethren in whatever work was most pressing, but occasionally they would be given a special task. Once when rats had again become very numerous and destructive, the boys were told to clear out the corn-crib and kill the pests. As years before, when Martin helped on a similar occasion, the undertaking was most successful, and when the great hunt was over the boys proudly exhibited one hundred and twenty tokens of their prowess.

When the wild grapes were ripe in the fall the Brethren and boys took holiday and went to the woods to gather them, and the wine made from them, together with the currant wine made in mid-summer, was a welcome addition to our pantry.

As I look back across the years, this period seems to me the time when our village most deserved its name Bethabara, "House of Passage."

In addition to the casual visitors who came and went, there were others who stayed with us for a brief period and then passed on to homes of their own which they established in the neighborhood. There were more Single Brethren; who stayed for a while and then moved into the Brothers House in Salem. There were more boys, sent for the same destination, and among them Gottlieb Schober, who was to become one of the prominent figures in Salem, but who first caught our attention by his musical ability. Brother Graff gladly gave instruction to several boys who wanted to learn to play the organ, and the little Schober was the first to attain sufficient proficiency to be allowed to play the accompaniment for the singing of one of our liturgies. For the rest of his life he loved the organ and was one of our best players.

Some of the families coming from Pennsylvania rented or leased land near Bethabara or Bethania, and became associated with one of those congregations; others went south of the Wachovia line and took up or bought land not far from Adam Spach. This latter group was too far from our villages to make church attendance easy; so they asked for help from the Brethren here, and after they had built a combination residence, school-house and meeting-hall, Brother and Sister Bachhof were transferred from Bethania to teach the school and hold the services for the South Fork Society, later called Friedberg congregation.

A much larger group came to us from what was then the Colony of Massachusetts, now the state of Maine. We first heard of them from Brother Graff, who in turn had heard of them from Brother Soelle while he was in Pennsylvania.

"Brother Soelle has been greatly interested in the group of hearers that he has gathered on the Broadbay Plantation in New England," he told us.

"Where is the Broadbay Plantation?" I interrupted him to ask. "Is it on the coast of New England?"

"No, about six miles inland, where the little river Medomac widens into what the New Englanders call a broad bay—we would say the river flows into a lake and out at the other end of it."

"And there are many settlers around the Broadbay?"

"Yes. The story is that a certain Samuel Waldo, General Samuel Waldo, secured a rather extensive grant of land there, and proceeded to advertise it widely abroad, especially in the Palatinate. Many families came over, but found things far different from what they had been led to expect, the ground being rocky and not fertile, and the winters very cold. Soon war with the French and Indians broke out, and the men were forced to join forces with the English troops to protect themselves."

"What became of their families?"

"Some of the women accompanied the army, I hear, and others went to Boston, the Plantation at Broadbay being deserted entirely."

"And after the French were defeated?"

"Many of the families returned to their farms at Broadbay, and others joined them there."

"How did Brother Soelle find them?"

"Brother George Soelle is truly what he calls himself, 'a free servant of the Lord.' On one of his missionary tours in that direction he heard of the Broadbayers, went to see them, was made welcome, and was asked to come again. In spite of the distance from Bethlehem he made repeated visits and finally became pastor of a group of interested men and women. Last year I heard that a company of them were speaking of leaving New England and coming to Wachovia, of which Brother Soelle had told them."

We had heard nothing more about this plan, but in November, 1769, it was reported that a company from Boston had reached Wilmington and was coming to Bethabara by way of Cross Creek. That proved to be true, and they reached us on November the 9th.

They had left Boston in the middle of August, but their schooner ran aground off the Roanoke and two families lost all their goods, though no lives were lost. In another schooner they reached Wilmington, where many of them had been ill, and some were still having fever. They were housed in the tavern until some of the cabins at the mill could be repaired for them.

A few days later more arrived, and several of them also had fever. As they were being escorted to the tavern one of them, a Mrs. Hahn, asked, "What is the text for today?"

"Cast all your care upon Him, for He careth for you," was the answer, and the good woman rejoiced greatly that she was among the Brethren, as she had long desired to be, and that she had reached us on a day which had so auspicious a text.

Shortly after their arrival there was a conference between our leaders and the leaders of their party, and it was decided that two families should stay at the mill, where the men could work; that two should go to Bethania; and that the rest should move into the partly finished houses in Salem, where the men could be employed in building.

"I had been hoping that we could move into one of those houses until our own was built," I confided to Christian, and again he counseled patience, pointing out that the additional help would make building go faster.

Early in the next year two Single Brethren arrived by way of Charleston, coming direct from Europe and bringing important letters and papers. One of these Brethren stayed two years and then went on to Bethlehem, in Pennsylvania; the residence of the other among us was but six months.

This Brother, Johann Klein, had been sent as business manager, and entered upon his duties with interest and energy. Finding that salt and other things were needed for the store he decided to go to Cross Creek himself, to become acquainted with the merchants there. Soon after the middle of August he went on horseback, taking with him about £30 proclamation money, besides some pocket change.

On the 2nd of September, just before bedtime, Brother Meyer took to the Congregation House an acquaintance from Abbotts Creek, Mr. Hans Lapp, who brought most distressing news.

"Mr. Graff," said Mr. Lapp sadly, "I am sorry to tell you that Mr. Klein has been drowned in Little River on his way to Cross Creek. Here is a letter from Justice Seal, who lives five miles from Little River, and I have brought back the horse Mr. Klein rode."

Such news spreads rapidly, and by the time Brother Graff had finished reading the letter Christian and other Brethren hurried in, and it was not long before I heard what little was known of the matter.

"Justice Seal said that two days after leaving here Brother Klein stopped at the home of Isaac Hill and hired a horse, as his was lame. A man at Hill's house suggested riding with him, but Brother Klein, perhaps distrusting him, rode on without him. The man followed, and later turned Brother Klein's hired horse and the saddle-bags over to a man, saying that he found them and that they should be returned to the owner."

"Oh, Christian, did the man murder Brother Klein for his money?" I cried.

"That is what we would like to know," returned Christian in a troubled tone. "Lapp knew nothing except that as he was returning with his wagon from New Bern he heard the story, found that the body had been discovered two or three days after the accident, caught in a tree in the edge of the water, and that immediate burial had been necessary. The men who found him had a letter taken from his pocket, and from it Lapp was able to tell them who he was. Justice Seal then asked him to bring back the horse and the small amount of money found in Brother Klein's trouser pocket."

"Were there any signs of foul play?"

"Justice Seal was not at home at the time and no jury was summoned; so no one could answer that question."

"It looks suspicious."

"It certainly does, especially as only about £5 was found in his pocket."

Everybody was restless that night. In the morning Hans Lapp was given a reward for his service in the affair, and the Brethren Charles Holder and Jacob Steiner were sent to see whether they could learn anything more, to pay any expenses that had been incurred by the man who had buried him, and to bring back his saddle-bags if they could be found.

A week later the Brethren returned, bringing the saddle-bags and the money which Brother Klein had put in them, which was all there. This relieved us from the fear that he had been murdered, and calmed us with the thought that his end was of the Lord's ordering. The miller who buried him had enclosed the grave with boards; and two years later the remains were brought to Salem and quietly re-interred in God's Acre here.

On the very day which relieved our minds of the worst trouble about Brother Klein, we heard the remarkable story of the adventure of the Brethren Toego Nissen and Andreas Broesing, which taught us that a man might drown in a small river when the Lord's hour for him had come, and that the Lord could withhold the key to the grave when he wished.

They had landed in Charleston, coming from Europe to Wachovia, and had made their way to Salisbury without special incident. There they hired a wagon for the last part of their journey, but when they came to the Yadkin River they found the ferry out of order. In spite of warning from people near, the driver decided to drive across, as was often possible when the water was low.

"He should have listened," said Brother Nissen, "for we were scarcely in the river when the horses began to swim, and the wagon turned over twice."

"How did you escape?" asked Brother Graff.

Brother Nissen looked at Brother Broesing, and they both smiled.

"I hardly know," said the latter, "but somehow we managed each time to avoid being caught by the overturn, and to climb on the top side of the wagon."

"The boy who was with the driver was less fortunate, and was drowned," said Brother Nissen, "and so were three of the horses, but the wagon drifted to the edge of the river and caught there. We had to wait nearly two hours for rescue, but finally men saw our plight, and came for us in a canoe. In a near-by house we were kindly treated and allowed to dry our clothing, and the packages of letters we were able to save."

"How did you come the rest of the way?" asked Christian.

"A friend of the Brethren in Salisbury heard of the accident," said Brother Broesing, "and he at once took horse and rode along the river until he found us. He guided us to Salem and lent his horse to Brother Nissen, who had been ill; he and I walked."

"I felt ashamed to be obliged to accept their kindness," said Brother Nissen, "but thanks to their thoughtfulness I am feeling much better, and have not been made worse by the exposure and strain."

Before the year was out we heard still another story of a hard journey. Another company of Broadbayers arrived, including Philip Vogler and eight sons and daughters, but no wife.

"Mrs. Vogler sailed with us," said Brother George Soelle, who came with this party to remain in Wachovia. "During the voyage she was not well; on the way up the Cape Fear she grew worse rapidly, with what we recognized as yellow fever, and in Cross Creek she was released from suffering."

"Whatever will the poor man do without a wife?" I said to Sister Graff, and we decided that he would be forced to marry again, in order to have a woman to look after his home and his younger children. Until there was time and opportunity for this the other Broadbayers gave him what help they could; and the houses in Salem remained full to overflowing, and my lesson in patience was not yet ended.

Count Nicholas Louis von Zinzendorf

From an engraving in the Salem Moravian Archives.

The Reverend Frederic William Marshall

From a pencil sketch in the Salem Moravian Archives.

16.

WE BUILD

W HEN BROTHER MARSHALL CAME TO WACHOVIA ONE OF HIS
chief concerns was the building of the central town, and the
progress of Salem occupied much of his time and thought. It was at
his suggestion that Christian measured the fall from springs north
of the town and higher on the ridge, and the result led to the
decision to move the Square seven building lots or one block farther south. A similar change was made in the location of God's
Acre, but as there had been no interments, that made no difference
except on the town map.

Houses in the first group were either complete or in course
of construction, and the change placed them one block farther
from the Square; but since it would be possible to build the second
group in the intervening block, that was no hindrance.

"I always did like the new site better," Christian confided to
me. "The ground is more level, and I think the main houses will
look better there, but I did not have enough objection to No. 2
to protest when others decided on it for the Square. Shall I try to
move your lot also, my wife?"

"No, Christian, I have built my dream house on that corner
too often to change it," and he patted my shoulder to show that
he understood the longing that was ever with me, and this time
he made no reference to "the pioneer's daughter," and her desire for
solitude.

With the definite locating of the Square there came plans for
the building of the Brothers House, the first large undertaking of

the Salem builders. "We ought to have an architect," said Brother Triebel. "It has been a simple matter to build the little family houses, and even the two-story house, but for such a structure as the Brothers House we need someone who knows more about architecture than I."

"I am in the same position," said Brother Rasp. "I can lay a wall or build a chimney as well as anybody, but we need someone who can plan the house as a whole, inside and out."

"Brother Reuter is a fine draftsman," said Charles Holder. "Can he not draw a house too?"

"Drawing a house is not designing it," said Christian. "I could do less with that than any carpenter or mason."

"How about Brother Nils Petersen? He knows what rooms a Brothers House needs."

"But not how to put foundations under them and a roof over them," said Brother Petersen, shaking his head.

"Ask Brother Marshall to draw the plans for you," said Brother Bagge, who had been listening silently to the conversation.

"Brother Marshall! He is a preacher, not a builder."

"Wait a minute," said Brother Triebel. "Brother Marshall did tell us how to construct the walls for the family houses."

"He has always been interested in architecture," said Brother Bagge, "and has made quite a study of it in the lands which he has seen. As he has lived in Germany, Holland, England, and Pennsylvania, his opportunities have been good. If he draws the plans I will guarantee that the house will not only look well on the outside but will be substantial and durable. He is the sort of man to consult with each of you about the details of which you will be the best judges."

So Brother Marshall was asked to draw the plan for the Brothers House, and was so successful in pleasing his associates that thereafter no question was raised; if a large house was to be built we looked to Brother Marshall to serve as architect and chief supervisor.

The Brothers House was placed on the main street, facing

the northwest corner of the Square. It was decided that only half of it should be built at first, and that the construction should be the same as for the first family houses, with strong framing filled in with laths wrapped with the straw-clay mixture, protected by wide eaves and a narrow roof between the stories, the walls to be weather-boarded later. From the front door the narrow hall ran back the width of one room and then turned at right angles, planned to connect with the second section when it should be built. The stairway to the second floor rose from near the door, and ascended again to the third floor, which was under the high pitched roof but with ample space for use as a sleeping-hall. The foundation walls were of stone, massive and firm, and because of the slope of the hill the rooms to the west were above ground and could be used for kitchen and dining-room, while on the east there were good cellars on the same level. The heavy timbers were raised safely in May, 1769, and when the last one was in place the trombonists mounted to the ridge-pole and played our favorite hymn of thanksgiving:

Now thank we all our God.

On November 19th, of that year Christian, Sister Krause, and I rode to Salem to stand sponsor for the infant Anna Maria Baumgarten when she was baptized. It was the first baptism in the new town and took place in the meeting-hall on the first floor of the two-story house, with Brother Utley officiating. The parents lived on a farm two miles away; so the little one had to divide honors with wee David Holder, born six months later, who is recorded in the church register as "the first child born and baptized in Salem."

It had been some time since I was there, and after the service we walked about, looking at the buildings that were entirely or nearly finished.

The two-story house stood on a corner, with the meeting-hall on the first floor and living quarters above. Next to it stood the first house erected on the main street. "The loom and the saddlery are still in it," Christian told us. "Until the Brothers House is finished all these houses will be used by the Brethren who are working here."

"Where are the outside workmen lodged?"

"In the smaller log house near the branch. We will go there presently."

So we walked north to a narrow cross street, with Brother Aust's potter-shop on one corner and Brother George Schmid's blacksmith-shop on the other, and turned into it, presently seeing the two log houses which sheltered the first town-builders.

"Now let us get our horses," said Christian, and we went back to the two-story house where the horses were tied. We mounted them and rode across the branch, over a low ridge, and to the tanyard, which was on another little branch. "We think this is far enough from town that the tanning vats will not be objectionable," said Christian, "and yet it is near enough to be convenient for Brother Henry Herbst, who will run the business."

We returned to the main street and paused at the Brothers House, which was so nearly finished that Christian could take us over it. Then we rode to the southeast meadow, where all summer the men had burned brick for the huge chimneys in the Brothers House, and the smaller ones in the family houses. This of course took us the length of the new Square, and by my lot, still waiting for me. On the other side of the Square, as we returned, Christian pointed out the site of the Congregation House, for which plans were being made and which was to be built the next year.

As we rode to the Brothers House once more, I saw Brother Triebel on the corner and asked him whether the Bethabara saw-mill had been able to supply all the lumber needed. "No," he said, "we have had to supplement with boards cut at David Allen's mill on the Yadkin."

"That was quite a distance to bring them."

He smiled. "We resorted to an old lumberman's trick and floated the boards down the river to Isaac Free's landing. The real difficulty was there, for Free had a field in cultivation between the landing and the road to Bethania and we had to wait until he had gathered his corn before he would allow us to drive across."

"Did it delay the work?"

"Not seriously, for we had ordered the boards early, not knowing how long it would take to get them."

Afterwards I asked Christian: "Did Free do that because he was a Regulator and had a spite against the Brethren?" I remembered that the Regulators had met at Free's house about the time the disturbance began, but Christian could not tell me why the man was so disobliging.

In December the Brothers House was finished, and the Single Brethren moved in with appropriate ceremonies. As the Broadbayers arrived at about the same time and were sent to Salem temporarily, the houses vacated by the Single Brethren were quickly filled, though early in the following year it was possible to arrange lodgings for Brother Utley and his wife, when he was appointed pastor for the Salem residents until the congregation should be fully organized.

Daniel Schnepf and his wife moved into one of the family houses to open a kitchen for feeding the outside workmen. The Brothers House had its own kitchen, for with this move came the beginning of the breaking up of the common housekeeping which had served so well for the pioneer period in Bethabara. Brother George Holder and his wife moved into a small new house across the Wach, where he began a farm, to raise produce for marketing in Salem.

While the building activities of Wachovia were largely centered in Salem some things were done elsewhere. The South Fork Society erected a community house, containing a meeting hall, a school-room, and living rooms, and Brother and Sister Bachhof were sent thither from Bethania. Brother Jacob Ernst was selected for Bethania, and a marriage was arranged for him with Sister Juliana Carmel, who was serving as cook in the community kitchen.

Jacob himself was serving as cook in the kitchen of the Brothers House, and I wondered whether he could fill the place of teacher and lay pastor, but Brother Marshall knew the preparation which Jacob had received in his youth, and made no mistake now. Of course he consulted with Brother Graff, and from Gertrude I heard Jacob's story.

"He was the youngest of thirteen children," she told me, "and was born in Arau, Switzerland, where his father was pastor. One of his older brothers was studying theology, and his father destined Jacob also for the ministry, and gave him careful education in the local schools, where among other things he learned Latin and Greek and Hebrew. At the age of fourteen he went to a higher school in Berne, and ultimately to the Seminary of the Unity at Marienborn."

"It seems odd that a Lutheran pastor should send his son to a school conducted by the Moravians."

"Pastor Ernst learned to know one of the Brethren and was much attracted to him; and was eager for the associations that Jacob would have among them."

"How did his congregation take it?"

Gertrude smiled. "To avoid criticism and advice Pastor Ernst made his arrangements secretly, and Jacob was told to stay at home from church one morning, slip away quietly, and go to a man who was in connection with the Unity. From there he went on in company with one of the Brethren."

"And his father never regretted the move?"

"On the contrary he later expressed regrets that he had not known the Brethren ten or twenty years earlier, in which case he might have joined them himself. He was so much pleased with the Seminary when he visited it that he sent another son there also."

"If Brother Jacob was trained for the ministry how does he happen to be a cook?"

"It seems that at one time he somewhat lost interest in his studies, and the Brethren advised him to take up a trade. He worked in different crafts, as tinsmith, first, and then in a bakery and kitchen."

"That was quite a change!"

"Indeed it was; but you know among the Brethren all work is honorable, and if a man or woman is doing something that needs to be done the task is considered equal with the other tasks, no matter what it be."

"Yes, that is true. We lay little stress on the nature of the work, but much on whether a person is industrious and honest."

"At the same time education does count, especially for teaching and preaching; and Michael and Brother Marshall were glad to know that they had a well-prepared man to send to Bethania."

"He ought to be ordained."

"Of course that cannot be at the moment, since we have no bishop resident here, but I feel sure it will follow as soon as the necessary arrangements can be made."

So the banns for Jacob and Juliana were published the three times required by English law when no license was procured: once in Bethabara, on the same day in Bethania, and again in Bethabara one week later. Two days after that Brother Graff spoke the words that united this pair, in the name of the Holy Trinity, and the church's blessing was pronounced upon them.

One of the advantages of our official recognition by the English Parliament was our right to publish the banns and to have our members married by our own ministers. For many years only rectors of the Church of England and ministers of the Moravian Church had this right in the Province of North Carolina, which must have been very annoying to other denominations. For this reason our pastors were careful to perform the wedding ceremony only for communicant members of our town congregations, for we did not wish to flaunt our privilege in the face of our neighbors. Our justice of the peace, or some other justice, officiated at the wedding of members of our country congregations, which was in accordance with the custom of the country at that time.

Publication of the banns was different, for there the only matter of importance was the public notice, twice repeated. It was expensive in time and money to go to the county seat, sign a marriage bond affirming under heavy penalty that there was no lawfull hindrance to a proposed marriage, and buy a license to wed. Banns were always published for our members in town or country to save this expense, and the neighbors frequently asked that such notice should be given for them. When such request was made with the knowledge and consent of the parents on both sides, the service was rendered willingly by our ministers.

Shortly after Brother Ernst and his wife moved to Bethania the congregation there began the erection of a new Congregation House, which was their major interest until it was finished. Like all such houses it contained the meeting-hall, school-room, and living rooms for the pastor and his wife, and so became the center of the life of the congregation.

Through Juliana I heard two or three stories which I hesitated to repeat to Christian, in view of his life-long dread of snakes, though I could not keep him from knowing that snakes were unusually plentiful that year, and that many persons in the neighborhood had been killed by them.

"One of the children was going to the spring," said Juliana, "and she inadvertently stepped on a snake, which instantly coiled around her bare leg. Of course she screamed, and one of the Sisters, who was not far away, ran to her assistance, grasped the snake with her bare hand, tore it from the child's leg and threw it from her, and one of the Brethren who came hastily killed it with his hoe."

"That took a lot of courage," I said. "I wonder how many of us would have been brave enough to seize the snake?"

"Probably the danger to the child gave her the needed courage," said Juliana.

On another occasion a woman living outside Bethania had a disagreeable experience.

"The night was hot," she said, "and the children and I had no cover over us; my husband was not at home, and we were alone in the house. Suddenly I was awakened by feeling something drop on my foot. 'Just a rat,' I said to myself, but the next moment something else fell on me and lay still, and this was cold and certainly no rat. I kicked it aside, got up and uncovered the fire and lighted a candle, and there on my bed was a large black snake with a rat in its mouth! That was too much for me, and I hurried the children out of the house, and to a neighbor, who took us in for the rest of the night."

"And it really was a snake? How could it get on your bed?"

"Next morning some of the Brethren investigated, and found the snake still on my bed, with the partly digested rat making a lump in its throat. They assumed that the snake must have been chasing the rat along one of the beams overhead, and when the rat jumped it followed and happened to fall directly on the rat and on me."

"Horrible!"

"It was pretty bad, but the men killed the snake, and the snake had already killed the rat; so neither of them will bother me again." Such courage does life on the frontier beget!

In the fall we were again reminded that we were on the edge of the settlement, for bears came over the mountains and into our neighborhood, though they did no great damage. And lest in the future the first days of Bethabara should be forgotten, a memorial stone was set in the field on the site of the hut that Martin and his company found, and on it was chiseled the date, *November 17, 1753.*

In several respects the year 1771 was noteworthy in Wachovia.

Very early in January, the Assembly divided Rowan County by an east-west line, giving to the northern part the name of Surry. Our Brethren had used all their influence to preserve Wachovia intact, but neighbors turned a deaf ear to their arguments, caring nothing for the inconvenience which a division of our land would cause, some of them probably thinking this a good chance to deprive us of the privileges we enjoyed as a separate parish with our own vestry. The action of the Assembly assumed that Earl Granville's land was eighty-four miles wide, and placed the line forty-two miles from the Virginia line, with no regard to where it struck Wachovia.

"This is going to be very inconvenient," said Brother Marshall. "We will have to go first to one county seat and then to the other, with deeds and other instruments divided between the two."

"It leaves me without a parish," said Brother Utley. "I understand that Dobbs Parish is not mentioned, and Wachovia will be partly in one parish and partly in another, and neither of them our own."

"Don't worry about yourself; we will find plenty of work for you to do," said Brother Marshall consolingly. "I think the home mission service can be continued, regardless of county lines."

"The enmity and lack of courtesy the men have shown irritate me," said our usually calm and kindly Brother Graff. "We gave them shelter when the Indians threatened, and this is a poor return to make."

"The end is not yet," said Brother Bagge, with the trace of a smile on his lips. "Counties must have money to pay their bills, and look what they have done for themselves. They have run the line in such a way that Salem remains in Rowan County, leaving the new county of Surry with only scattered farms and the income they can draw from Bethania and what will be left in Bethabara. Just wait until they count the cost, and see what happens!"

And indeed it was only a short time until the men who had refused to consider us came begging that we would consider them. "We simply cannot support a county government without Salem," they argued. "Please, please don't ask to stay in Rowan; please unite with us in a petition to have the line moved far enough south that Salem will fall into Surry."

"Our taxes would probably be less in Rowan," said Brother Bagge, whom they were trying to enlist on their side. "It might be wisest for us to protest the dividing of our land and ask that the whole of it be left in Rowan County."

"That would ruin Surry County," the men cried in dismay. "Just agree to join with us and we will do all in our power to see that Wachovia remains a whole, even if the line has to run around it!"

"Well, I will talk with the other Brethren," said Brother Bagge, and it was finally decided that we would send a petition to the Assembly asking that Wachovia be placed all in one county, without naming the county, and further requesting that Dobbs Parish be reëstablished. Our petition was bitterly opposed in the Assembly, though some of the Surry leaders supported us because they hoped we would be placed in the new county.

Also early in the year the Broadbayers decided upon the site for a new settlement about six miles southeast of Salem. Christian ran the lines for them, and at their request the farms were made long and narrow, so that all the houses could be placed along a road on the north side of the farms and at no great distance from each other. Brother Marshall selected a place for their meeting-house and graveyard, for which no charge was made. Following the example of the South Fork settlers they united in a Society and built a community house.

As soon as arrangements could be made Brother Toego Nissen married and moved there as school-teacher and lay pastor. In the course of time a congregation developed and received the name Friedland.

"The moving of the Broadbayers releases room in Salem," I remarked one day, half hoping that Christian would decide to take advantage of the fact for us.

"That is true, my wife," he answered, "but it seems to me that for the present we are more comfortable here."

"A house has been built for Brother Miksch in the block between the two-story house and the Brothers House."

"But in addition to the Congregation House the men are working on the grist mill and a house for the miller, and on the tavern, so their hands are full."

"Very well, Christian, I will say no more, and you can tell me when you think our time has come," and I could see that my leaving it to him gave him pleasure.

Of the visit to Wachovia of Governor Tryon and his army I have already spoken, but it should be noted that as the army marched through Salem the officers rested for a while in the Brothers House, and one of their number, who was quite ill, stayed there for six days. Brother John Birkhead, one of the hosts when Governor Tryon made his first visit to Salem, was sick this time, and departed this life on the very day on which the birthday of the King was celebrated with such pomp in Bethabara, his interment being the first in our Salem God's Acre.

Plans for the organization of Salem congregation took shape gradually, and in mid-summer Brother Paul Tiersch and his wife arrived, accompanied by Brother Hans Christian Alexander von Schweinitz and his wife. Brother von Schweinitz was to serve for many years as manager of the affairs of the Unity in Pennsylvania, and he and Brother Marshall had much to discuss and plan. Brother Tiersch was called to become the preacher for Salem congregation, as soon as the meeting-hall should be ready.

In September we had still more distinguished visitors, namely the Brethren Loretz and Gregor, who came from the Unity Elders Conference to see how matters were progressing in the American congregations of the Unity. This was the first official visitation from the governing board of the Moravian Church to the American provinces. With them came Bishop John Ettwein, formerly pastor of Bethabara, and Ludwig Meinung who was to remain in Wachovia as book-keeper.

"I want to see your little organ," was one of the first requests made by Brother Christian Gregor.

"It is very small in comparison with your fuller organs," said Brother Graff modestly, "but it has given us much pleasure."

"Of course it has," said Brother Gregor, seating himself at the instrument, and during his stay he often played for us, and taught us several of the new chorales which he had recently arranged.

"Are all these tunes your own composition?" asked Brother Graff.

"Not all, but some of them. Others are adaptations of popular tunes, rearranged to make them suitable for use in church services. I like the harmony and dignity of the chorale, and enjoy increasing our store of that type of music."

I knew but little of the official business that the visitors transacted, but their personal friendliness and Brother Gregor's music brought us all into closer touch with the Brethren overseas.

Brother Ettwein was much interested in the progress that had been made since he left us, and especially in what was being done in Salem. The visitors made several trips to the new town, being entertained in the Brothers House, and inspecting the Congregation House, rapidly nearing completion.

The Congregation House was of considerable size, larger than the Brothers House, and faced the Square across the east street. The foundation was of stone laid up in clay; the rest in our type of straw-clay and framing, protected by wide eaves and a narrow roof between the first and second stories.

"The effect is not particularly pleasing," said Brother Marshall, "but when we are able we will cover the outside with good plaster and paint it, and at that time we will cut back the eaves and remove the narrow roof."

"Just now we are anxious to finish it far enough that the interior can be used," added Brother Graff.

"How will you use the rooms?" asked Brother Loretz.

"By putting two doors facing the Square, we are serving a double purpose," said Brother Marshall. "The rooms on either side of the north door will furnish apartments for Brother Tiersch and myself and our wives; and the Brethren will use that door to reach the meeting-hall on the second floor. In the south end the Single Sisters will have their rooms, and the Sisters will use the south door and stairway to go to the meeting-hall. We considered using the two-story house for the Single Sisters until they can build a house of their own, but the two-story house is on the main street, where there is much passing, and we felt that they would be safer with us than exposed to the rudeness of some of those who come to our villages."

"Where do you plan to build the Sisters House?" asked Brother Ettwein.

"In this same block, facing the other corner of the Square."

"What are you putting on the third floor of the Congregation House? I see you have the high-pitched roof that provides much place there."

"At the north end we have two or three guest rooms, and the rest is the sleeping-hall for the Single Sisters. On the second floor, besides the meeting-hall, we have conference rooms and rooms in which the lovefeast preparations can be made."

"Will you bring your little organ here?" asked Brother Gregor.

"No, we plan to leave that in Bethabara, and have another and somewhat larger organ made for Salem. There is a man named Bullitschek living near Bethania who is a trained organ-builder, and we expect to have him build an organ for us, and probably one for Bethania also."

"When do you expect to consecrate the meeting-hall?"

"We think the hall will be ready by November, but we have waited to set the date until we could consult with you."

It seemed too bad that our visitors could not be with us for the consecration. After much deliberation the thirteenth of November was selected, as this is the day on which the Unity of Brethren takes special note of the fact that the Lord Jesus Christ is acknowledged as the Chief Elder and Head of the Moravian Church, and that all members are Brethren working together under His direction. The visitors decided not to wait for the services, as they did not want their return trip to Pennsylvania to be too late in the winter, but when they were delayed by bad weather until less than a week before the consecration some of us felt that they might have waited a few days longer, and regretted that they felt obliged to leave before the important day.

At ten o'clock in the morning of the thirteenth all the Brethren and Sisters in Wachovia, all the members of our congregations and societies, assembled in the new meeting-hall, and after singing:

Give us Thy blessing, God our God,

Brother Marshall offered the prayer of consecration: "Oh our Lord Jesus Christ, Head of the Church, forgive our sins and give us grace anew to become Thy property. Let Thy presence be deeply felt amongst us. Hear our petition that all gatherings here to be held in Thy name may be aware of Thy presence, that each heart which here shall cry to Thee in need may be graciously heard and richly blessed. . . ."

At noon there was a lovefeast at which more than three hundred were present, including the children. Brother Graff presided, and during the service he read from our Text Books the important texts which applied to Wachovia and to Salem:

Nov. 17, 1753, when the first colony of Single Brethren took possession of the little hut at Bethabara: *I know where thou dwellest.*

Feb. 14, 1765, when the site for Salem was chosen: *Let thine eye be open toward this place day and night, even toward the place of which thou hast said, My name shall be there.*

Feb. 19, 1766, when the first eight Brethren moved to Salem: *I will be sanctified in them which come nigh me.*

April 17, 1770, when the foundation stone of the Congregation House was laid: *Sing unto the Lord a new song, and his praise in the congregation of saints.*

Nov. 13, 1771, when the meeting-hall in the Congregation House was consecrated: *The Lord is in his holy temple, let all the earth keep silence before him.*

Then Brother Marshall announced the congregation officers. "Brother Marshall will be general pastor, assisted by Sister Marshall. Brother and Sister Graff will have special oversight of the married people, and for the present will continue to live in Bethabara, serving that congregation and Bethania. Brother Paul Tiersch will be the preacher in Salem. Brother Richard Utley will be the treasurer and business manager of Salem congregation."

This service was closed with a song service, specially arranged, with the ministers, congregation, and choir singing in turn.

The afternoon service was touching in a quite different way. Brother Graff spoke on the text for the day, and then announced: "My Brethren and Sisters, in connection with the consecration of this new meeting-hall the Lord has given us a poor Negro, Sam, into whose heart He has placed a longing to be washed from his sins in the blood of Jesus through Holy Baptism." There were many moist eyes as the profession of faith was heard and the sacrament of Baptism was administered, the man's name being amplified into John Samuel in token of the new life now beginning, which was to be lived among us worthily for many years.

In the evening a meeting for the communicants closed the never-to-be-forgotten day.

Two days later Brother and Sister Tiersch moved to Salem, staying in the two-story house until December, when their rooms in the Congregation House were ready. On Christmas Eve the first Christmas Eve lovefeast was held at six o'clock in the evening. On New Year's Eve there were three services in the evening, Brother Tiersch presiding, the last one marked at midnight by the singing of the hymn:

Now thank we all our God
With heart and hand and voices.

In the early part of 1772 there was much moving. Henry Herbst and his wife went to the Salem tanyard. Charles Holder and his wife moved into a house which he had rented from the congregation. Brother Bagge moved the store to the first floor of the two-story house, and followed with his wife and child. Jacob Meyer and his wife moved also, ready to take charge of the tavern as soon as it was finished. Valentine Beck and his wife moved into one of the houses on the main street, where he continued his trade as gunstock maker.

It was the first of March when Christian came in smiling, with the question, "Wife, how soon can you be ready to move to Salem?"

"In three days, Christian, but what has happened?"

"The Brethren want me in Salem now, and I think that if we are there I can soon start work on your house."

Map of Wachovia, 1766, with some additional Surveys

Drawn by P. C. G. Reuter. Original in the Wachovia Historical Society Museum.

Sister Gertrude Graff

From a portrait in the Bethlehem Archives.

Needless to say I was happy, even if it meant crowded quarters for a while, and on March 4th the move was made, Brother and Sister Marshall and Brother and Sister Bonn following within two weeks.

The Single Sisters, meanwhile, had made several trips to Salem to start their garden, and by the end of the month they too had taken possession of their rooms in the Congregation House.

Before summer came we had duties enough. "I hardly have time to go to see how the house is progressing," I said one day. "As chief among the women serving in the meeting-hall I must be there at all services, and there are the additional calls to attend the meeting of the Helpers Conference."

Christian laughed. "I am not exactly idle myself. I go to the Helpers Conference with you; the Brethren have appointed me to look after all visitors to the town; and now I have been made forester, in addition to my duties as surveyor. At the recent meeting of the citizens I was elected one of the vestry and then one of the two church wardens; and now I have been authorized to draw up any legal papers that may be needed and have been given a scale of the prices I may charge."

"I hope the prices are high enough, Christian, we shall have our house to pay for."

"I have arranged for that, my wife, don't worry about it, just enjoy the prospect of moving in." In such a happy spirit of companionship and service the weeks passed, and on the seventh of September we shared in the covenant day of the married people, held for the first time in Salem.

To this service Brother Matthew Stach and his wife came from Bethabara. They had arrived in Wachovia two weeks before, and Brother Stach had undertaken to teach the school in Bethabara, though he was no longer a young man. As we came to know him better it was fascinating to hear him tell of his experiences as our first missionary to Greenland, where he had landed in 1733 accompanied by two other Brethren. After hardships, trials, and heartbreaks they had the joy of seeing the fruit of their labors, and when he was obliged to retire because of age he left a well organized field with several Christian congregations gathered from among the Eskimos.

It was our custom to take up a semi-annual collection for foreign missions, the collector making a house to house canvass. After the arrival of Brother Stach the duty was assigned to him, and he counted it a rare privilege that so he could continue to serve the mission cause.

Remembering our lack of schools in Pennsylvania I have always been interested in the way schools were founded in Wachovia even when the scholars were few in number. Bethabara and Bethania schools I have already mentioned, and the desire for schools in the Friedberg and Friedland neighborhoods had much to do with the organization of the Societies there. Salem was led by highly educated men. The Brethren Graff and Tiersch had been students at the University of Jena and Brother Marshall at the University of Leipzig, but instead of making them despise the needs of little children it had made them so alive to the value of education that they started schools for the boys and girls of Salem as soon as there were children who were old enough to learn their letters. A school for little boys and a school for little girls were begun in 1772, the latter in one of the rooms in the Sisters part of the Congregation House with Sister Elisabeth Oesterlein as teacher, and the former in a room in the house which was built by Brother Triebel on the corner opposite the Brothers House. When one plants a seed it is interesting to watch it come up and grow and develop, and I am glad that I have lived to see the growth of those two schools into a vital part of our congregation life.

"Why Gertrude, where did you come from?" I exclaimed one day in October, when Sister Graff came to my room.

"From Bethabara, with Michael," she replied. "He has come down to help Bullitschek tune the organ for the meeting-hall."

"Oh good!" I cried. "Is it really ready, and what does Brother Graff think of it?"

"He says that it is a success; it has two stops, is neatly made, and has a very good tone, the organist can see the minister through it, and in general it is very well arranged."

"It will be a great addition to our meetings, especially the song services, and thanks to the lessons Brother Graff has been giving we have several young Brethren who can play it well enough to accompany the hymns, even though they do not play as well as your husband."

"Since the wind instruments have been divided and the trombones have been brought to Salem, you are in good shape for music," said Sister Graff, who knew my fondness for trombones and the organ.

Another glad day followed soon after when Christian came in with the news for which I had been waiting: "The white-washing of the walls is finished, my wife, and you may move as soon as you like."

"This is Saturday. We will move on Monday if you will ask one or two of the Brethren to help you with the heavier pieces of furniture."

"Gladly; but, Wife," and a serious tone came into his voice, "remember that it is only a little house into which you are going. When I think of what you have told me of your father's farmhouse I sometimes fear that you will feel cramped in this one."

"No, Christian, it is just exactly what I want. If it were larger it would take more time than I can well give to housekeeping with my other duties, and I feel confident that we can be entirely comfortable."

It was indeed but a small house, with two rooms and a hall on the first floor, and one room under the roof. One end of the back porch had been cut off for a kitchen, so we had four rooms, which was quite enough for two people. Under the house there was a cellar; and back of the house there was space for a garden, where I expected in the spring to have vegetables and flowers. We could use water from the little branch for wash-day, and could bring our drinking water from the fine spring in the grounds of the Brothers House; Christian took pride in keeping the bucket full, so that I need not carry it.

Yes, it was a little house, and the November weather was dreary enough, but indoors a happy and contented wife sang at her tasks.

17.

HELPERS

———————

THE HELPERS CONFERENCE HAD NO EXECUTIVE POWERS. IT WAS composed of the Elders, the Supervisors, five other persons ex officio, and nine elected Brothers and Sisters, and we met each Monday morning at eight o'clock. We were told that it was our duty to bring to the Conference any matter which we thought might benefit the church and community, or anything which we feared might be injurious, and all these things would be discussed freely. If it was decided that they merited further consideration they would be referred to the Board of Elders or the Board of Supervisors or the Congregation Council for action.

I found these discussions very interesting and enlightening. The economic set-up in Salem was so different from the common housekeeping in Bethabara that there were many questions to be asked and answered.

"Why do we need a Board of Supervisors, if each man is to support his own family?" asked Brother Charles Holder.

"We are not giving up coöperation in abolishing the common housekeeping," said Brother Marshall, smiling. "You can see how inconvenient it would be if we found ourselves with ten shoemakers and no tailors, or with five stores running in competition and all at a loss. A board is needed to keep the balance, and to see that each man has a fair chance to succeed."

"I have been given the tools I need for making gunstocks," said Brother Beck, "and have been told that I must pay for them as soon as I am able. Have all the craftsmen been treated in that way?"

"Yes, all of them," said Brother Utley.

"I think we should have a definite understanding of how the general expenses of the congregation are to be met," said Christian.

"Four industries have been reserved for the benefit of the congregation at large," said Brother Utley, "the store, the tavern, the pottery, and the tanyard. Each branch will pay interest on its stock, rent for the house or houses, ground rent, and in addition will make a contribution from the profits. The Brother in charge will receive a salary."

"Your mention of ground rent brings up another question," said Brother Bonn. "I want to buy my house from the congregation, but understand that I cannot get a deed to the lot, but must hold it under lease."

"The quit rent agreement under which we bought from Lord Granville is still in force," said Brother Marshall. "As you know the land on which Salem stands is part of the general Wachovia tract to which title rests in James Hutton of London, as Proprietor, or trustee. Salem leases its three thousand acres from Brother Hutton, and in turn leases lots to individuals, and so the amount needed for the quit rent is made up."

"Then if I put money into a house I am in danger of losing it, if for any reason the Board of Supervisors, or you as Administrator of Unity affairs, decide to cancel my lease."

"Your contract protects you from such a danger," said Brother Marshall. "The house is definitely yours, and if your lease is cancelled arbitrarily you will get back what you put into it, or what appraisers fix as a just amount. You are at liberty to sell, if you choose, on the one condition that it be to a person agreeable to the Elders and Supervisors."

"That is a wise provision," said Brother Tiersch. "It certifies that no one can become a house-holder in Salem who is not in sympathy with our principles and purposes."

"Is it allowable to mention individuals and their problems?" I asked.

"Yes," answered Brother Marshall. "It is of course understood that everything said here is confidential, and not to be repeated."

"Then I would ask what can be done to help Brother Miksch. His wife was talking to me yesterday, and she is much worried. He has no handicraft and is too old to learn one, and she does not see how they are to live."

"I too have been thinking about him," said Brother Utley, "and would be glad for suggestions which I could pass on to him."

"He might raise vegetables, gather seeds, make cucumber pickles, and start a nursery for fruit trees," said one Brother, "only that means no income for months."

"Meanwhile he might make candles, sell oil, and prepare smoking tobacco and snuff," suggested another.

"Sister Miksch makes delicious gingerbread," said Sister Polly Tiersch.

"And she always dries fruit in the summer," Sister Utley added.

"I need a chain carrier when I am surveying," said Christian. "Perhaps I can employ him from time to time."

"We will refer these suggestions to the Board of Supervisors," said Brother Marshall, who was presiding over the Conference.

This was done, with the result that Brother Miksch gratefully accepted the suggestions and opened the small shop that the Board allowed, and began at once to clear and cultivate the Square, which the Board put at his disposal for the time being. Sister Miksch was pleased with the compliment to her gingerbread, and it became one of the standard delicacies of the town and a steady source of revenue.

As my membership in the Helpers Conference gave me opportunity to learn much about economic conditions in the community, so my service as chief chapel servant on the women's side of the meeting-hall brought me into close contact with all that went on there.

Besides myself there were four Sisters in this group, Felicitas Aust, Ann Beck, Magdalena Herbst, and Anna Minster, the latter a Single Sister. These four took a week apiece, in turn, but we all helped at lovefeasts and on other occasions when many persons were present. The general supervision fell to me, including the oversight of the cleaning of the hall, which was done twice a week. Each member of the congregation was obligated to serve in turn as cleaner, but if one or other did not wish to do this work he or she might pay one shilling, with which someone else was hired. Brother Gottfried Praezel was chief on the Brothers side, with his own assistants, and conferences were held whenever necessary so that uniformity and smooth service might be secured.

Christian's election as church warden and his appointment to look after visitors brought him into contact with all sorts of persons, from beggars to the Governor of the Province of North Carolina. In August, 1772, Governor Josiah Martin spent four days in Salem, and Christian saw much of him.

"In his suite are Colonel Nash, the lawyer Canon, and Secretary Biggelson," Christian told me, "and they have been much interested in the Brothers House and the work shops."

"Are they going to Bethabara?" I asked.

"Yes, tomorrow we will escort them to Bethabara and Bethania; and here arrangements will be made for them to see the Congregation House. They plan to attend the evening services while they are in Salem, and Brother Tiersch thinks our song services will give them most pleasure."

"That explains why Brother Praezel has called a conference of the chapel servants for this afternoon," I said. "Everybody in town will want to attend the service when it is known that that will be a chance to see the Governor. And tell me something else, Christian, will the Governor give us any help toward having the county line re-run and our parish reëstablished?"

"He had me show him exactly where our lines are, and promises his assistance," said Christian. "He had with him a copy of the first map of North Carolina I have seen, and he promised to try to get a copy for us. He tells me that the first draft was made by our friend William Churton, but after Mr. Churton died the work was continued by a Captain Collet, whose name appears on the map."

"Is Governor Martin more popular than Governor Tryon?" I asked.

"I fear not. From what I hear he is not at all conciliatory with the Assembly, and insists that England has a right to lay such taxes as she pleases, and to allow or forbid the holding of courts, no matter how much the lack of them may inconvenience the people. He seems unconcerned over the trouble made in the seaports by the stamp act and the tax on tea, but if courts are not held it will be a province-wide calamity."

"But he is pleasant socially?"

"Yes, very pleasant, which makes the unpopularity he is gaining seem the more unfortunate."

During the Assembly session of 1773 the matter of our boundary lines came to a climax. The Brethren Marshall and Bagge went to New Bern, and exerted all their influence to secure the passage of a new act in our favor. Finally they were called into the Council meeting, and the Governor asked them point-blank: "In which county do you want to place Wachovia?"

"We left that for you to decide," replied Brother Marshall, "but it would seem more logical to place the Wachovia Tract in Surry County, since the act of 1771 left less than half the acreage in Rowan."

"Good," said the Governor; and before many days the bill had passed its third reading, and our point was gained, including the re-establishment of Dobbs Parish.

One of the most interesting matters of these months was the activity of Brother George Soelle as an itinerant minister. When the Broadbayers moved from Salem, he remained, living in the Brothers House and going out from there as opportunity offered or the spirit moved him, not only to the Broadbay settlement but north, south, east, and west, covering the field more thoroughly than had yet been done. He always came back with something interesting or amusing to tell, and we always gathered about him after service to hear the latest report. He was not a good horseman and preferred to go on foot, but the doctor had forbidden that; so he did the best he could, but often the question: "Well, Brother Soelle, what have you done this time?" would bring a chuckle and the reply, "You could count on my doing something stupid, couldn't you? Well, my horse got away again overnight, but the good people sent me on with one of their horses, and had mine ready for me as I returned." Or the answer might be, "Oh, I lost my way again, but a friendly stranger found me and took me in for the night; people are always good to the old man."

The fact was that he made friends easily and everybody loved him, or at least nearly everybody, for now and then he was poorly received and told us, "I made no appointment to go again; if they want me they may ask me." Once at least the opposition took open form. He had made an engagement to preach at a certain place where there was a new meeting-house, and a good audience had gathered. "I went to the table to open the service," he told us, "but before I could begin a man commenced to sing, then another spoke, and finally one man said plainly that I was not allowed to preach there. Others protested that the house had been built chiefly for my use, but I asked my friends not to discuss it but to go with me to a friendly house near by, where I would preach for them. The large majority went with me, and my opponents were left with an almost empty house."

"Served them right!" exclaimed several at the same time, but Brother Soelle shook his head gravely, saying, "It is not for us to judge them."

Such incidents were rare, and as a rule he was warmly welcomed and asked to come again. Young people, especially boys, were attracted to him, and that he liked them was manifest in his passing remarks: "The boy is wild, but I loved him for his open-heartedness"; or of another boy of seventeen years: "His parents thought he cared nothing for religion, but of his own accord he brought me the Bible and asked me many intelligent questions." Parents told him their problems, their hopes and fears; the sick of soul found comfort and strength in his words. At several places he was offered a pastorate, but he declined with courtesy, saying that he could not be bound to any one congregation.

Once he attended a Baptist service, where four were immersed. "If they had had on white garments it would have made a pretty picture," he told us, and added that one odd thing had happened. "Before the first meeting began I was standing in a doorway talking to a man when a young fellow came up, who very plainly had had too much to drink. 'Make me repentent if you can,' he sneered. 'I know I am drunk, and I made myself drunk on purpose.' I said nothing, but the other man told him that if he had come to disturb the house of God the hand of the Lord would be laid heavily upon him. A moment later such a severe attack of colic came upon the young man that he was completely sobered, and had to be carried to a bed where he lay all day in great pain."

Frail as Brother Soelle was, and often greatly fatigued by his trips, he persevered in his efforts, and had built up a rather extensive field in his home mission work, when he was called away from his earthly labors, and went "as gladly as a man to his marriage," as he himself expressed it. He had been visiting in the Friedberg neighborhood, and was ill when he reached the school-house. Brother Bachhof rode to Salem with him, where all possible was done for him, but the next day, May 4th, 1773, he passed into the joy of his Lord.

This was our second serious loss of the year, for in January Bethabara had been obliged to give up Brother Jacob van der Merk, one of her few remaining leaders. "It was impressive, my wife," said Christian, returning from his funeral. "There were five justices of the peace there to attend the funeral of one of their number."

"Five?"

"Our justices Jacob Bonn and Charles Holder were there, of course, but the ones who surprised me were Gideon Wright, Moses Martin, and Malcolm Curry. Mr. Curry asked, with tears in his eyes, that he might help carry the coffin to the grave, saying that he had loved Brother Jacob."

Grieved as we were to give up such valuable members it was almost worse to lose others because of their own wilfulness. The marriage customs in Salem take it for granted that members are fully devoted to the Lord and desire to be led by Him in all things, His will being revealed to us through the *lot;* but alas, sometimes one or another refuses to be led and goes his own way. All through the years we have had cases of this, but the spirit of self-will began about the time of which I am speaking, and one instance remains in my memory. One of the Single Sisters (I will call her Smith because that was not her name), had gone to help Sister Steiner at the mill and while there had learned to know a young man who lived in the neighborhood. Rumors began to drift back to Salem and found their way to the Helpers Conference.

"I hear that Sister Smith has been seeing too much of a certain young man," reported Sister Bonn.

"Do you know anything about this, Sister Quest?" asked Brother Marshall.

"No," said Sister Quest, looking worried, "and I do not like to believe it."

"If there be truth in the report it is a matter for the Elders," said Brother Marshall. "I suggest that you take Sister Tiersch with you and go to the mill and have a conference with her and with Sister Steiner."

"Is there any objection to the young man?" I asked.

"Not that I know of, but there is every objection to a clandestine engagement to marry, if it has gone that far."

That was entirely true. We all knew that the Moravians considered marriage as an honorable estate, not to be entered into lightly or unadvisedly, but reverently, discreetly and in the fear of God, and with due regard for the rules of the congregation. A secret engagement was the opposite, and could not be tolerated.

A few days later we heard that Sister Smith was in Salem; still a few more days and we were told that she had been dismissed from the fellowship of the congregation and had returned to the home of the miller, where she was to be married to her young man.

"Sister Quest was very kind to her," Sister Tiersch told me afterwards, "and explained the situation to her carefully, offering that all would be forgiven and forgotten if she and the young man would break their secret engagement and she would return to the Sisters House pledged to keep the rules."

"And they would not do it?"

"From what Brother Steiner could learn I have an idea that the man would have let the matter drop, but after considering it for a few days Sister Smith refused obedience; so there was nothing to do but send her away."

"And Sister Steiner took her in?"

"We did not want any harm to come to her; so we arranged that she should return to Brother and Sister Steiner, and be married under their care."

"If she should ask to be reinstated would the Elders receive her?" I asked.

"That would depend on the circumstances, but if they settle near us and live upright, honorable lives, and then ask for readmission, I imagine that some arrangement will be made for them to join one of our congregations," said Sister Tiersch, and the events of the next years proved that she was a good prophetess.

As we had made arrangements in the meeting-hall for the attendance of Governor Josiah Martin, so also we planned for the services of Easter Sunday, April 11, 1773. The year before, because of rain, it had been necessary to hold the sunrise service in the hall, but this year the weather proved to be fine. The usual meetings were held during the week, and early on Easter Sunday the congregation gathered in the meeting-hall. After the Easter greeting and the singing of a hymn we went in procession to God's Acre, only two blocks away. Standing around the graves of those of our number who rested there we prayed our Easter liturgy, claiming the promise of our risen Lord: "Because I live ye shall live also," and praying: "Keep us in everlasting fellowship with the Church Triumphant." It is a solemn and yet a triumphant service, which through the years has laid a blessing upon an increasing number of souls who have come to share with us in our testimony to the Resurrection.

Early in May Brother Graff set out on a journey to Pennsylvania, taking Brother Lorenz Bagge with him.

"I know why Brother Graff is going," I said to Sister Tiersch, "but why is Brother Lorenz going?"

"He needs a wife, and it has not been possible to arrange a suitable marriage for him here," she replied. My thoughts flew back to another man who made a similar journey for the same purpose, and I wished for this Brother good success and longer happiness. They returned in the middle of July, bringing the new Sister Elisabeth Bagge, and we were officially informed that on July 6th, 1773, Brother Graff had been consecrated a bishop of the Unity of Brethren for service in North Carolina.

While they were away preparations were made for rooms to be occupied by Brother and Sister Graff in Salem. It was in the Helpers Conference that I first heard of the plan to build a new house for the store on the corner opposite us, and of the preliminary building of a new skin-house behind it, so as to release the former skin-house as a residence for Brother Graff. "Didn't you know of it?" I asked Christian. "Why didn't you tell me?"

"We had joked so much about building a house away from others that I thought it might grieve you," he answered.

"I have come to feel differently about that," I told him. "It may bring more people near us, but that is sure to happen as the town grows, and besides I will feel rather safer when you are away and strangers in town are as rough as they are sometimes."

"That relieves me greatly, my wife," he said. "I often think of you when I am away all day, and when you have Brother and Sister Bagge across the street I shall not worry."

"Besides," I added, "I would put up with more than that to have Gertrude Graff in Salem, and I know that there has been no place for them to live. When the skins are moved to the new place, and the old skin-house is freshened up and arranged for them it will be very pleasant to visit them. You and Brother Graff can discuss the affairs of the congregation, and Sister Graff and I can talk about our own problems."

That was not entirely a joke, for keeping house did bring to me problems that I had not considered when others were caring for the common housekeeping in Bethabara. The store did its best for us, but sometimes so necessary an article as salt ran short, and we hailed with joy and relief the arrival of salt wagons from Cross Creek. At certain seasons of the year butter was scarce and expensive; fresh meat was always a problem, as we had no market-house and the number of residents was still so small that meat might spoil before it could all be used if a large animal was killed during the summer. It cost us eight pence each time our chimney was swept, and it always made much dirt for me to clean up. If I needed help in my household tasks I must pay one of the Single Sisters two shillings a day for working in the garden or for washing, or one shilling six pence if the work were lighter and indoors. If she stayed with me all week it cost seven shillings, and I must give her breakfast and supper; she went back to the Sisters rooms for dinner.

Nor was the cost the only thing, for to pay bills one needs money, and at that time we had various kinds of currency, and must try to remember the relative value of each. "You will have to figure this for me," I said over and over to Christian, who was good at reckoning, while I was not.

"One Spanish dollar equals eight shillings of proclamation money, and that equals four shillings six pence sterling," he would repeat patiently.

"But that does not tell me how much to pay for two pounds of meat," I would say pleadingly, and he would make the calculation for me, so that I could use whatever currency we had on hand.

Early in October the skins were moved into the new skin-house, and the old house was put into good order, and on the 15th Brother and Sister Graff moved to Salem. Two days later there was a most impressive service in the meeting-hall, or rather a series of services, beginning at nine o'clock in the morning with a sermon by Brother Graff. Then in a meeting of the Elders, Brother Graff received as akoluthes four Brethren and two Sisters who had been in the service of the congregation for some time, but had not been so received for lack of a suitable opportunity.

The second public service was at noon, when the entire company assembled for a lovefeast, for which we had made ample preparation, the members of all our congregations and societies having been invited. Brother and Sister Graff were welcomed as future residents of Salem, and the buns and tea took the place of a noonday dinner for most of us, the choirs singing appropriate anthems while we ate together as one large Christian family.

The climax of the day came at two o'clock, when we witnessed the first ordination in Wachovia. The Doxology for ordinations was sung and then the Brethren Bachhof and Ernst were ordained deacons by Bishop Graff, assisted by Deacons Utley and Tiersch. Then the Doxology was sung again and the Sisters Bachhof, Ernst, and Elisabeth Bagge were ordained deaconesses by Bishop Graff, assisted by Deaconess Gertrude Graff.

"It was the most impressive service I ever saw," I told Gertrude afterwards. "It thrilled me through and through to see you at the table, assisting your husband, and giving to the new deaconesses the kiss of peace."

"It meant much to me," she said humbly. "Since Michael's consecration as bishop I have felt my responsibilities more than ever before. It seemed to me that Sister Marshall should assist instead of me, for she is older, both in years and in the service, but she insisted that she wanted me there beside my husband. It was good of her, for she probably guessed how much it would mean to me."

"I have never felt that I knew her well," I said. "Do you like her, Polly?" for Sister Tiersch lived across the hall from her, and knew her as none of the rest of us did.

"She is dignified and a bit reserved, but always kind and ready to help if needed," was the reply. "She is punctuality itself, and frequently strikes the hours on the big bell, when Brother Marshall is not at home. I fancy that it was partly on her account that Brother Marshall ran that rope from the bell-tower on the Square to their room, so that the bell could be struck without her going out of doors." Our town bell had been cast in Bethlehem for Salem and was used for giving notice of hours of work and for religious services, as well as for telling the time.

As yet we had no town clock, and it was difficult to keep the various watches and house clocks together; so Christian was asked to make a sun-dial. After ascertaining the noon line, he placed the sun-dial on a brick base in the Square, and the citizens found it a great convenience.

When I told Christian of my conversation with Gertrude and Polly he reminded me that Sister Marshall assisted her husband in many ways, besides striking the hours for him. "She is a member of the congregation Board of Elders," he reminded me, "which gives her many things to think about. Then when the Board of Provincial Elders was organized last year she and Sister Graff became members of that important board along with their husbands and the Brethren Utley and Tiersch."

"That does throw a good deal of responsibility upon her," I agreed, "and possibly she helps Sister Quest with the Single Sisters and older girls more than any of us have realized. On at least one occasion I know that she confirmed two of the girls for their first participation in the Holy Communion, assisted by Sister Quest, who is an akoluthe but not authorized to confirm."

"We may be quite sure that her heart and her hands are full enough, my wife, even if you do not happen to see as much of her as some of the others," said Christian. "In the meetings of the Helpers Conference she does not say much, but her words are always wise and worth consideration," which was certainly true.

One month after the chapel servants were organized some of the Sisters in Salem decided that they wished to systematize the nursing needed from time to time. After much informal discussion among ourselves we took the matter to the Helpers Conference, which approved our proposals and referred them to the Elders. They appointed as midwife Maria Bonn, who had already had training along this line and could count on the assistance of her husband, Jacob Bonn, our community doctor. Felicitas Aust agreed to serve as chief sick nurse, with the help of Ann Beck, Magdalena Herbst, Polly Tiersch, Sallie Utley, Susanna Schnepf, and myself, who as sick-visitors were on call in turn a week at a time. One of the Single Brethren was nurse in the Brothers House, and the Single Sisters had their own arrangements for nursing, so that these appointments put us in quite good shape for taking care of any need that might arise.

In spite of the best of care, persons pass out of time into eternity, and in our small, crowded houses it was difficult to manage properly during the interval between a departure and the interment. Brother Bonn brought to the Helpers Conference a suggestion which met with hearty approval, and that was the building of a Corpse House on the Square, not far from the Congregation House. "I think," said he, "that a house of two small rooms will be sufficient, but they should be well ventilated. When a death has occurred the body can be placed there, where friends can visit it, and where it can be placed in the coffin when that has been made. At the close of the funeral service in the meeting-hall, the coffin can be placed on the bier to be borne in the procession to God's Acre."

This idea met with general approval and was carried into effect within the next month; as was another suggestion made by my husband to the Helpers Conference.

"Our God's Acre," said Christian, "is intended for the interment of our own members only, but at any time we may be faced with the need of providing burial space for a traveler passing through or some outsider working here or tarrying here under the care of Brother Bonn. I suggest that we lay out a parish grave-yard, so that in case of need we may be ready."

"I am heartily in favor of that plan," said Brother Utley. "Where would you suggest placing such a parish graveyard?"

"It would be possible to extend southward the street in front of the Congregation House," said Christian. "There is a suitable place lying east of the tavern that could be reached easily in that way."

"Wouldn't that put it on our main street?" asked Brother Utley.

"I meant a place east of the continued street," replied Christian. "That would leave an entire block between it and the main street."

"I recommend that the plan be referred to the Board of Super-visors with our approval," said Brother Bonn, and very soon Christian received instructions to lay out the parish graveyard and have a neat fence built around it.

18.

CONTRASTS

———————

"**W**IFE," SAID CHRISTIAN ONE DAY, "I SAW GEORGE HARTMANN, OF the South Fork settlement this morning. He asks whether you would be willing to take his eleven-year-old daughter, Elisabeth, and let her help with the work for the privilege of attending our school?"

Such an arrangement had been made at intervals ever since 1765 when Adam Spach took his nine-year-old daughter Maria to Bethania for the school opportunities there. Now, however, the South Fork settlement had its own school, taught by Brother Bachhof; so I asked, "Why does he not send Elisabeth to the Friedberg school?"

"He says our Salem school is better, and besides he wants her to learn something of town ways under your care," said Christian.

"I liked the girls of that age when I taught in the school in Pennsylvania," I said reflectively, "but will you like to have a young girl in the house, with its possible interference with our movements?"

"On the other hand, she will relieve you of some of the work, and will be company for you when I am obliged to be away. Do as you like about it."

"Then suppose we leave it to the Elders. If they approve we can give her a trial. Will Brother Hartmann pay the school fee or will we be expected to do that?"

"Probably he will expect us to bear that expense, as well as

food and lodging, but he will clothe her. We shall have to find out
how much it will be."

So we referred the matter to the Elders, and they approved,
letting her come on trial; the school fee was fixed at four pence a
week, for the hours which she would be in school. The three
smallest girls, of whom Sister Oesterlein took care all day, were
paid for at the rate of one shilling each a week, while two somewhat larger girls, staying not so long a time, were charged six
pence. This seemed fair to us, and we found the child an agreeable member of our household, and willing to do all that we asked.

Through her we heard of the Marcus Hanes and Martin Ebert
families who had recently come from Pennsylvania and had bought
land in the South Fork settlement. Two of the Ebert sons could
play the violin, and Elisabeth said that Brother Bachhof was allowing them to play accompaniments for the singing in the meeting-
hall, which was giving the congregation much pleasure.

More families had come from New England and had joined
the Broadbayers; and Christian was called upon to lay off land for
a company of English people from Carroll's Manor, in Maryland.
They wanted to be near a stream so that they could fish, and they
decided to settle not far from John Douthit, on the farther side of
Muddy Creek. There they ultimately built a school-house, meeting-hall, and parsonage, and organized the congregation of Hope.

Salem had come to have roads leading in all directions, as I
had good reason to know, since Christian had been appointed road-
master by the court, and was responsible for seeing that they were
kept in good repair, and that each man did his legal amount of
work. Sometimes very annoying situations developed, when heavy
rains washed away a bridge and there was trouble in getting it
replaced, or when one or another man objected to doing his share,
but the advantage of good roads was great.

"You help Salem when you give us good roads," said Brother
Bagge. "It brings more people to trade with us, as well as facili-
tating our bringing in of goods for the store."

"It helps Brother Utley in his preaching trips," said Sister

Bagge. "He does not have nearly as many accidents as Brother Soelle did, though of course that may be partly because he rides better."

"Neither does he go to as many different places," I said. "He gives more regular service to certain places, but his field is not so wide." And privately I confided to Christian that I did not believe that Brother Utley was as popular as Brother Soelle had been outside of our Moravian groups, but that of course we did not say to others.

The increased trade in our town had one visible effect which gave Salem a more business-like aspect, and that was the placing of signs at various points—the tavern, the tanyard, the shoe-shop, and the pottery, among others. Brother Aust, the potter, made a large and ornamental plate for his sign, which attracted much attention, though even without that his shop was always a busy place. There were other potter shops in our neighborhood, but his ware was so much better that people preferred to trade with him, and he was always alert to improve the product. A visitor to town gave him instructions for the making of queensware, and soon after a journeyman potter asked for work, saying that he could make queensware. This suited exactly and a beginning was made with it, Brother Aust learning the art from the man he employed.

"We have another distinguished visitor," said Christian one day in the spring of 1774. "Herr Rebsdorf, Governor General of the Danish West Indies, has arrived, accompanied by Captain Bang."

"What can bring them to our retired little town?"

"They are journeying through the English Colonies and say they heard of the Moravian settlement and wanted to see what it was like."

"What do they think of us now that they have seen us?"

"They are very friendly, and we will do all we can to make their stay pleasant. The trouble is that they counted on hiring from us horses and a guide as far as Maryland, which is not at all convenient just now, with the spring farm work pressing, but we will do our best for them. I think we may be able to let them have three horses, and Henry Stair, with the understanding that another arrangement shall be made at the first opportunity."

Henry Stair was a young Brother who had a desire for matrimony, and as soon as he returned from this trip he had a conference with Brother Gottfried Praezel and asked him to take the matter to the Board of Elders.

"How does he stand in the Single Brethren?" was the first question asked.

"Brother Heinzmann has been worried because he is behind with his payments for board and room in the Brothers House."

"Then tell him that we will not consider his application until he has paid his debts. We will not allow any Sister to be placed in the position of marrying a man who is known to be careless about what he owes. Henry is getting his wages regularly, and he must learn to manage the spending of them properly before he undertakes to support a wife."

This message was duly delivered, and had a most beneficial result, for it was only a month until he had paid everything and his marriage was allowed to proceed.

But life in Wachovia was not all progress and development. One day in the early fall Brother Jacob Steiner and his wife came in from the Salem mill and stopped to see us. "How is the grain situation?" asked Christian.

"Not good. The grain fields recovered from the spring freeze beyond the expectation of anybody, through new shoots sent up, but the delay in the time of ripening brought it to the season for mildew and the wheat is scant and small. Rye is nearly all straw. Barley is scant and small and will not grind well."

"I hear that oats and flax are about as usual. There was only half a crop of hay at the first cutting, but prospects are good for the second crop."

"We have had no fruit," said I, "either to use or to dry for winter, and if flour is short what will we do for bread?"

"Most people will have to live on corn," said Brother Steiner.

"We have built a bolter for cornmeal at the mill, which will give a finer meal, and that will have to be mixed with wheat flour to make bread."

"Owing to the spring frost there is neither mast nor forage in the woods," said Christian. "The larger and smaller wild creatures, field mice, squirrels, raccoons, possums, bears, and the feathered tribe, have been driven into the fields, and have done much damage, especially to the corn."

"Sister Bagge told me recently that the one hundred pounds of powder which the last wagons brought from Cross Creek was all sold in a few days," said I. "She told me people said that besides bears they had seen panthers, which had followed several persons, though no one had been attacked."

"Even as the fields teem with thieving creatures so it goes among men," said Christian sadly. "Brother Bonn brings from court the report of robbery, murder, the stealing of horses and swine, and the counterfeiting of paper and of hard money, so that there is no kind which has not been counterfeited. The present unrest permits the turbulent spirit to increase greatly, and we may thank God that we have remained undisturbed except for a few minor incidents."

The stealing of a few shillings from the rooms of the Single Sisters in the Congregation House did indeed seem a minor matter when October brought us the loss of Brother Tiersch.

Christian had left me saying that he was going to the Stockburger farm, but only half an hour had passed when from the window I saw him returning, walking rather rapidly. Sensing that something must have happened I went to the door to meet him, and was greeted with the advice: "Wife, you had better go to the Congregation House and see what you can do for Sister Tiersch."

"Oh, Christian, is Brother Tiersch worse?" I knew he had not been well for several days, but had hoped that it was a passing indisposition.

"I met Brother Bonn coming from the Congregation House. He is worried over Brother Tiersch, and was on his way to the

Brothers House to make arrangements for nursing; several of the Brethren will stay with him in turn, day and night."

"Do you think I can help?"

"I came by his room for a moment. He looks very badly, and Sister Tiersch looks completely worn out, and as though she had not slept for twenty-four hours. By this time one of the Brethren will have gone to wait on him, and perhaps you can persuade her to lie down a while."

Of course I went at once, and for the next days Sister Marshall, Sister Graff, and I relieved her of all household cares, and made her rest as much as she could. On the ninth night Brother Tiersch had a hard chill, and by noon of the next day it was apparent that the end was approaching and the last blessing was given to him; then our dear Lord permitted His servant to rest from all his pain.

Since the new Corpse House was not yet ready, his body remained in the Congregation House. All the next day many called, and soft music and sweet liturgies were rendered from time to time. So many gathered for the funeral that the procession stretched from the Congregation House almost to God's Acre; and after the casket had been lowered into the grave the usual prayers from our church liturgy were read.

Sister Tiersch accepted her unexpected sorrow with true Christian resignation, nor did she fret over giving up her comfortable rooms in the Congregation House. "There is nothing else to do," she said quietly, when I protested that she should not be disturbed. "Brother and Sister Graff must come here, of course, for the archives are kept in these rooms, and he will have to take over Paul's work in the congregation."

"What do they plan for you?" I asked, half rebelliously.

"The Supervisors are going to arrange a room in the half-story of Brother Meinung's house, and he and his young wife have been to see me and have offered to do anything they can to make me comfortable. Don't worry, dear, it is for only a little while, for as soon as the opportunity offers I shall go to Bethlehem and enter the Widows House there." Remembering a day when I had wanted to do just that, I could not argue against it, though it doubled our loss to give her up.

She stayed with us through the next Easter. She heard the grand *Hosannah* chorus sung by two choirs on Palm Sunday; she heard her husband's name read among those who since the last Easter day had gone to join the Church Triumphant; then with another widow she set out with Brother Casper Heinzmann for Pennsylvania. Brother Heinzmann had come from Europe a few months earlier to become business manager of the Single Brethren, and he was going north on business and could take them to Bethlehem.

Before she left we had lost two more important members of our congregation, for a longer time than we expected though not permanently. Brother and Sister Marshall left early in February for Europe, whither Brother Marshall had been called to attend a General Synod of the Moravian Church. They expected to return within a year, but it was nearly five years until we saw them again. In preparation for his absence he turned over all his business matters to Brother Graff, who became our able leader during the troubled years which followed, showing a wonderful mixture of firmness, tact, and wisdom, which aroused my unbounded admiration.

My intimacy with Gertrude Graff was increased by their moving to the Congregation House, for my duties as chapel servant took me there nearly every day and I saw her often. I usually walked across the Square, which was improved this year by the planting of trees and grass, Brother Miksch having been given other ground for his garden. The services in the meeting-hall followed the accustomed program—daily services of one and another kind, special days of the general Christian Church, special days of the Moravian Church, special days for the groups of old and young, married and single and children. As a rule there was peace in Salem, though in the world at large there was much distress.

At Salem we had a rather unusual custom, borrowed from

early days in Herrnhut. We called it the association for Hourly Intercession, and members divided the hours of daylight so that someone was always engaged in prayer for the blessing of the Lord upon us, our missions, or for aid in whatever difficulty might be most pressing. As the clouds grew darker we studied the text: *When ye shall hear of wars and rumors of war be ye not troubled,* and Brother Graff urged us not to be needlessly worried over the warlike state of the land, for our business was to pray and leave the results to the Lord. So we prayed for our rulers, we prayed for the Continental Congresses as they were held, we prayed for the Convention in Hillsborough, we prayed for our Unity the world around, we prayed for ourselves and were comforted and strengthened from on high.

On May 8th, 1775, Brother Bagge finished moving the store into the new building just across the street from us and with his family took possession of the living rooms on the south side of the house. By an odd coincidence it was on this very day that we heard by rumor of what was to be the beginning of years of war. Christian and I went over to call on Brother and Sister Bagge and give them welcome, and one of the first things Brother Bagge said was: "A report has drifted in that there has been a skirmish in New England between British soldiers and a group of Americans."

"Any particulars given?"

"None. It was just a general rumor brought by several lawyers stopping at the tavern, but in view of the growing unrest I fear it is all too true."

"But how can it amount to anything except local measures to subdue those who have been most active? New England has no troops except the militia, and what can they do against trained soldiers?"

"One wonders. The American colonists are a hardy folk and may be dangerous if aroused, but they are unarmed and untrained. England has armed and trained men, but the Atlantic lies between her and her American Colonies."

"Perhaps the rumor is false," I said hopefully.

"Time will show." But nine days later we knew it to be a fact. Christian Conrad, of Bethania, had been to Pennsylvania, and in returning he brought us letters and newspapers. The letters were dated April 25th and May 1st and confirmed the report that on April 19th there had been a skirmish near Boston between the royal troops and the provincial militia. This was bad enough, but in addition the newspapers stated that the Congress held in Philadelphia last year had been declared by the British Parliament a proof of rebellion although that Congress had vehemently declared its loyalty to the king.

Throughout the rest of this year and part of the next there was the strangest contrast between the phraseology in vogue and the acts of men.

"I cannot understand it," I told Christian, "How can men claim loyalty to the King and rebel against the King's ministers, against the government of which the King is the head?"

"The leaders do not want war," he answered, "and are trying to keep open a channel through which they may find redress of their grievances and keep the peace."

"But it is illogical for rebels to issue summons 'in the King's name,' and try 'King's causes,' with the 'King's attorney' prosecuting the cases," I said, for I had been visiting Sister Bonn, and she had heard about the recent sessions of the county court of which her husband was presiding magistrate, and had told me of the contradiction between these terms and the anti-English attitude of the men who used them.

"It is just part of the general confusion," answered Christian. "If the rebellion becomes general those terms will be changed, but meanwhile they mean nothing politically; they are simply a convenient form of speech."

"Then you do not think that Mr. Evan is trying to stand on both sides of the fence when he continues to use his title of King's attorney, and tries cases under King's laws, and at the same time goes as a delegate to the Hillsborough Congress, which has been forbidden by Governor Josiah Martin?"

"No. Whatever happens the province must retain the old laws against murder, theft, and the like, whatever they are called. The term used matters not at all."

But before the Hillsborough Congress was held, on August 20th, 1775, many things had happened. To begin with, the unrest affected the Negroes; of this we had two evidences, one of which might have been serious. Three of our Single Sisters had been to Bethabara, and on their way back they were met by a run-away Negro who attacked them and one of them was knocked down. They gave him four shillings and succeeded in getting away and came home badly frightened. The same man met another Sister and attacked her with a big knife, but as one of the Brethren hurried to her assistance she jerked the knife from the man and ran. The next day the Negro was captured beyond Bethabara by two travellers to whom Brother Bagge had told what had happened; they took him to Bethania, and Brother Michael Hauser sent him bound to Salem, where he was tried before Justice Bonn. He denied having done anything wrong, but the money taken from the Sisters was found on him, and a whipping was ordered and administered; then he was sent to his master, from whom he probably received additional punishment provided by law for running away.

One of the Negroes in Salem also ran away, but after three weeks was captured near the Catawba River and returned to his master here. He was tired and hungry, apparently glad to be back even though it meant trial and a whipping, which he took meekly and patiently.

Governor Josiah Martin did not exactly run away, but he "retired" to Fort Johnston and went aboard an English ship lying there. Thence he issued orders and prohibitions to which the North Carolinians gave no heed, and finding himself worse than helpless he sailed for Charleston, South Carolina.

In our county sentiment was divided for and against the government. On March 25th, an election had been held at Richmond, the new court-house of Surry County, and James Clan and Robert Lanier had been chosen for the Assembly, the former being in favor of the Governor and the latter among those who opposed him. At the vestry meeting on the Monday after Easter, Christian was not reëlected church warden, but that office had ceased to be of much importance and before long was dropped entirely. Brother Bagge became more and more prominent, partly because of his position as merchant and partly because of his grasp of public affairs.

"Here is another interesting paper for my collection," he told us in the latter part of June.

"Your collection?"

"Yes. I am saving the letters and papers that come to me, which deal directly with public affairs. Brother Graff saves all Unity and congregation papers, but he approves my suggestion that we make a separate collection of papers of this sort, which may be of value some day."

"What have you now?"

"A printed circular containing the *Proceedings of the Committee in New Bern.* It came addressed *To the Inhabitants of the Moravian Towns,* and was brought by a man from Virginia who was yesterday at the court-house of Guilford."

"What is it?"

"It prints a circular letter, dated April 27th at Charleston, South Carolina, which announces that Parliament has declared America in a state of rebellion, and says that the King has ordered troops and ships sent to Boston. Further, it publishes minutes of a committee meeting in New Bern on May 31st, telling of 'the bloody and barbarous action committed by the army under General Gage on the inhabitants near Boston, until they were met by a few companies of provincials who forced them to retreat to their fortified city of Boston'; and accompanies these minutes with an appeal to the several committees in this province to take measures for our common safety and defense."

"Who sent the circular to us?"

"No name was given, and the man who brought it did not know."

"I believe our county has no committee to which it should be referred."

"That is correct, and the Elders have decided to ignore it and await developments. It is reported that Mecklenburg County has already acted, unseating the magistrates appointed by the government and putting their own Select Men in their places, but we need not be in a hurry."

About two weeks later I was standing at the door talking with Gertrude Graff, who had been drinking chocolate with me, when we saw a man on horseback come down the main street and stop in front of the store. He looked travel-worn and tired, and in a moment Brother Bagge came out to speak to him; then the man dismounted and Brother Bagge showed him in, going through the house door, not the door into the store. For a while the horse remained tied in front of the house; then the man remounted and rode away, waving his hand in friendly adieu to Brother Bagge. My curiosity was aroused, and I was glad when Brother Bagge stopped us after the evening song service and asked us to go with him to Brother Graff's room.

"I had an interesting caller this afternoon," said Brother Bagge. "Captain Jack, who had been sent *express* from Mecklenburg to the Continental Congress meeting in Philadelphia. He brought me a circular signed by our representatives in Congress, the circular being an appeal that people take up arms. He also brought a call for a day of fasting, humiliation, and prayer."

"Did you get any further particulars about the action taken in Mecklenburg?"

"It appears that when the news reached Charlotte that the British had fired on the provincials near Boston, feeling ran so high that resolutions were passed declaring independence from Great Britain, and eleven days later further resolutions were adopted replacing the magistrates with men of their own choosing, as we have heard. Captain Jack was at once sent to Philadelphia to take word of their action. Congress thought the declaration of independence premature, but advocated the forming of Committees of Safety and the arming of additional militiamen."

"What did you tell him?"

"That it was our policy to take no part in political matters, but that the circular should have due consideration. Then I gave him food and drink and urged him to rest a little, but he was eager to be on his way."

Brother Graff was never a man to act hastily; so it was five days until he called a committee to discuss the circular brought by Captain Jack. Its serious import was realized by all, and it was known that at any moment our Brethren might be called upon for a definite statement whether they held "with the King or with Boston," as the saying was. After much talk Brother Graff drew their attention to the fact that the circular was addressed to the *Committee appointed to bring to Execution the Resolves of the Continental Congress.*

"But we have no such committee," said Christian.

"Neither has Surry County," said Brother Bonn.

"Then it seems to me that we might do nothing except file the circular with my other papers," said Brother Bagge, and that conclusion satisfied all the members present.

"Thick clouds are gathering, and it looks like a storm," said Brother Graff, in dismissing the committee meeting. "Use all your influence to prevent the giving of offense; warn all our members to be on their guard against careless word and incautious expression of opinion. That course saved us during the trouble with the Regulators and must be our method now."

Friends outside our Moravian circle urged Brother Bagge to run in the election for delegates to the congress to meet at Hillsborough in August, but he refused. In spite of that, he and George Hauser and Jacob Blum were appointed to the newly formed Committee of Safety for Surry County, and some ill feeling developed when they declined to serve. However, when the Brethren Bagge and Bonn waited upon members of the Committee to explain their reasons they were courteously treated and their excuses accepted.

Salem Congregation House

From an old print made before the House was taken down in 1854.

Friedland, the settlement of the "Broadbayers," near Salem

Colonel Alexander Martin

*From a pastel portrait painted in Philadelphia; now in possession of
descendants of his brother, James Martin.*

The Hillsborough congress authorized the enlisting of many additional militiamen and also offered premiums for certain goods if they were made in this country, for foreign trade had practically ceased. "I insist that the Moravians be debarred from competition," one man is reported to have said. "They will take all the premiums." But Colonel Martin and several other gentlemen refused their sanction to such restriction, and his suggestion was not accepted.

That our store and our craftsmen continued to function created some jealousy against us, and also brought us demands which were often difficult to fill. These demands began in September and continued for years, Brother Bagge becoming virtually though not officially a purchasing agent for the militia officers.

The organizing of the Committee of Safety in the county did little to replace the county court; and as the laws were not enforced theft and robbery increased.

Salem again must give up one of her leaders, for Brother Utley was called away in the early part of October. Like Brother Soelle, he returned ill from a preaching tour, and suffered but a short time until release came. His body was the first to tarry in the new Corpse House, and then was laid to rest in our God's Acre.

A severe thunder-storm; the issuing by North Carolina of large amounts of paper currency which rapidly depreciated in value, further injuring commerce; hopes for peace fading; fear of war increasing—such was the story of that November. Then came December, bringing our beautiful Christmas services with their reminder of the Infant Jesus, who came to earth to redeem the world and bring brotherhood to all believers. What a contrast between human need and divine love!

19.

STORM

═══════════

BROTHER GRAFF'S PROPHECY WAS ALL TOO LITERALLY FULFILLED, and during 1776 storm swept the English Colonies in North America from end to end.

Wachovia was not exempt. Indeed we had troubles which did not touch those who held publicly with one or the other party, for in our effort to remain apart from politics and to maintain our freedom from military service we were suspected by both sides, though we gave help readily to the American cause and withheld it absolutely from the Tories. Among our own group opinion was divided as to how we should assist the American cause, some enlisting in the militia, and others refusing to bear arms but pledging themselves to any service not against their conscience.

"Gertrude," I asked, "does Brother Graff think it possible to keep such a congregation as Bethania from splitting? Men like the Hausers have no inherited scruples against military service, while Brother Ernst and his followers honestly think it would be wrong for them to bear arms."

"Michael is worried, of course, but he thinks that the leaders of each group in Bethania will respect those of the other, and he hopes that respect and Christian brotherhood will prove stronger than differences of opinion as to worldly matters."

"Does he intend to try to influence those who enlist, or subject them to church discipline?"

"No. He has taken as his motto: 'Allow each man to be guided by his own conscience.'"

"That is easy to say, but exceedingly difficult to do!" And yet he did do it, and saved our unity of fellowship throughout the war.

Beginning in January the Tories made three separate attempts to draw us to their side.

"Captain Henry Herrman came to see me today," said Brother Bagge. "First he tried to draw me into a discussion about present conditions, and then asked me outright whether we would not join his party."

"Five or six years ago he was an active Regulator, making a nuisance of himself in Bethabara, and threatening us because we would not fight the English Government."

"I understand that a good many of the Regulators are now Tories. Perhaps it is not as illogical as it sounds, for then they were opposing the government, and now they are opposing government still—only it happens to be another government."

"Do you suppose they feel bound by the oath that Governor Tryon forced them to take?"

"Some of them may, but I doubt whether many of them care for that, judging by what I know of them. It would be too easy to argue that an oath obtained by force was not binding."

"Then you think they are simply against the power that can lay and collect taxes?"

"Oh, the Tories are not all alike. Some of them are honestly in favor of the King and his government, and are entitled to all respect if they adhere firmly to their allegiance in the face of the trials which are heaped upon them by those who have joined the Association to support freedom. These are trying times," said Brother Bagge, "and the confusion is increased by the constant rumors of which no man knows the foundation."

"At least Christian will not be involved in this controversy," thought I to myself, for he was growing feeble. I was much worried about him and sought such comfort as I could find in knowing that he was beyond the draft age, so that the question of his enlisting would not arise.

"What did you tell Captain Herrman?" I asked, and Brother

Bagge replied, "I told him that it does not accord with our character as Brethren to mix in such political affairs; that we are children of peace and wish peace with all men. With this answer he left, but I fear others may be more insistent."

Fortunately for us Martin Armstrong, colonel of this district, and Henry Smith, who was elected captain, were men who could understand our position and showed us all the consideration possible, of which we soon had great need.

In February there was a very unpleasant occurrence. George Hauser, Jr., had been to Cross Creek and had bought a rather large amount of salt, for which he arranged to send wagons. There was also salt lying there which had been bought by the Salem store, and Brother Bagge decided to send for some of it. Nine wagons left in company, and with them went Christian Heckewelder, Brother Bagge's clerk in the store.

About the same time a message came to Brother Bagge, purporting to be from Governor Josiah Martin, calling Brother Bagge to come to a certain place to confer with Tory leaders, but he refused to go. When it was reported that Governor Martin would be at Cross Creek many Tories set out to join him there, and Colonel Alexander Martin led his militia to oppose them.

Those wagons set both parties against us! The Tories stopped them, cursing the drivers and threatening to throw the salt on the ground so that it might not help the "rebels," but some of the calmer heads persuaded them to let the wagons go, which they did twenty-four hours later. The incident was misrepresented in Salisbury, where it was made to appear that the Moravians had sent nine wagons to help the Tories, the salt being just an excuse. The result was a formal investigation in which Colonel Martin Armstrong and three captains took part, guarded by fifty militiamen.

The interview took place in one of the upper rooms in the Salem tavern. After requiring a solemn affirmation that our Brethren would tell the truth, Colonel Armstrong asked:

"Have you received ammunition from Governor Martin and are you keeping it for him?"

"No."

"Why do you not accept the new Congress money?"

"We do not refuse to accept it, but we would feel differently about it if we could be sure that it was not counterfeit, and if we could feel certain that we could pay it out again."

"Will you sign the Test prepared by Congress?"

In answer to that Brother Bagge explained why the Brethren did not feel at liberty to sign the Test, because of the way in which it was worded, and asked that in place of it Colonel Armstrong would accept a declaration which had been drawn up and signed by the leaders of Bethabara, Bethania, and Salem, including Brother Graff, Christian, and himself, which pledged the Brethren "to support the country," and in no case whatever to do anything "that shall be detrimental to the good province we inhabit." The declaration promised "the paying of taxes and anything else that is not against our own conscience," which was virtually claiming exemption from military service for those who asked it on the ground of conscientious scruples, but pledging coöperation in all else, and this became the standard by which all future action was measured.

Colonel Armstrong accepted the declaration in the spirit in which it was offered, and in turn gave the Brethren a certificate that he had received "full satisfaction," a paper which did us good service on several occasions.

But rumors continued to trouble us. We heard that the Boston party planned to destroy Salem; we heard that Governor Martin was in Salem; we heard that the King's standard had been raised; we heard that Governor Martin had landed at Wilmington with two thousand trained soldiers. No wonder Brother Graff took as his text one evening: *Say to them that are of a fearful heart: Be strong, fear not.*

> Unafraid and undismayed
> Will Christ's man
> Ever stand
> Let what may assail him.

At last we heard for a fact that the Governor had not landed, that the Tories had been defeated, and this quelled the rising for the time. The victorious militia were authorized to seize a bushel of salt for each man from the Tory stores in Cross Creek, and the share of Captain Smith's company was distributed in Bethabara on their return.

March was full of petty annoyances, with one terrific storm which did great damage in Salem, blowing down a stable, unroofing houses, and throwing down fences. Brother Graff was called to Salisbury "to open a package from England in the presence of the Committee of Safety," but he was courteously treated, and when he looked over the letters and assured the Committee that they were on church business only, he was allowed to bring them back with him. Salem was full of militiamen time after time, and also during the Passion Week, but we were able to hold our usual services and most of the men left before Easter Sunday, so that our early service on God's Acre could take place without interruption.

April brought word of an Indian outbreak in Transylvania though the rumor seemed of doubtful authenticity. It also brought the Halifax Convention, where duly elected representatives of the people of North Carolina passed resolutions urging the Continental Congress to declare independence from Great Britain. The Convention authorized another large issue of paper money, and from this time hard money disappeared leaving us to wrestle with four kinds of paper: North Carolina, South Carolina, Virginia, and Continental.

Now everyone came to spend his money where things could still be found, and very few would take change. If there was some part due on a bill they wanted to spend, they would say, if in the tavern, "Give me a dram for it"; in the store, "Give me some thread, needles, tape, sugar," or whatever; to the tanner it was, "Give me a strap, a pair of soles"; to the potter, "Give me another pipe," and so on. Our businesses found it a real problem to spend the money they were obliged to take; and even among ourselves there was murmuring on the part of those who had to live on their wages, for prices were higher and wages did not cover expenses.

The Halifax Convention also enacted in regard to the Brethren that "as they did not bear arms their guns should be taken, but politely, and at an appraised value, and that they themselves should not be forced to serve," which protected the Brethren of Salem and Bethabara but was little observed by captains of other districts.

In May the taxables from Friedberg, Friedland, and Hope settlements were called to Steiner's mill and their names were taken as enlisted. This created much consternation in Friedberg, where men like Adam Spach were with the Salem Brethren in their conscientious objection to military service. His also was an inherited objection, for his father had come to America when war in Europe seemed imminent, bringing the boy of thirteen with him, and contact with the Brethren had strengthened Brother Spach's feeling.

"I shall not attend muster," he said firmly, "and I will endure patiently whatever this may mean for me. If all men felt as I do they would meet weekly for prayer, instead of meeting monthly for drill." It required courage to take such a stand, but he never wavered, and like ourselves he contributed food whenever it was asked by the American forces and paid the fines and special taxes without a murmur.

Friedland could not honestly claim such scruples; indeed some of their older men had fought during the French and Indian war in New England, and on the 10th of May some of the young men were called out for service. This time they returned the next day, but during the war the same thing happened from time to time and for longer periods.

May was also a month of heavy thunder-storms, and of bad news from the front. At one time it was reported that Lord Cornwallis had landed on the Carolina coast with seven thousand soldiers. Everywhere it looked doubtful whether General Washington's raw and undisciplined troops could possibly hold out against the Hessian and other mercenaries that England hired and sent over. In addition there were renewed reports of preparation for war with the Cherokees, who were said to be led by white men sent by the British.

Even the more trivial incidents of the month had a grim side. Sister Meyer told of visitors to the tavern, "including a Scotchman who went into the garden, found a rather large black snake, picked it up, wrapped it around his neck, let it bite him, and played with it as though it were a tame creature."

"As between the two I had rather risk the lightning," I said, referring to an experience which Lorenz Vogler and Andreas Kremser had during a recent storm, when they were on the Bethabara road hauling fire-wood. Lightning struck a large tree just behind them, shattering it and throwing branches all around them, making it difficult to hold the frightened horses.

"The bite of a black snake does not seem to be poisonous to man," she said, "but one bit a little dog and its throat swelled badly."

"When was that?"

"A few days ago. A snake glided between the feet of a Sister who was on her way to the well for water. It did not attack her but bit the little dog, which was saved, however, by pouring milk warm from the cow on the wound; this drew out the poison and saved its life."

In June we had more storms, several of them so severe that in the woods trees were torn up by the roots, and in our orchards fruit trees were uprooted or broken. On the twenty-second there was a most unpleasant occurrence in Salem, with one exception my most dangerous experience of the war.

I had been to the kitchen and stopped on the back porch to hang up some dish-towels when I glanced across to the store stable lot and saw Christian Heckewelder hurry out, throw a saddle on the horse, and ride north at full gallop. More than a little alarmed I went in to tell Christian, and as we were discussing it we heard shouts and cries and shots down toward the tavern. Christian started toward the door, which just then burst open and two of the

Brethren darted in followed by a shower of stones, one of which narrowly missed me. Christian pushed me into the bedroom and bolted the door, while we heard stones smashing one window-pane after another, with threats and curses hurled along with them.

Almost before we could draw breath the crisis was over, and we ventured back to ask the Brethren what had happened.

"We were near the tavern," one of them said, "when four scamps who had been drinking there tried to pick a quarrel with Brother Meyer over their bill. Seeing their condition, he refused to argue, and let them have their way, and they went to their horses. But as soon as they had mounted, they rode their horses into the public room and made insolent nuisances of themselves. Thinking of his wife and child, Brother Meyer slipped into the family living room and bolted the door; then they turned on Brother George Frey, who had taken no part in the discussion, threw him down, held him by the throat, and wounded him twice on the head with a gun barrel. His wife saw her chance and hid two of their guns, and while they were looking for them George slipped out of the back door, which made them that much more violent. They broke down the living-room door, swung tomahawks around the heads of Brother and Sister Meyer, stamped into the cradle, from which the baby had just been lifted, and hacked the dining table through the cloth."

"How did they happen to attack you?"

"George Frey saw us and called for help. He told us what had been done to him, and we rushed in to find them maltreating the Meyers. We tried to stop them, and they turned on us, knocked two of us down, and threatened us with their tomahawk and guns, and we ran for our lives."

"How did Brother Heckewelder hear of it?"

"He was with us, and when we went in he hurried to tell Brother Bagge."

It developed later that Brother Bagge knew that muster was being held at Bethania, and he sent Heckewelder at full speed for help, while he hurriedly closed and bolted the doors and shutters at the store. Seeing this, the scoundrels did not stop there but went on to the Brothers House.

Brother Heinzmann, hearing the commotion as the other Brethren rushed into the Brothers House, ran to the door and tried to prevent the rioters from entering, but they seized him, hurt his eyes, kicked him, tramped on him, and gave him two wounds on the head with a tomahawk. Then they thrust their loaded guns through the windows, smashed other windows, broke doors and furniture, beat about them with guns and tomahawks and clubs and a pair of fire-tongs they found, and badly injured five Brethren, and two others less severely. The house residents and two married Brethren who came to their assistance, though unarmed, finally overpowered the miscreants and bound them, and then sent for Brother Bonn to come and dress the wounds of those who had been hurt.

By the time things had quieted a little Captain Smith and some of his men arrived, having come at full speed as soon as they heard the news. The men were kept under guard all night, and in the morning they were bound hand and foot, placed on horseback, and Captain Smith took them to the Surry County jail at Richmond Court-house. The Brethren Bagge and Bonn made out a statement of the damage the men had done and gave it to Captain Smith to take to Colonel Armstrong.

The next afternoon the four prisoners were brought back by Captain Smith and Colonel Armstrong, under a strong guard. "I have never seen a man more moved," said Brother Bagge afterwards. "When Colonel Armstrong saw the damage done to the Brothers House and saw the wounded men the tears not only came into his eyes but trickled down his cheeks."

"Are the men still so violent?" I asked.

"They tried to lie out of their part in the affair, but two visitors, who are members of the Committee of Safety, asserted that they had been here and had not only seen it all but had written out a full account and had signed it before a justice. That cowed the prisoners, and they have agreed to pay for the material damage done, though Brother Bonn refuses to make a bill for his services, saying that if he accepts pay from the prisoners he makes himself legally responsible for the lives of the wounded, which he is not willing to do."

"That sounds bad!"

"It is bad. He hopes they will all recover, but he cannot be sure yet."

"Who are the men?"

"None of the names are familiar to me, and may not be their true names. Three claim to be from South Carolina and one from North Carolina, and Captain Smith suspects them of being deserters."

"What will be done with them?"

"Our Brethren are to guard them tonight, and tomorrow they are to be sent to Salisbury for trial." This was done, and there they were released under bond, disappeared, and we never heard of them again.

Two days after Lorenz Vogler and the others returned from taking the prisoners to Salisbury, Brother Heinzmann was suddenly attacked by diarrhoea and cramps and was very ill, but after he was bled twice he improved and ultimately recovered from his wounds and from this attack. When all the injured had recovered Brother Bonn estimated the amount due himself for services, and a collection was taken up in the congregation to cover it, the general feeling being that the attack was aimed against the whole town, and that we all should assist those who had suffered most greatly.

The material damage at our house was nine window-panes and one window frame broken and two bad cuts in the weatherboarding, the repairs being paid for out of the amount secured from the prisoners.

The leading question during July was whether we would or would not bear arms, for preparations were made for an expedition against the Cherokees. Later it was the custom to draw lots for as many as were needed for the assigned quota, but now the officers took all they could get. All the young men of Friedland were called to muster to hear when they should march. Lorenz Vogler, a Friedland youth, left Salem to join the company of Captain Smith. Four young men went from Bethania: George Hauser, Jr., John Hauser, Samuel Strub, and Abraham Transou. Several were called from Friedberg but hid in the woods to avoid being taken forcibly until their fathers could make proper arrangements for their excuse.

In August a young man who had been working in Salem left to join Captain Smith, and the projected expedition against the Cherokees finally took place, Salem furnishing much food to be carried by the "Bag-horse men."

When we received word of the action of the Continental Congress in declaring independence, the name of King George was dropped from our church liturgy and thereafter we prayed "for the rulers of our country."

The rest of the year was less exciting. Seven members of the Council of Safety spent several days in Salem and were very friendly. General Rutherford's troops returned from the Cherokee expedition and were paid and disbanded, except one detachment which was sent to Virginia for further service against the Indians. For these the Salem store must supply many things, including six hundred flints. Brother Ernst and Daniel Christman went to Haw River, where the former preached several times, and the latter visited his relatives. Brother Fritz took charge of our Maryland settlement, preaching for them frequently. There were many visitors to the town, sometimes a hundred being fed in one day at the tavern.

Brother Wallis, who had been treasurer of Salem congregation for several years, went to Pennsylvania because of ill health, and Christian was asked to take the office until a new treasurer could be secured.

"I am sorry they have asked this of you," I told him. "With so much confusion as to the currency, especially the 'Congress money' issued in North Carolina, I wish you did not have the responsibility."

"What I can do I gladly do," he answered, quoting a line from a verse of which he was very fond, and I did not venture to say more, for I did not want him to know how far from well I thought him.

In retrospect the next year is largely a dark blur, my concern for Christian dwarfing even my anxiety over national affairs. I knew, of course, that the North Carolina Assembly had passed an act which made all men between the ages of sixteen and fifty liable for muster and militia service, and there were many calls to muster which Salem Brethren ignored; but Adam Spach and other Friedberg fathers must pay £10 each for sons who were called and did not go, their fathers forbidding them to take up arms against the Cherokees in an expedition sent in April. Peter Sehnert enlisted as a continental soldier and returned in safety when his time expired. Peter Strub became an ensign and died in the South Carolina campaign.

But my thoughts and cares were within the four walls of my home, not with our militia, nor even with General Washington, highly as he was regarded. For some time Christian had been troubled by salt-rheum on both legs, which spread to other parts of his body, so that for three years he had seldom been able to go out to measure land. On January 12th, 1777, he had a stroke, and his home-going was feared. A Brother was appointed to watch with him during the night, but in three days he had improved so much that it was evident that the danger was over for the moment. By the end of the month, though not able to be out, he was able to send business messages to the Supervisors, recommending that care should be taken of various vacant gardens in town.

That his helplessness worried him I was sure, more because he could not attend to his tasks than because of himself; so I was not surprised when he began to talk about a successor. "But you are better, Christian," I said, trying to be encouraging.

"A little better, wife," he answered, "but I will never be well again. The Brethren have been wonderfully patient, but I have done little for them these years past, and now I would like to help them find some man to take over the work I am no longer able to do."

At the bottom of my heart I knew that this was what the Elders wanted, for Gertrude had given me a tactful hint; so I asked, "Have you anyone in mind?"

"Ludwig Meinung perhaps might do. He is good at figures, and writes a neat and legible hand. He can easily prepare the legal papers, having my forms to copy, and if he is willing to undertake the surveying I will be glad to teach him, if I am spared long enough."

This I encouraged, thinking that it would furnish him with a new interest. I brought him paper and pen and he wrote a letter to the Board of Supervisors offering to instruct Brother Meinung if they desired. The proposal met with the approval of the Supervisors and of the Elders, Brother Meinung was willing to be taught, and Christian had many happy hours with his apt pupil.

Another thing that interested him was the building of the waterworks, which he had had in mind from the beginning of Salem. Unable to go out, he had several conferences with Brother Johann Kraus, who undertook to look after the project, Brother Triebel being employed to bore the pine logs for the pipes.

"It is an excellent idea to do it now," he told me. "We need to keep this paper money in circulation and it could be used in no better way than for the permanent improvement of the town; and incidentally it will furnish work for some of the Brethren under Brother Kraus's direction."

"Will they use the springs you walled in several years ago?"

"Yes, and will in general follow the route I planned for the line of pipes."

"Will the water come to us?" I hoped so for with Christian sick it was quite a task to bring all we needed from the Brothers House spring.

"Yes, one of the standards will be placed in the Square," and until March, when the task was completed, Christian kept himself informed as to its progress, and watched with intense interest the placing of the Square standard, where the water spouted to a good height from the top of the pipe until that vent was plugged and a more convenient outlet arranged on the side. At first we had to let a barrel fill overnight if we expected to need any considerable quantity of water, but later in the year a water-hole was dug and walled, from which we could dip the water we needed. As this was at the corner of the Square nearest me, it was a great convenience. Other standards were placed across the main street from the two-story house, at the Brothers House, the Congregation House, and the tavern; so the town was well supplied.

In spite of its serious side, the whole congregation laughed over an episode of the first week in April. The constantly rising prices and depreciation in the value of currency produced a situation that demanded attention, and after mature deliberation it was decided to raise all wages and all charges. This was announced at a meeting of the Single Brethren, and no one said anything except one young man who was not in good standing at the moment, and he objected that the wages were too low.

"You are not in position to talk," said Brother Graff, looking at him steadily. "If you do not like it you may leave us and seek a wider field, for in a congregation of the Brethren things are arranged for the good of all, not to suit individual wishes."

Nothing more was said then, but after the meeting there was much arguing and complaining in the rooms; and the next morning eight or nine of the young men left town, going to Bethabara and elsewhere, hoping to force an increase in their wages and to make the officials dance to their piping. In the evening they returned, only to find themselves the laughing-stock of the town, and this hurt them worse than any scolding could have done.

Called before a committee of the Elders and Supervisors one young man offered the excuse: "We did not realize that what we were going to do was so bad!"

"Eve gave the same excuse when she was tempted by Satan," observed Brother Graff, and several of the young Brethren looked sheepish, and the next day sent letters of apology saying that they were ashamed of their childish behaviour.

Early in May Gertrude Graff had a narrow escape from death. About two o'clock in the afternoon the horizon was filled with thick, heavy clouds and suddenly the wind became a hurricane, without rain, such as no one remembers to have seen here. It lasted only five or six minutes, but did much damage to the fences around the Square and Congregation House garden, to the roofs and in the woods. It tore the heavy roof and roof timbers from the wood-shed of the Single Sisters, and threw part of it into the garden behind the Congregation House more than a hundred paces away.

"It was a terrifying experience," Gertrude told us. "I was in the garden when the wind became so strong, and was hurrying toward the house when suddenly the air was full of flying timbers, and part of the roof fell just where I had been working. How I escaped I do not know."

"The hand of God shielded you," said Christian calmly, and we knew that he was right.

Brother Bagge was very good about coming to see Christian, telling him of anything that he thought might interest him; so we heard that he had been notified of his appointment as one of the "overseers of the poor" for Surry County.

"That means that our parish no longer exists," said Christian. "At least the county has taken over the duty of caring for the poor, which is that much to their credit."

"Did you hear how Colonel Armstrong came to the assistance of Brother Aust?" asked Brother Bagge.

"I had not heard that Brother Aust was in trouble."

"You know how people have been crowding into town whenever they have heard that a kiln of pottery has been burned." Christian nodded. "Well, recently the number was unusually large. Brother Aust foresaw trouble, and instead of opening the door he served customers through the window, and they pushed and pulled to get early chance at what there was, guessing that there would

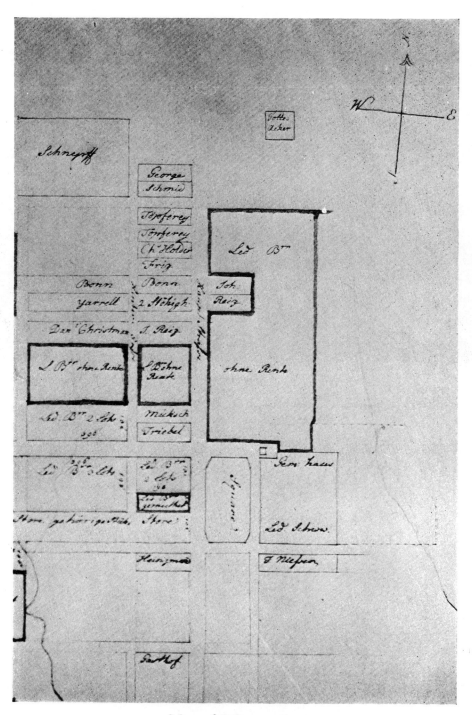

Map of Salem, 1783

Original in the Salem Moravian Archives.

A View of Salem in Carolina, 1787

From a painting by G. von Redeken, in the Wachovia Historical Society Museum.

not be enough to go around. Colonel Armstrong was in town, and seeing the situation he went to the pottery, drew his sword, and took command, letting it be known that he would use his sword if his word was not sufficient."

"We are fortunate in having so good a friend among the military leaders," said Christian; but even his kind intentions could not protect us from all difficulty.

Brother Graff went to Bethabara, and on his return reported that he had met Brother Michael Hauser, a justice of the peace in Bethania, who was on his way to Salem with a message from Captain Smith. A new draft was about to be made, and Captain Smith proposed that we might take up a collection here, and from the money raised he would enlist eleven men and not call on us.

"We met this morning," Brother Graff told Christian. "All the Brethren were asked for their opinion and their unanimous declaration was: 'We Brethren do not bear arms, nor will we enlist others to do it for us, but we will not refuse to bear our share of the burden of the land in these disturbed times if reasonable demands are made.'"

Some of the Bethania Brethren thought this meant we would be willing to pay for substitutes; so Brother Bagge was sent to explain to Colonel Armstrong and Captain Smith, who at first were puzzled, for they had thought their suggestion would be a good way to satisfy our consciences. "When they understood how we felt they promised to do their best for us," said Brother Bagge, "and the Brethren Michael and Peter Hauser have themselves given money to Captain Smith to be used as he thinks best, so that the crisis has passed for the moment. The Brethren Heinzmann, Herbst, Bonn, and I have been appointed a committee to look after anything further that may come up in connection with this or any other political matter, of course conferring with the Elders."

On the last day of August Christian had another stroke, and while he rallied again his speech was impaired, so that others had difficulty in understanding him, though I could always follow. It hurt me to the quick to see him so unlike himself, and one day when he began to speak of his desire to go to his heavenly home I broke down, and falling on my knees by his bed I sobbed, "Oh Christian, must you go and leave me alone in these dreadful times?"

For a moment he said nothing, then I felt his hand on my shoulder in the familiar gesture, and heard him say, more distinctly than usual, "The Lord has cared for you from childhood, my wife, and He will not desert you now." It was almost as though he spoke with prophetic vision, and strangely quieted and reassured I reached for his hand and kissed it and laid my cheek upon it, resting.

The giving up of his legal and other work reduced our income, and it began to be very difficult for me to manage. Salt was rising to three, to four, to five pounds per bushel and other things in proportion, and I did not know what to do. I said nothing to Christian but he guessed, and succeeded in making Brother Graff understand the situation. He and Gertrude had been having the same trouble, and it was not long until I was informed that a certain sum would be paid to Christian monthly, as an increase in salary, which was a brotherly and thoughtful way of putting it. It was the last service Christian was able to do me, for he began to fail more rapidly, increasing deafness rendering it the more difficult to speak to him, and the harder for him to understand, or perhaps his mind was failing, for the salt-rheum had left his feet and body and had attacked his head. Finally it attacked his chest, and either that or another stroke made him perceptibly worse early in December, though he lingered until December 30. The end was hard, hard for him and hard for those of us who stood by helpless, but finally it ended and he lay with all the lines smoothed from his face, resting as sweetly as a little tired child who has fallen asleep and has a happy dream. "He was loving and beloved," said Brother Graff as he stood beside him, and who could ask for a finer epitaph?

His burial was held on the first day of the new year and was attended by a rather large number of people from our various congregations. Three days later I again received the white ribbon of widowhood; and soon after that service we had a lovefeast for all who had helped me during these hard months. That meant all of the married Brethren, many of the single Brethren, all the members of the Board of Elders. It was a service of affectionate remembrance of the departed, and some of the more interesting parts were read from his autobiography. The entire paper was read to the congregation in three meetings several days later. A number called it a remarkable autobiography, and I agreed with them, though it was not new to me, for Christian had let me read it when he wrote it some years before.

Brother Henry Herbst was appointed to succeed him as temporary treasurer, and I turned the cash box and papers over to him. Christian's will left everything to me except his surveying instruments and maps, which he willed to the congregation. Certain items which he had not specifically included in the bequest but which would be of use to his successor the congregation bought from me.

Everybody was most kind, and Gertrude especially insisted that I continue with my work as chief female chapel servant, which made me a member of the Congregation Council though I no longer belonged to the Helpers Conference. Elisabeth Hartmann was still with me, and a great comfort, and in March Brother and Sister Jacob Steiner asked me to take their little daughter Anna so that she could attend school in Salem as the distance from the mill to town was too great for daily travel. In mid-summer her younger sister Betsy was brought to me for a while; and in the fall when Brother Lorenz Bagge lost his wife he brought his little daughter Susel to me, and I cared for the child for more than a year and until her father married again.

"You never tire of taking care of little girls, do you?" said Gertrude, and I made answer that my training in Pennsylvania had helped me in many ways, and that a woman with no children of her own needed to borrow some at times, especially when she might otherwise be a prey to unendurable loneliness.

In May smallpox broke out in Salem and my little girls took it, but recovered without lasting ill effects, and in nursing them I had no time to think of myself. They had plenty of company, for the children were not in the least afraid of the disease and often visited the sick, indeed felt rather out of fashion if they did not take it.

The smallpox was brought to Salem by a detachment of Pulaski's Legion, which spent a little more than four days in town the preceding month. The soldiers behaved well, attending the evening services in the meeting-hall and joining heartily in the singing of such hymns as

> Now I have found the solid ground
> Which holds my anchor fast for aye.

A corporal and several privates were called from the hall one evening, and next day Sister Bagge told me that three deserters had been arrested. The leader was held for a higher tribunal, but the other two were made to run the gantlet in the Brothers House yard.

"I could not watch them," said Sister Bagge. "The soldiers formed two lines, each armed with a stirrup-strap, and the two men were forced to run between them, taking all the blows that reached them, until they were ready to admit their wrong-doing."

"Were they members of the company?" I asked.

"I understand that they were not regularly enlisted men, but were helping with the baggage."

"Any reason given for their desertion?"

"They are said to have stolen a number of things and then to have sold them."

"Then they deserved what they got," said I, with the lack of sympathy we are only too ready to give to those who do wrong and suffer for it.

"Poor hurt men," said little Anna bursting into tears, for we were talking before the children, not thinking how it might affect them, and the conversation ceased while I tried to comfort the tender little heart.

Forty-one residents of Salem suffered before the epidemic ended, and of these three passed away. The sickness dragged out endlessly, for we dared not shorten it by inoculating those who were liable to take it, because of threats made against us if we did inoculate. John Snead, of Richmond Court-house, was the worst in his threats, but all the neighbors were afraid of the town, and took all sorts of precautions if obliged to come in. A tobacco leaf, rolled and stuffed in each nostril; tar smeared on the forehead and under the nose, were the preventives most in favor, though whether they really did any good I do not know. One result was that fewer demands were made for supplies for the militia, and in spite of the cases of illness the harvests were gathered without outside help. In September a lovefeast was held for those who had recovered, so that due thanks might be rendered to our great Physician, for His help in our need.

Also in September Brother Graff brought me a request from the Elders that I would undertake the task of looking after the ladies visiting our town—Brother Bagge had taken Christian's place with visiting gentlemen. Feeling that in this way I was carrying on Christian's work I said yes.

20

ENCIRCLED BY DANGER

O N NOVEMBER 5, 1779, BROTHER AND SISTER MARSHALL REJOICED our hearts by their return to Wachovia after an absence greatly prolonged by the war. Indeed their return journey had taken more than a year, for they had left Barby in September of the preceding year, had gone to England, and had finally secured passage to New York, which they reached in April. They were accompanied by Bishop Johann Friedrich Reichel and his wife, who had been sent by the Unity Elders Conference to visit the American Moravian congregations and advise with them in their present difficult circumstances. The party had remained for some time in Bethlehem, Pennsylvania, and the Bishop and his wife were still there, and would visit Wachovia later.

That Brother Marshall had many questions to ask and that Brother Graff had much to tell him may easily be imagined. All the incidents of the years of war were to be related, especially those which concerned the Wachovia land.

"You will be interested to know that Brother Hutton transferred to me the title to Wachovia," said Brother Marshall, "and as I have been an American citizen for many years we have hoped that this would solve some of the problems."

"We need help," said Brother Graff, "need it badly. Acts have been passed by the Assembly, confiscating the property of non-resident owners, and claim has been made that this includes all of our land since Brother Hutton is an Englishman. It has gone so far that entries have been made on our land by many persons; some of our own members have entered, fearing to lose their farms, and a number of those who do not feel kindly toward us have entered the land on which our villages and mills are built, as well as our unsold land."

"Do you have a list of those entries?"

"Yes, we had a copy made, and I have it ready for you. I think it will be necessary to go to the Assembly to have our land made safe, and the transfer of title to you will help, I feel sure."

"What about the Oath of Allegiance?"

"That is finally adjusted satisfactorily. The Assembly passed an act prescribing a form which we are willing to subscribe, and those of our members who had not already taken the Test Oath appeared before Justice Dobson, took the Affirmation, and received certificates."

"How about service in the militia?"

"Some of our members outside Salem have enlisted, but for others inside and outside Salem fines were paid, first of £10, and last year £25, for each young man who refused to serve. The last act of Assembly freed those of us who would register as having conscientious objections and would agree to pay the taxes threefold. It is a heavy burden, but we were glad to have the matter so arranged."

"I will go before the Committee this month and take the Affirmation," said Brother Marshall, "and notify them that I am now the legal proprietor of our land. Tell me about the financial situation."

"It is bad and our losses are heavy. Perhaps the shortest way to state it is to say that today salt costs £3 in hard money and £80 in paper money per bushel."

Brother Marshall threw up his hands, then asked rather grimly: "What about crops?"

"A late freeze killed all the fruit and hurt the grain badly."

"Anything else unpleasant?"

"There are many deserters lying out in the woods, stealing at every opportunity, and others take advantage of this and pilfer when they can, trusting that the blame will fall on the outlyers."

"For example?"

"For example our Negro Jacob. He was a provisional member of the congregation, and we thought of him as a reliable man and took every care of him when he contracted smallpox in the last epidemic, but he had hardly recovered when we began to miss things, at the tavern, at Sister Reuter's, at the Brothers House. We suspected this stranger and that, then suddenly discovered that Jacob was the thief. Of course he was whipped, and that night one of our horses died of poison. He was forced to admit that he had killed it out of spite, and was whipped again, but it did not lead him to repentance; so he was sold to Robert Lanier, who lives twelve miles away near the Shallow Ford of Yadkin River. At least that is one problem with which you will not have to deal."

"What did you get for him."

"One hundred bushels of oats, two hundred and fifty bushels of corn, one hundred and thirty bushels of rye, six bulls, two thousand pounds of hog-meat. Half is to be paid before the end of this year, and half next year. Barter is far more satisfactory than money these days."

"How about health?"

"It has been about as usual. We had an epidemic of mumps, one of dysentery, the usual colds, and the epidemic of smallpox following the visit of Pulaski's men."

"How have you personally stood the strain?"

"Very well, though I had a rather bad accident in February of this year. I was on the way to Bethabara and at the Petersbach my horse shied and threw me. I rode on to Bethabara, where I was bled and put to bed, and Brother Bonn was notified. His medicine seemed to relieve me, but on the third day I felt greatly oppressed in my chest, and my back was very painful. Brother Bonn bled me again; and the Brethren Heinzmann and Herbst manufactured a litter to be swung between two horses; in that I was brought to Salem with a minimum of suffering. I stood the trip very well and gradually recovered."

"One more question. What about the spiritual life of the Brethren in the midst of these distresses?"

"There at least I can give you a more favorable answer. As was to be expected there has been much discussion, the expression of differing opinions, some grumbling, but on the whole our people have done wonderfully well. Our regular services have been maintained, and many visitors have attended them and have said that they received benefit. Preaching has been continued in our country groups, with some service at more distant points. We have lost leaders, as you have heard, but some of our younger Brethren have developed nicely, and on July 14th of this year I ordained Gottfried Praezel and Valentine Beck as deacons, the latter as pastor of Friedberg and the former to help here. Others are doing well in managing the businesses of the congregation, and Brother Traugott Bagge has won our confidence and the trust of the county and militia officials. The cleavage between those who have refused militia service and those who have enlisted has not resulted in splitting any of the congregations; in Bethania, for example, the Hausers have made things easier for those declining active service. The Friedlanders have been unsettled, but in general have accepted enlistment. When fines have been demanded and paid in Salem and in Friedberg the amount was largely raised by subscription, so that it did not fall too heavily on any individual; the brotherly willingness to help was gratifying. In short, the Saviour has proved Himself our Leader, our Shield, our Chief Elder."

"Thank God!" said Brother Marshall. "In Him will we continue to put our trust."

Of this divine assistance we had greater and greater need in the months that followed. General Washington held the British forces in check in the north, but South Carolina and Georgia were overrun, Charleston was captured, and the Americans under General Gates were defeated at Camden. The Brethren in Wachovia faced difficulty and danger on every side, and nothing short of Almighty Power could have brought us through without disaster. As Brother Graff expressed it: "God protected us numberless times, and through His angels often turned away the misfortune which the Evil One planned and intended."

The year 1780 opened not so badly. The boys school was reorganized in January with eleven scholars and with the Brethren Christian Heckewelder and Gottlieb Schober as teachers. My Elisabeth was received as a provisional member of the Salem congregation, her father, George Hartmann, having come from Friedberg for the ceremony. The county court of Surry answered in the affirmative our request that our Brethren might pay only the provincial tax threefold and might pay the county tax straight.

In the latter part of February the lawless spirit began to manifest itself in our neighborhood. Several young men from the English settlement, sons of good friends of ours, threw stones at Brother Heinzmann for pure wantonness, and also threw a stone into the shoeshop, which missed the workmen but broke a tile in the stove. They had no grudge against us, and their fathers were distressed and promised to speak seriously to their sons, but it was typical of the restlessness and irresponsibility of many.

In The Hollow, some miles north of Wachovia, there were many outlyers, and a company of Guilford County militia marched against them, but without much result. We had a very hard thunder-storm, with a terrific wind and a roaring sound like an earthquake, but the Lord protected us from harm.

With June the constant passing through our towns began. From my window I saw them, on foot, in wagons, on horseback, largely coming from the south. "They are fleeing from the English armies," Brother Bagge told me. "Since the American defeats in Georgia and South Carolina the people feel very unsafe, and are going elsewhere, chiefly toward Virginia."

"Will they be safer there?" I asked.

"At present there is not much military activity in Virginia, but who can tell how long that will last? A new draft has been called; the young men from Friedland and Hope attended the muster, and Philip Green has been drafted."

"In which direction are they to go?"

"To the south, where a new effort is to be made to check the British."

"Is there any late news from the south?"

"A soldier who has passed through Salem within the last days tells of a particularly bloody engagement between the troops of the Continental officer Buford and Colonel Tarleton. He says that Buford's men laid down their arms in token of surrender, and then, as the English came near, one man jerked up his gun and fired. The English went wild and killed right and left without mercy; 'Tarleton's quarters' is likely to become the name of all merciless slaughter of unarmed men."

"Will more of our men be called?"

"Many more, probably. Brother Graff tells me that three of the Friedlanders came asking for certificates that they are members of our Society, but he refused to issue the certificates, telling them that they have waited too long to register as conscientious objectors who desired to pay the threefold tax, and that they will have to serve."

Into this confused situation came Bishop Friedrich Reichel and his party on June 15th. Their trip had been uneventful, except that north of the Potomac River a coffer had been stolen, and this was serious, since it contained the deed from Hutton to Brother Marshall transferring title to Wachovia. It had been impossible to wait for the uncertain finding of the coffer, but a suitable reward had been offered, and there was hope that this would induce someone to bring it in. Arrangements were at once made to send a messenger for it, and fortunately it was recovered.

Taking heart from the British successes, the Tories in our neighborhood now became very active. Over on the Yadkin, Captain Samuel Bryant headed one party, and Captain Henry Smith called out his company of militia to meet them. "Brother Nissen reports that Michael Vogler, George Lagenauer, and other men from Friedland have gone," Sister Graff told me, "and he fears that the fact that Salem is sending none will make trouble for us."

"It is a critical time!"

"It is indeed. The Tories have risen in the Abbotts Creek settlement, and Frederic Miller has come here to stay a few days, fearing that they will raid his house as they have been doing elsewhere."

Brother Reichel made no complaint at having been sent to America at such a time, but instead he did all that he could to keep up our spirits and our courage. Speaking on the anniversary of the founding of Herrnhut, he took as his text: *The Lord hath done great things for us, whereof we are glad.* "Think, my Brethren," he told us, "think of Herrnhut, founded fifty-eight years ago, and of the many other congregations which have arisen since, and remember how the Lord God himself has brought them through all kinds of dangers from within and without. In truth we can apply this text to ourselves and say: The Lord hath done great things for us."

On another occasion, speaking to Congregation Council, he told us: "It is not only wisdom but our duty that as children of peace we keep quiet during these days of turmoil, without partisanship, but our Brethren should not permit themselves to be called Tories, which slanders them, and they have proved the contrary. We must bear our fair part in the calamities of the times, and must not think that as children of God we shall escape the general trials of the country. If the Saviour will only hold us together and let us keep our homes in these turbulent days we will have great reason to give Him thanks and praise."

"It is all right to tell the Brethren that they should repudiate the hated name of Tory," I said afterward to Sister Graff, "but he did not tell them how they can force evil-minded men to hold their tongues!"

"Richard always said that you could not force men to be fair," said Sister Utley, who was also a member of the Council.

"At least some of the leaders mean to treat us justly," said Gertrude. "Brother Bagge told Michael that when Major Joseph Winston left a few days ago, after spending the night here with his light-horse, he drew up his company in front of the store and gave his and their thanks to Brother Bagge for the good treatment they had received."

"We can count on Colonel Martin Armstrong, Colonel Alexander Martin, and a handful of others, and the only thing is to hope that the rest will be prevented from harming us," said Sister Marshall, who had come up while we were talking. The trouble proved to be that the best of the officers had little control over their troops, most of them short-term men who came and went, with no respect for military discipline.

In addition to his public addresses Brother Reichel and his wife had a personal conversation with each member of the Moravian Church in Wachovia, making a study of the situation within our ranks. Certain changes were suggested, and one of them took me utterly by surprise.

It seems that Brother Heinzmann had stated that he would like a change, having been the business manager of the Single Brethren for more than six years. He had been doing some preaching during that time, and it was suggested that he might be placed in charge of Friedland, where a congregation was to be organized, allowing Brother Nissen and his family to return to Salem. I told Gertrude afterwards that she might have given me a hint, but she only laughed and said she did not repeat official matters outside the Board of Elders; so when I answered a knock at the door and found Bishop Reichel standing there I had no idea why he had come.

"Sister Reuter," he said, after a few passing remarks, "I bring you a call from the Elders. It is planned to send Brother Heinzmann to Friedland as pastor, and you are called to marry him and go there as pastor's wife."

"But I am quite content with my life here, taking care of my little girls, and supervising the chapel servants, and looking after visitors," I said, rapidly thinking of the various reasons why I might refuse.

"This is a call to more important service," he said calmly. "Think it over carefully, and I am sure you will not feel at liberty to decline."

"But you have said nothing about Brother Heinzmann's wishes in the matter."

"He has said that he will be glad to have you accept the proposal, and the Elders feel that you and he are well suited to work together in that field."

"I will let you know this evening," I said, but there was little doubt in my mind, for it was indeed a call to wider service, and having grown up among a farming population I had no doubt about making myself at home in a country congregation such as Friedland was coming to be.

Four days later, in the afternoon, we were betrothed in the room of Brother and Sister Marshall. Brother Reichel had been quite ill with an attack of flux, and though he was better he was not able to be present.

Eight days later Brother Heinzmann turned over the cash box and the account books of the Single Brethren to the Brethren Petersen and Samuel Stotz, who were to succeed him. The next day, July 23rd, the Single Brethren had a lovefeast in which they bade farewell to Brother Heinzmann, thanking him for his faithful service of six and a half years, and at the close he showed his love for each Brother by giving to each the kiss of peace.

That evening, in the meeting-hall, Brother Reichel spoke on the text for the day, with special reference to us, and the choir sang the marriage liturgy:

> Lord, Lord God, who Thyself didst marriage institute.
> . . . Thou has desired that this our Brother, this our Sister,
> in the bond of holy wedlock shall united be, that together
> they may serve Thy congregation and may serve Thee.
> . . . Oh anoint them as a priestly couple, and reveal Thy-
> self to them in every way . . . and teach them how to live
> according to Thy will, until all has been done, oh Lord,
> to which Thou hast appointed them.

I had heard the liturgy often, but never with the meaning that it had that evening, as Brother Reichel pronounced the blessing of the Lord upon us.

I returned to my home, and Brother Heinzmann went to the Congregation House; four days later Elisabeth and little Anna moved to the Single Sisters and Casper came to my house, where we remained until the 10th of August, when we moved to Friedland and the Nissen family took my house, with the stipulation that the room upstairs should be reserved for us, to be used whenever we spent the night in Salem.

On September 16th a solemn ordination service was held in Salem, and Bishop Reichel, assisted by Brother Graff, ordained the Brethren Heinzmann, Fritz, and Friedrich Peter as deacons of the Unity of Brethren, Casper for service in Friedland, Brother Fritz as pastor of Hope congregation, and Brother Peter to serve as secretary of the various boards and assist in the ministerial service as needed. Four Sisters were received as akoluthes, and of them I was one, so receiving the stamp of approval of the church upon my call to assist my husband. In this ceremony the Sisters Marshall and Graff took part, and as I gave my hand to Gertrude and felt her warm and loving clasp I felt a new impulse to dedicate myself to do my best, with the help of the Lord.

My new husband was a man a little above medium height, slender, not given to many words, but a man in whom others felt confidence; so it was not long before we had made friends with our parishioners, sharing with them in their anxieties of which the war was bringing not a few. Several wagons had been pressed for Continental service, taking flour and meal and other supplies to the army in South Carolina, and when word came of the defeat at Pinetree (later called Camden), friends of the waggoners were much worried about them. Casper went to Salem to see whether he could get news and came back to report: "Colonel Armstrong was in the battle, but escaped. Many soldiers are passing through Salem, on foot, hungry, without money, and our Brethren are having their hands full feeding them."

"Did you hear anything about the wagons?"

"Only that horses have been taken wherever they could be found by the soldiers, and that while the wagons were not captured by the English many of them are standing along the road, unable to move because the horses are gone."

This was confirmed a few days later when Peter Schneider and George Lagenauer arrived, saying that they had left their wagons thirty miles away, all right except that two of their horses had been stolen. Arrangements were made at once to send other horses to bring the wagons in, and Casper went to Salem to take the good news. When he returned he told me, "The Society members from Friedberg, Bethabara, and Bethania have also come back without personal injury and have recovered most of what they had lost."

"How is Salem faring?" for by our transfer to the country we were escaping the constant confusion on the main street of that town.

"A number of Virginia cavalry were there yesterday, under Colonel Campbell, accompanied by Colonel Martin Armstrong. They took possession of the tavern meadow for camp-site and pasture, but made requisition only for bread. They behaved in an orderly manner and many of them attended the evening service in the meeting-hall."

Next day Colonel Campbell and his men came through the Friedland settlement, ordering grain, but at a fair price. One of the men said that after his company left Salem he had been sent back on an errand, and found that a few men had arrived who were behaving in a manner which he called brutal. "They ought to have given one fellow a ball in his head," he said indignantly.

Brother Reichel took a somewhat different view, telling the Congregation Council: "It is a cause for thanksgiving that we suffered no harm from the soldiers who were here yesterday. In spite of all the insolence which people give us during these times we must remember that in war nothing is done that is right and praiseworthy, and must thank the Saviour that we have been shielded from serious harm. He will make known to all men that we are loyal to this country, even as we have taken the Affirmation in the sight of God."

When every day brought its story of turmoil and confusion,

of requisitions, of abuse, of danger, of strife between Whigs and
Tories, it is impossible to remember or relate all that happened. A
few things one can never forget, such as the account of the Whig
encampment at Bethabara in September, when punishment was
meted out to Tories who had been arrested and brought in. Man
after man was whipped, one receiving as much as one hundred
lashes. One was hanged, but before he died he admitted that he
had committed highway robbery and deserved his sentence.

Bad as that was, one felt more indignation at the incident of
which Brother Fritz told us when we met him at the Conference
of Country Ministers, which Brother Reichel had organized and
which met each month.

"Last night about ten o'clock we were already asleep," he
said, "when Captain Holston and sixteen men arrived, and burst
through the door. They ordered us to open our chests, and when
we demurred they drew their swords and forced us to do their
bidding. Then they took our clothing and linen, even tearing the
shirt off my back."

"You knew the men?"

"Several of them, and they knew me. Finally I found courage
to ask Captain Holston if they were not ashamed to act like Tories
and to abuse people whom they ought to protect? That touched
the captain and several of the men, and they begged me not to
worry, saying that the crowd was drunk, and they would see that
everything was returned. Finally the captain found pluck enough
to order his men to give back what they had taken, and this was
done, with the exception of one piece of linen, which the captain
found later when they were asleep, and which he sent back to me
in the morning."

"It is just such barbarous and unjust treatment that has driven
to the Tories many who would have preferred to remain quiet,"
said Casper, and I could easily see how that might happen, though
it did not make it less distressing when neighbor was arrayed against
neighbor, each trying to be more brutal than the other, and each in

turn venting his spite on those unfortunate enough to fall into his hands.

In October the two parties had a sharp skirmish near the Shallow Ford of the Yadkin, and several were wounded. A call was sent to our Brother Bonn to come and attend to them. He sent his apprentice Joseph Dixon, who found one man so severely wounded that he was afraid to treat him and Brother Bonn was obliged to go. The wounded men were then taken to Bethania, where Brother Bonn visited them from time to time until they recovered.

Much worse for our towns was the bringing of the English and Tory prisoners to Bethabara after the battle of King's Mountain. "More than two hundred Tory prisoners were herded like cattle in a small, fenced-off space, where they spent nineteen days and nearly starved," Brother Lorenz Bagge told us. "The English soldiers were lodged in an empty house, and the English officers in some of the family houses. As no arrangements had been made for caring for so many, the burden fell on Bethabara, with only a little help from outside."

"I came up to see what I could do for you," said Brother Marshall.

"Your visits in all the homes meant much for the encouragement of our people," said Brother Lorenz. "I was thinking of the material side, of the large amount of food that was needed, of the difficulty we had in procuring it, and of the great loss in cattle and meal which we sustained."

"They seem to have made much difference in their treatment of the Tories and the English," said I.

"Apparently they considered the English as fair prisoners of war, while they hoped to force the Tories into serving with the American troops as the price of pardon and release. The plan succeeded, for most of them did that very thing, though their officers remained with the English officers as prisoners."

"I heard something about a service on Sunday for the prisoners," said Casper.

"It was a remarkable service. A Baptist minister, named Hill, preached to the prisoners a long sermon of thanksgiving for the victory over the Tories, though one can hardly imagine that the poor fellows agreed with his point of view!"

When the Tories had promised to enlist in the American militia they were allowed to return to their homes for a few days, and the prisoners, the sick soldiers, and their doctor, passed through Salem on their way to Salisbury. Bethabara rejoiced in the lifting of the burden, and Salem was glad that the twenty or so English officers who spent a week in Salem behaved well, which was more than could be said of the many parties of militia who came and went daily. Thinking back on that time I have often wondered how the comparatively few Moravian Brethren managed to feed and supply with leather and other necessaries the uncounted hordes who made demands upon them. "Out of six troubles has the Lord saved us, and in the seventh no evil has befallen us," quoted Brother Graff, and that alone can explain why our membership did not starve, why our towns were not destroyed.

If Bethabara was sorely oppressed in the late fall of 1780, Salem and Bethania had their worst times early in the following year. We heard frequently of their serious difficulties, but there was nothing we could do to help.

It was on the last day of January that Casper said to me, "Catharine, the Elders are to meet in Salem today, and there are several matters on which I would like to consult them. I hesitate to leave you here alone, and I am almost afraid to take you with me, because of the disturbed condition of the town."

"Take me with you," I said. "That is no more dangerous than it is everywhere these days." So we saddled our horses and rode thither, without misadventure.

We were a little early, and found Brother Graff at his table, writing. "Just making entries in the diary," he explained, "I dare not skip a day, for events crowd so closely upon each other's heels that I must put each down as it happens. I wonder sometimes what someone who may read these pages a hundred years from now will think about all this," and he turned the closely written pages almost lovingly.

"Give us a sample," I begged, and with a smile he read bits here and there, skipping more than he read, for it was nearly time for the meeting.

"*Jan. 1.* Major William Campbell and one hundred and five volunteers from Boutetourt County, Virginia, arrived. This Major Campbell kept good order, and we hear that the soldiers wish to behave better than the Virginia troops under the Colonel of the same name who were here some time ago. In the evening they attended our song service and were attentive and respectful.

"*Jan. 5.* A messenger came from Colonel White's Virginia cavalry to arrange for quarters, provisions and forage for three officers, twenty sick cavalrymen, and thirty or forty horses. They will probably be here for two months.

"*Jan. 12.* The Brethren Traugott Bagge, Johann Reuz, Peter Yarrell, and Samuel Stotz have been appointed a committee to look after war matters.

"*Jan. 16.* A Sergeant came from General Greene's army with twelve men and a wagon loaded with gunpowder. On *the 20th* two more wagons arrived, with a guard, and a Conductor who will make up ammunition here. It was decided to put up a log house for the purpose, outside the town. Next day two more powder wagons came.

"*Jan. 23.* Colonel Armstrong has been ordered to call out half the militia.

"*Jan. 30.* All the militia is to be called out. Gottlieb Spach was helping raise the magazine and had a bad fall, fortunately was not seriously injured."

"And as you came in," added Brother Graff, "I was recording the arrival of two more ammunition wagons."

We returned to Friedland when Casper had finished his business, but news spreads with astonishing rapidity, and we heard that on February 2nd Salem had to furnish grain and salt, and Bethabara and Bethania meat, for militia guarding the prisoners captured at the Cowpens in South Carolina, who were being taken to Virginia. Two days later the Continental Hospital was brought to Salem, the two-story house being emptied for the use of the sick men. On the same day wagons gathered from the neighborhood came to haul away the ammunition, among the teamsters being our friend Adam Spach and his son, who were kept busy for ten days with this aid to the Continental army.

The hospital, too, moved on, and when the guards were withdrawn the conduct of the visiting men became more disorderly. The Wilkes County militia, as usual, were very boisterous, making many threats against the town. Their captain, William Lenoir, encouraged their bad behaviour, declaring that "the Brethren are my enemies, but for the time I will not harm them, but they must give us what we need and demand."

"Why does Captain Lenoir hate us so?" I asked, for this was always the attitude of the Wilkes militia.

"A guilty conscience causes hatred toward the party injured," Casper replied. "For years he has been the leader of the men who have settled on the Moravian land known as the Mulberry Fields. They are squatters and have no legal title to the land, but they have refused to move, and so they hate us."

On top of this came the English army under Lord Cornwallis. They had followed General Greene from Salisbury to the Trading Ford of the Yadkin, where Providence interfered, sending a heavy rain just after the Continentals had crossed, and raising the waters so that the English could not pass through the ford. Impatient of the delay the army turned north and came up the river to the Shallow Ford, and followed the road to Bethania, where they camped during the night of February 9th. It was a night of terror and of loss, of which Brother Ernst gave us a vivid description. His own personal safety was due to the fact that one of the officers was a Swiss by birth, and protected Brother Ernst when he learned that he also was Swiss.

Next morning the army moved on, passing through Bethabara without stopping; indeed the officers posted guards at the gate leading into the village, and at the distillery, to prevent their men from straying and delaying. This was done for their own purpose, but was greatly to the benefit of the village.

In Salem there was some straggling and some stealing, but the main body of the army marched through the town and camped some miles to the south. Lord Cornwallis and some of his staff sent word that they would stop for a while with Brother Bagge, which surprised him until he found that Governor Josiah Martin was with the General, and of course he had known Governor Martin in happier days. Brother Marshall went to assist Brother Bagge, and the visit passed off well, for Lord Cornwallis and Governor Martin were gentlemen even if they were on the wrong side of the struggle.

That night our turn came. The Friedland people living near the English camp lost nearly all their cattle and forage. Men forced their way into the schoolhouse, and we gave them food as long as we had any. I had not been feeling well all day and finally said to Casper, "My back is paining me so that I will have to go to bed," to which he answered, "Go by all means, Catharine. I will turn out the light, for surely no more will come."

The hope was vain; about nine o'clock six or eight more men came, demanding food. "We have no more," said Casper, but they refused to believe him, fiercely insisting that food they must and would have, rummaging through the provision closet themselves to see what they could find.

In spite of the pain in my back I got up, and Casper made an effort to leave the house to call for help.

"Oh no, you don't," they shouted, one thrusting a naked bayonet at Casper's chest, ready to stab or fire, while others prepared to break open the clothes chest which we kept locked. I was nearly frantic with terror, and just at that moment the door opened and Samuel Stotz and three other Brethren rushed into the room. Startled, and not knowing how many might be following, the ruffians ran and we were saved. The Brethren in Salem had been worried about us and had sent us the help we so sorely needed.

When all was quiet two of our rescuers returned to Salem, but the other two remained with us overnight.

For the rest of the month things were worse than ever in Salem, with parties of militia coming and going, showing little respect for the efforts their officers made to control them, and sometimes the officers seemed even worse than the men. Again and again the Wilkes militia descended upon the town. Every day was a hard day, and hardly a house remained unrobbed. Twice Brother Bagge was in imminent danger, with a loaded pistol at his chest; twice he was saved from death. Others were in almost as great danger; for four days not a single service could be held in the meeting-hall. In the tavern men ate and drank like beasts, telling Brother Meyer to charge it to public expense; from the houses they stole any and everything they wanted; the woods swarmed with robbers, but they were no worse than the men who claimed to be patriots but were really unlicensed evil-doers.

On March 15th there was a battle near Guilford Court-house between the Continentals and the army of Lord Cornwallis, and the reports that reached us were that the army of General Greene had been forced to retreat, that he had been completely defeated by the English. An old man from the neighborhood was sent around with an open letter addressed to "all friends of the country" asking for old rags, meal, and brandy for bandaging and feeding the wounded. Among us we made up a bundle of bandages and old rags, which two of the Brethren took to the Continental hospital at Guilford Court-house.

21

PEACE, THE GIFT OF GOD

T**HE BATTLE OF GUILFORD COURT-HOUSE HAD LITTLE EFFECT AT** the moment, except that large military operations moved away from Wachovia. The English army had held the field, but apparently Lord Cornwallis did not care to face another engagement and marched eastward. The next definite news that we had he was at Haw River. General Greene moved to the south, and one of his men passing through Salem said mysteriously, "You will hear something before long!"

Members of the militia had been wounded in the skirmishes that preceded the battle and had been sent to Salem for care. Brother Bonn looked after their wounds and was most successful; only one man passed away, and he was in a dying condition when he was brought in. Some of the men had relatives who came to wait on them; others the Brethren nursed. All expressed their thanks for the kind attention shown, and it was hoped that the religious impressions they received might be for their lasting good. The magazine put up for the army was used as a small hospital for these men.

The weather was so peculiar that it could not be forgotten. There had not been a single snow during the winter, but a snowstorm came on April 16th, killing most of the fruit, and badly hurting the rye. Four days later there was a storm with hailstones as large as hickory nuts; and as late as May 11th there was a heavy frost which ruined the gardens. The gardens were of course replanted, and contrary to all expectation the harvest was a bountiful one, refilling the granaries which had been emptied by the incessant demands.

Throughout April there was constant passing through our towns, with large requisitions charged to public expense. Fortunately it proved possible to use the tickets and receipts in the payment of taxes; so the loss was not as great as it might otherwise have been, though there was much taken by individual militiamen for which no return was made. One rather unusual demand was for dressed deer-skins, of which one hundred and fifty-three were pressed, to be used in making clothes for Colonel Lee's dragoons.

Brother Bagge said that the behaviour of the militia passing through Salem was "fairly peaceable and modest," but Christian Frey, of the Friedberg settlement, had a different story to tell.

"Men called at my door," he said, "and John Wolfesberger, who was working for me, went to the door. The men asked whether there were strangers within, and when he said no, they seized him. He jerked loose and ran into the house, and then they broke a window and forced their way through the door. I spoke to them gently and one of them hit me on the head, while another struck my wife on the shoulder with the flat of his sword.

"Finding a large stone somewhere, they used it to break the paneling in the cupboard, and with their sword cut the wood around three locks, taking all our money and whatever else they wished. I attempted to stop them and was given another cut on the head; then I tried to slip out of the house, but the guard at the door gave me such a blow on the chest with his gun that I almost fainted. Finally I did get out, and ran, shouting for help. They shot after me but missed me. My poor wife, who had hidden behind the door, sank on her knees when she heard the shot, and when the four rascals finally left she was overjoyed to find me living."

"Who were the men?"

"I have no idea. They may have been Whigs, they may have been Tories, they may have been plain robbers, claiming no connection with either side."

Indeed at this period there was a great deal of trouble with robbers, highwaymen, and petty thieves. At Salem it got so bad that one man was shot by the nightwatchman in the garden of the Single Sisters behind the Congregation House. The man got away, but from blood-stains found the next day it was assumed that he had been badly wounded. Finally appeal was made to the militia of Surry County, who turned out and scoured the woods, finding the remains of their camp though they did not capture the men. Perhaps the robbers moved into an adjoining county, for a little later we heard alarming tales of conflict between Whigs and Tories, of robbery and plundering.

One result of the movement of the militia was the spread of another epidemic of smallpox. Casper and I visited a number of patients in the Friedland settlement; Salem inoculated all who had not had the disease, so shortening the time of the epidemic and giving it in a lighter form; Friedberg reported a total of ninety-six cases; in Bethabara several were seriously ill, and many were inoculated. When it broke out in Bethania William Grabs was taken to Salem to have it there, and it did not spread widely, though both of the Sehnert children took it. Their father was also ill at harvest time; so Brother Ernst took several of the younger men to the Sehnert farm and cut the grain for him.

In April the Indians began murdering on the upper Catawba River, driving many families away. In mid-summer the refugees in Virginia began to return to their homes in South Carolina, only to find themselves in more difficulty, and many men who had been rich found themselves very poor.

In July the militia were called out again, and Casper went to Salem to consult with the ministers there about the giving of membership certificates to men belonging to Friedland Society who had asked for them.

"In my opinion," said Brother Marshall, "if they behave like Brethren and pay the threefold tax, they will not need the certificates to secure exemption from service."

"Tell them that you can give certificates only to those who

qualify on these points," advised Brother Graff, "and that even then you will issue certificates only if the militia officer asks for one."

"Please write a letter which I can read to the congregation," said Casper, which Brother Marshall did, stating the case very plainly.

In the middle of that month we heard that Tories had captured twenty members of the Assembly, but had released them on parole; also that the rest of the Assembly had taken to the woods, but had succeeded in holding their sessions. Quite at the end of the month Major Winston dismissed his men in Bethabara. "They were wild with joy," said Brother Lorenz, "and fired their guns, and broke window-panes at the tavern, and took fruit and vegetables from our gardens."

In September half the militia were called out again, which brought up the question of certificates another time, but the Conference of Country Ministers decided to abide by the rule already established, and in addition resolved not to receive anybody into our Societies for a while, lest it should look as though we were depriving the land of able soldiers.

"Some of the men claim that their names have been placed on the muster roll without their knowledge," said Casper.

"Then they must take the matter directly to their captain," said Brother Marshall. "We can do nothing about that."

Matters in the eastern counties were still in great confusion, and the Tories under Colonel Fanning captured Governor Thomas Burke and held him prisoner. At Eutaw Springs, on the Santee River, there was a bloody battle, and a messenger was sent to Brother Bagge asking that bandages and rags be sent to Charlotte for the care of the wounded, and we all helped in gathering them.

On October 30th we heard that Lord Cornwallis had surrendered at Yorktown in Virginia, and the next day Casper went to Salem to see whether the report was true. He came back looking sad, and I asked:

"What is the matter, Casper, more bad news?"

"The report of the defeat of the English seems to be true," he answered, "but our Brother Bonn has found peace before the rest of us."

"Surely you do not mean that he has been called home; I did not know he was ill."

"He had not been. It was a stroke, and he passed blessedly and quickly to the Saviour. A beautiful way to go, Catharine."

"Beautiful for him to be spared a long illness and perhaps much suffering, but hard for his wife and his friends."

"We must think only of his side, now. Later you will do what you can for Sister Bonn."

So on the second day thereafter we went to Salem for the funeral, which was attended by all of Brother Bonn's local friends and perhaps two hundred from the other congregations and from the neighborhood.

His departure left Wachovia without a doctor, except his partially trained apprentice Joseph Dixon. Word was at once sent to Europe, asking for a successor for him, but it was two years before his place was filled, and then not very satisfactorily.

In November, Salem had the stupendous task of entertaining the Assembly of North Carolina. Notice had been given well in advance; so the potter had made a quantity of chocolate cups, bowls, and plates, additional knives and forks were bought, food supplies were gathered, and arrangements were made for boarding and lodging the Assemblymen, their horses, their servants, and the militia guard of two companies.

Sixty-three members arrived, but that was not enough to form a house. They waited and waited for twenty days in the hopes that more would come, but finally adjourned without having been able to do any business. As Governor Burke was still a prisoner, Alexander Martin was acting Governor; he was lodged in the Congregation House.

During this time our services in the meeting-hall were continued as usual, except that the special services for communicants were omitted, and all were open to our guests, who attended in number and seemed much impressed. There was also time for many conversations concerning the Moravian faith and practice, and the favorable impression made on these leading men of the state was worth the trouble and expense their coming caused.

Shortly before the Assembly adjourned there was an alarm given that the Tories were coming. Guards were set on all roads, with orders not to let anyone come or go without a pass, and a special guard was drawn up in front of the Congregation House to protect the Governor, but nothing happened.

So much pleased were the Assemblymen with the way they were treated that they decided to meet in Salem in January. Our Brethren were loath to go through all the trouble again, but agreed to do their best to make them comfortable. Colonel Sheppard told Brother Bagge that it was said some of the members had stayed away because of the expense.

"It should be possible to overcome that difficulty," said Brother Bagge. "The cost per day would be six shillings, good money, or its equivalent in paper, but we would be entirely willing to accept food stuffs of various kinds at definite prices."

"Will you come before the gathered members and explain that?" asked Colonel Sheppard.

"With pleasure," said Brother Bagge, and all seemed satisfied with this suggestion.

The day after the Governor and his guard left Salem the Wilkes militia camped near Friedland, one hundred and fifty in the company. We were alarmed, knowing their reputation, but except for shooting two cows they committed no excesses, and left the next day, Tory hunting.

A month later highwaymen broke windows and stole horses in our neighborhood and committed various acts of violence, but the inhabitants succeeded in overpowering them and took them to Bethania, where they were released with a caution as to their future behaviour. Three days later a report that they were threatening to return to Friedland in eight or nine days led Casper to warn the house-fathers to be on their guard, but fortunately they did not come.

On December 26th Brother Christian Lewis Benzien, who had come to Wachovia in August, was ordained a deacon by Bishop Graff, with prayer and the imposition of hands, and the choir sang the ordination doxology.

January, 1782, brought the Assembly back to Salem, but with fewer members than in November. They therefore adjourned after eight days, with nothing done. It happened that those in attendance this time were largely men who had not been in Salem last time; so more learned to know the Brethren and left with friendly feelings.

A number advised that Brother Bagge should run for the Assembly in the next election, and it was decided that it might be advantageous for us to have one of our Brethren there, especially as the question of the title to our land was to be presented. Many went to Richmond Court-house from our three towns, and two of our Brethren wrote ballots to be distributed as opportunity offered. Several of our Friedland Brethren went to vote for Brother Bagge, and on their return one of them told us:

"It was the most disorderly election crowd I have ever seen. The rougher element were drunk and made a great commotion. One good man was badly abused, and Brother Bagge was harshly threatened though he escaped actual injury."

"Who was elected?"

"Colonel Sheppard received most votes for senator, instead of our candidate Colonel Martin Armstrong, but Mr. Cummings and Brother Bagge were elected, in spite of the opposition to them."

This "rougher element" continued to give trouble for some time, and several of our Friedberg Brethren were badly treated. Three rascals fell on John Hanes in the road near his house, bound him, and held him and his wife powerless while they robbed his house, and with pistols at the breasts of their victims threatened to shoot them. The same thing happened to two others, and frightened us not a little.

There was also much passing of militia, mostly men returning from the camp of General Greene, having served their term of eighteen months. Others were prisoners of war who had been exchanged and released; and all must be given food and drink at public expense. They could pay nothing, for Virginia currency had entirely lost value, and North Carolina currency fell to eight hundred to one in specie, and then also dropped out.

The April session of the Assembly was held in Hillsborough, and Brother Marshall went thither with Brother Bagge, to secure the confirmation of the transfer of title to Wachovia from Brother Hutton to himself. In this he was successful, in spite of opposition of men from Wilkes County, and the fear of losing our land through the confiscation act was happily ended.

The Assembly gave Brother Bagge two additional offices at this time. He was appointed Auditor for the upper Board of Salisbury District, together with Mr. Bruce and Mr. Hunter, both of Guilford County, Brother Bagge representing Surry County. The Auditors sat in Salem, and many came to have their accounts with the government validated, so that they were busy for several weeks. Brother Bagge was also commissioned a justice of the peace, and qualified at the next term of Surry County court.

While General Greene was having considerable success with his operations in the south the English still held Charleston, and it was decided to send the Brethren Ernst, Shore, and George Hauser, Jr., to see whether it was possible to enter the city and secure payment of the tickets given by the army of Lord Cornwallis as they passed through Bethania. The trip was a very hard one, the ravages of war having made it almost impossible to get food for the horses, or shelter for themselves. "Most of the plantations that we passed were either abandoned or burned; now and then one was inhabited but they had nothing," Brother Ernst reported.

"On the seventh day we met a lieutenant of General Greene's cavalry, who said there was not a chance for us to get through the Santee Swamp, as there were more than three hundred Tories in it, and while they would probably not kill us they would rob us of everything we possessed."

So with nothing accomplished they had to retrace the hard

road, their disappointment lightened at one place by a report that
peace had been made between England and America.

On August 6th our dear Brother Graff had a severe attack of
pain in the body, which developed into dysentery. Casper and I
took the first chance of riding to Salem, and found him cheerful
but weak.

"I nursed him myself for several days," Gertrude told me,
"but as he grew worse the Elders arranged with Brother Adam
Koffler to take care of him during the day and help me, and at
night two of the Brethren watch with him, one a married and one
an unmarried man, different members taking turns."

"Does he suffer?"

"He does not complain. You know how patient and affectionate he has always been, and illness does not change that, I find."

"Is there anything I can do to help? I will stay with you if
you want me."

"Thank you, my dear, but we are getting along all right, and
I keep hoping that he will improve."

"I wish Brother Bonn were here!"

"So do we all, but we must leave our dear one to the Great
Physician since there is no human help available."

Another trip to Salem we made on the day after the festival of
the Thirteenth of August had been observed with the anniversary
Communion. We found that the Sacraments had been taken to
Brother Graff as the congregation was being served upstairs in the
meeting-hall, and he partook with his flock in that way, with
much joy. "Greatly has the Lord blessed the Unity of Brethren
since He poured out His Spirit upon the congregation of Herrnhut
on August 13, 1727," he whispered. "May He ever bless us!"

With tears in her eyes Gertrude told me that he had begun
to talk of leaving her, saying, "Now I have received permission
from the Lord to ask to be taken home," and prayers for this came
to his lips from time to time as weakness increased. One evening
when he seemed scarcely conscious he opened his eyes and looked

Bishop Johannes von Watteville

From an oil painting in the Herrnhut Archives.

Bethabara Church, built in 1788 by the Reverend Jacob Ernst

From an old drawing in the Wachovia Historical Society Museum.

around at the Brethren gathered near his bed. "Do you know us?" one of them asked.

"Oh yes, you are my dear ones," he answered. Then fixing his gaze on Brother Marshall he added, "I wish him a long life; mine is over."

The next evening he seemed passing away and Brother Marshall was called out of the meeting-hall to give him the last blessing. However, he rallied and lingered for some days. Strangely enough his hearing returned, and while he had been partially deaf for some time he now could hear even low-spoken words. Many hymns were sung in his room during these days and they seemed to give him pleasure, and sometimes he asked for a favorite verse.

On August 29th a messenger came to Friedland telling us that a little before two o'clock in the morning his soul had gone home, leaving the weary mortal remains to rest in peace.

The next day five or six hundred sorrowing friends gathered at noon for his funeral, which was held by Brother Lorenz Bagge, of Bethabara. In the procession to God's Acre his bier was borne by sixteen Brethren, representing all our congregations, the men wearing blue coats according to the custom of this country. They served eight at a time, as we followed the casket from the Congregation House to God's Acre.

He had left some notes and several poems, and his memoir was prepared by Brother Marshall and Brother Benzien, and a few days later was read to the congregation, while many tears were shed. It spoke of his twenty years of service among us, of his patience, humility, mildness, love, and of his outstanding characteristic that "among us he knew naught but Jesus Christ the Crucified, to whom he pointed all souls in public and in private conversation."

It was a year of losses in the ministerial ranks, for the pastors of Friedberg and Bethabara, and Brother Praezel of Salem, all must give up their helpmeets, making the work more heavy in general and in each part. Brother Friedrich Peter took the place of Brother Graff as preacher for the time being, and everybody helped where he could.

In Friedland life went on as usual. We taught the school; we tended the garden; we visited our members and friends; I kept the house in order and did our sewing and cooking; Casper prepared and delivered his sermons, administered the Sacraments, and gave counsel and help to many. A rather unusual incident took him to the home of one member who had been suffering intensely with his leg. A surgeon from Guilford was called in and decided to amputate the limb; Casper offered a fervent prayer for the success of the operation, stayed with the patient while it was being done, and had the joy of knowing that it was a success. Once a month we rode to Salem to the Conference of Country Ministers, where many things were discussed relative to the religious life of Friedberg, Friedland, and Hope. There it was decided that candidates for church membership should be named to the communicant members of the congregation, so that due information regarding the applicants could be given; also that the pastor and his wife should have a personal interview with each member once each quarter; this would give opportunity for intimate conversation on any problems which might be aided by sympathy and advice.

Our Easter services followed the general plan of those in Salem. On Palm Sunday in 1783 Casper began to read the story of the Passion Week, which was continued from day to day. On Maundy Thursday there was a lovefeast and blessed Communion. On Easter morning, before sunrise, the congregation was greeted with the words:

The Lord is risen,

and they answered in tones full of emotion:

He is risen indeed!

After singing a suitable hymn we went to God's Acre, singing most of the way, and there we prayed the Easter liturgy. At ten o'clock many were present to hear the reading and preaching concerning our risen Lord.

Easter Sunday fell that year on April 20th. The preceding day, April 19th, was the anniversary of the battle at Lexington which had marked the beginning of the Revolutionary War eight years before; and on that very day it was reliably reported in Salem that peace preliminaries had been arranged in Paris, and that the war between England and America was over. This was a wonderful blessing added to the observance of Great Sabbath, the day on which we remembered that the Prince of Peace rested in the grave after the mortal agony had ended on Calvary.

Also on April 19th Governor Alexander Martin officially announced the good news to the Assembly of North Carolina. Brother Bagge had failed of reëlection and was no longer a member of the Assembly, but such news spreads rapidly, and we soon learned that the Assembly had instructed the Governor to appoint the Fourth of July as a day of thanksgiving for the coming of peace. So far as I know we were the only state to take such action; the rest of the country observed a day of thanksgiving in December, after Congress had heard officially that the full Treaty of Peace had been signed.

Salem celebrated the Fourth of July with a rather elaborate program of hymns, choir anthems, and instrumental music. A number of the verses were written expressly for the occasion, the first one being:

> Peace is with us, peace is with us,
> People of the Lord,
> Peace is with us, peace is with us,
> Hear the joyful word!
> Let it sound from shore to shore,
> Let it echo evermore,
> Peace is with us, peace is with us,
> Peace, the gift of God.

In Friedland we were not in position to render such a program, but we celebrated the Peace Festival with happy hearts and voices, and commended to the Lord our entire land and especially His people whom He had planted therein.

All our congregations obeyed the proclamation of the Governor, inviting neighbors to join with us. Whether it was observed in any other part of the state I do not know; we did not hear of it.

With the strain of war relieved, life moved on quietly and happily until November. We had heard that Sister Graff had taken charge of the Sisters in Bethabara and would spend several days there now and then, and I was glad that she was in active service again. Wolves, panthers, and mad dogs had been reported from various places, but we had not been annoyed in our immediate neighborhood, and on the 20th and 21st the members came to us for their quarterly interview, and Casper was pleased with the good spirit they revealed as they talked with him.

On the morning of the 22nd Casper rose at his usual early hour, but lay down again immediately.

"Are you sick, Casper?" I asked anxiously.

"I feel faint, Catharine," he replied, and when he did not recover quickly I became alarmed and called Elisabeth Hartmann, who was visiting us, and sent her to a neighbor for help. The wife came at once, but there was nothing we could do. Once he whispered, "Oh Thou, dear Saviour," but about seven o'clock he quietly and blessedly fell asleep. He had spoken of the beauty of a quick home-going, and it was granted to him. One of our members took the word to Salem, and Brother Praezel came at once to see what he could do and to make arrangements for the funeral.

The next day was Sunday, and Brother Friedrich Peter came to hold the services. Brother Michael Vogler brought his infant son, born on the 21st, and asked for his baptism, the maternal grandparents to be the sponsors. I took the little John into my arms and carried him into the room where Casper rested so peacefully, after his life of service, and silently I prayed: "Oh Saviour, bless this wee boy, and let him grow up strong and faithful in whatever path Thou may'st appoint for him, that he may be as true to his duty and to his God as my Casper has been."

On Monday Brother Benzien came to hold the funeral of my dear husband. Many came from Salem, and the congregation here assembled and looked upon him with sorrow and bewailed their loss.

A few days later Brother and Sister Praezel came to celebrate the Holy Communion with the congregation, and brought me a message from the Elders.

"Will you continue to live here for the present and teach the school?" they asked.

"Will that be best?"

"The Elders think it will. You can send Elisabeth Hartmann back to the Sisters in Salem, and have Elisabeth Schneider live with you, and you can keep the house open for the Brethren who will come from Salem to hold the services."

"I hesitate to undertake to teach the boys."

"It will be all right if you take only the girls; and the women can continue to come to you as they have been doing for advice in many things. Other arrangements will be made as soon as possible, but meanwhile it will be a real service, and several of your members have asked that you may stay."

"If they want me I will stay with them, at least for this winter," I said, glad to do what I could to carry on the work, for the membership of the congregation had doubled under Casper's pastorate, and it did seem a pity to leave them alone.

22

AN INSISTENT CALL

―――――――

"SISTER HEINZMANN, THE SALEM TAVERN HAS BURNED DOWN!" exclaimed Elisabeth Schneider, excitedly, rushing in on the morning of January 31st, 1784.

"The Salem tavern has burned," I echoed in consternation. "What a catastrophe! Was anyone hurt?"

"I do not know. A man called to me as he rode past, but he did not stop and I had no chance to ask questions."

"Please saddle my horse, Elisabeth, while I get my wraps; I cannot stand it here without knowing."

So I rode to Salem at a swifter pace than usual. Stopping at the tavern site where the ruins still smoked, I called to one of the Brethren standing near, "Was anybody hurt?"

"Fortunately not," he replied; so reassured I rode on to the Congregation House, going to Sister Graff's rooms, where until a new preacher arrived for Salem she was able to remain undisturbed. From her I heard the story of the fire.

"We were wakened about three o'clock this morning," she said, "by the ringing of the fire-alarm on the bell, and everybody hurriedly dressed and ran out except the mothers with little children, who were obliged to stay with them. There was no need for anyone to tell us where the fire was, for the tavern was already burning fiercely, and seizing the largest bucket I had I ran thither."

"How did it catch?"

"Nobody knows. It was discovered by strangers from Wilkes County who were spending the night there, and they roused

Brother Meyer and his family, Brother John Holland, and the other guests. Fifteen minutes later their lives would have been lost; as it was they saved only a few of their personal belongings and the house clock. Most of the furniture was lost, and all of the grain stored on the upper floor. Some of the kitchen utensils were carried out, but that house burned also. We formed in double line to the well and to the cistern, the Brethren passing the full buckets and we the empty ones, but the best that could be done was to save the barns and stable. Fortunately there was no wind."

"It is a terrible loss to the town! What will be done about the many visitors who are in the habit of stopping here?"

"Brother Marshall has called a meeting of as many of the Brethren as can be spared from the scene of the fire, and they will decide"; and it was only a few minutes until Brother Marshall came down the stairs and stopped at Sister Graff's door.

"Sister Heinzmann," he said, "I saw you ride up and I am delighted that you are here. Will you approve our suggestion that Brother and Sister Meyer and the children take your house until the tavern can be rebuilt?"

"Brother Schober and his wife have been living there since Brother Nissen built. If it is all right with them I shall be happy to feel that my house is of service."

"Everybody must help now, and not mind being inconvenienced. We think Brother and Sister Schober will be willing to move in with Brother Nissen for the time being, Brother Meyer can take your house, and all the families in town will have to help care for travelers."

"How long will it take to get ready to rebuild?"

"There is a good deal of material on hand which has been prepared for building a Sisters House. The Sisters will have to wait, and we can use that for the new tavern."

It was hard on the Single Sisters, who had been looking forward to their own house with so much pleasure, but they took it well.

"It is an emergency," said Sister Betsy Colver, their treasurer, who had been one of the most active in the planning. "We cannot refuse such a call, even though it means self-sacrifice for us."

There was still time to fell additional timber, and sufficient brick was on hand for a start; so Brother Marshall drew the plans and work was begun immediately. As Brother Triebel and Brother Rasp were both in feeble health, younger carpenters and masons had to take the responsibility, consulting with Brother Marshall frequently.

This time the house was built for permanence, with massive stone cellar wall and brick above, making it much safer than the first tavern and much more sightly.

The burning of the tavern emphasized to the Brethren the lack of proper facilities for fighting the flames. Fire-buckets were supposed to be in every home, but a number of the house-holders had neglected to secure them, and at any rate they were insufficient in the face of a real conflagration when heat forbade a near approach. Immediate steps were taken to provide more buckets, and a subscription list was opened to cover the cost of two fire engines, a small one that could be carried and operated by two men, and a larger one on wheels requiring four men to pump it. As the engine parts had to be ordered from Europe it took two years to get them, but we felt safer after they arrived. The bucket brigade was still necessary, in order to keep the tanks supplied with water, but the distance to which the stream could be thrown helped a great deal.

"I wish you had been here last week," said Gertrude as I was starting back to Friedland on the day of the tavern fire. "Brother Martin Schneider has returned from his journey to the Cherokee country, and we listened eagerly to the account of his experiences."

"Perhaps Brother Marshall can let me read his diary," I said, and she promised to arrange it for me.

From the day that the Brethren moved to North Carolina they had wished to go as missionaries to the Indians, and now the way seemed opening. Brother Schneider had a very trying trip, but the story of it was most interesting; although he had not secured definite action on the part of the leaders of the Cherokee nation, it was an opening wedge.

When I told Gertrude goodbye I little thought that I would not see her again in life. Her health had not been good for several years, but the end came suddenly during the morning of February 21st. She was only sixty-two years old, but she was loved and respected as a "mother in Israel," and we missed her sorely.

There was a good deal of sickness that year, an epidemic of measles being followed by one of whooping-cough. We had no doctor until the latter part of June, when Brother John Lewis and his wife arrived and took over the apothecary shop and Brother Bonn's house, Sister Bonn going to live with Brother and Sister Traugott Bagge.

In April a shortage of food made itself felt, more acutely in the country than in Salem. Many thousand persons had to try to exist on roots and weeds, and they and their cattle suffered great hunger. Many of our Friedland Brethren had difficulty in securing food for themselves and their stock, and some of their cattle died; yet their suffering was not nearly as great as that of others. Of wheat there was only one-third of a crop, but there was a fine harvest of corn. Because of some peculiarity in the weather the apples bloomed a second time, and the fruit grew large enough to be used in the kitchens before it was killed by frost.

Added to these material troubles in the earlier part of the year was the anxiety felt in Wachovia over Brother and Sister Daniel Koehler and Bishop Johannes von Watteville and his wife, who were known to be on their way to America. Brother Koehler had been called as preacher for Salem, and Brother Johannes was coming on an official visitation to the Moravian churches in Pennsylvania and North Carolina.

They finally reached Philadelphia at the end of May, and Brother and Sister Koehler arrived in Salem on the 25th of September, coming in the small coach belonging to Bethlehem. The Brethren in Bethlehem had planned that the coach and horses should remain in Wachovia, but the leaders in Salem considered this inadvisable, and sent them back a few days later, Brother Bagge taking advantage of the opportunity to make a business trip to Pennsylvania.

The lovefeast to welcome Brother and Sister Koehler could not be held immediately because all the party were sick with fever when they reached Salem. When their recovery made the service possible I went to Salem, and heard the interesting story of their journey to America. The account would almost make a book, for the voyage was long and stormy, and included a shipwreck. Brother Johannes was nearly drowned while trying to enter the boat in which, with much difficulty, passengers and crew reached the shore of the Bahamas. There they were kindly treated by the Governor of the island, who entertained them in his own home and gave them free passage to Antigua. In this place they were detained for a number of weeks, but finally were able to take a ship bound for Pennsylvania. Brother Johannes and Sister Benigna had remained in Bethlehem, when Brother Koehler and his wife came south, but were to follow before long.

By the end of 1784 the new tavern was so far finished that Brother Meyer and his family could move into it; and on the 5th of February of the following year I came back to my own house, bringing Elisabeth Schneider with me. Brother Simon Peter and his wife, who had come with the Koehlers, were sent to Friedberg; Brother Valentine Beck and his wife went to Bethania; and Brother and Sister Ernst moved to Bethabara. Sister Ernst's service in Bethabara lasted only until August, when she was called by the Lord to her heavenly home. Brother Peter Goetje was sent to Friedland as lay pastor, having been married and having been received as an akoluthe.

The building of the Sisters House was the chief matter of interest this year. "The Sisters are thrilled to see work actually beginning," said Sister Colver. "I think they feared another delay."

"I enjoy watching from my window all the stirring around," I told her. "Do you find it difficult to keep the Sisters at work?"

Sister Colver laughed. "The Elders tried to rule that the Sisters should not go to the building site except on Sunday, and then only in groups, but the Sisters have discovered that it is very necessary for them to gather the chips where the carpenters are working!"

"Thriftiness is always commendable," I told her with mock gravity. "How did you arrange the matter with the Elders?"

"They agreed to let them go for chips, but only when sent. You can imagine that picking up chips has become a task greatly desired."

"If they behave properly it can do them no harm," I said. "It would be too bad if they were not interested in the progress of the work."

The house was placed as planned, facing the southeast corner of the Square, and on March 31st, 1785, the cornerstone was laid with appropriate ceremonies, Brother Marshall, Brother Koehler, and the officers of the Single Sisters, giving the usual strokes with the mallet. The brick walls were laid during the summer, and on August 19th, the trombonists played from the ridgepole as a sign of rejoicing that the work had progressed so far.

On the 18th of August, Brother Balthasar Christmann and a companion left for Bethlehem, taking two horses to assist in bringing Brother Johannes and his wife to Salem.

Two months passed, and we could not understand why we heard nothing from Brother Johannes, but at last a letter was received which explained that the party had been detained in leaving Bethlehem, but would be with us soon. The Brethren Reuz and Ackerman were at once sent to meet them, taking two fresh horses to help them on their further way. Three days later the Brethren Koehler and Benzien rode as far as Dan River, intending to meet the party, but Dan River was swollen by rain and they could not cross and were obliged to return.

On Sunday, October the 23rd, the travelers arrived, Brother Johannes and his wife, Sister Schlegel and Brother David Zeisberger the younger (a cousin of the missionary), who had come to wait on them, and Brother Christmann and Brother Gernand, who had taken care of the six horses. Brother Christmann drove, and

Brother Gernand rode one of the lead horses. The small coach was again used for this trip, and remained in Salem until they were ready to return to Pennsylvania in April of the following year.

On the day after they reached Salem, we had a happy love-feast for them; and in the weeks which followed they were busy with the usual activities of an official visitation. Brother Johannes visited all our town and country congregations, conversed with the members, and made such recommendations as he thought might increase the usefulness of the Unity of Brethren.

I, too, had been interviewed, but thought nothing of it beyond the interest of a more personal acquaintance with Brother Johannes and Sister Benigna, of whom I had heard so often but whom I had known so slightly.

I was a bit surprised therefore when I answered a knock at my door, and found Brother Johannes standing there. He was an affable man; indeed the Indians in Pennsylvania had dubbed him "John, the loving one," but he could also show an episcopal dignity, and some instinct told me that it was as the bishop that he had come to see me.

"Sister Heinzmann," he said, with few preliminary remarks, "you are called to wed Brother Jacob Ernst, of Bethabara."

"But I am sixty years old," I protested, "and I have already been married three times."

"I admit that Brother Ernst is six years younger than you, but he also has been married before, and at your ages a few years of difference do not matter."

"But I do not want to marry again, Brother Johannes; I want to live here quietly until I am called home."

"And do you want to go home, knowing that you have refused the call of the Lord?" asked the bishop, rather sternly.

"But Brother Ernst is often troubled with podagra. It seems to me that he should have a younger wife to wait on him."

"Brother Ernst himself suggested your name, and his choice was approved by the Lord. Brother Ernst needs you and the Lord needs you, Sister Heinzmann, dare you refuse both?"

Brother Johannes could well take that stand, for he himself never refused any call, no matter at what personal sacrifice, as witness this trip to America frail as his health was; so I could not resent the pressure he put on me, much as I would have liked to do so. He was one of those who put implicit confidence in the use of the *lot* to determine the will of the Lord, and to refuse to be guided by it seemed to him nothing short of treachery to the Almighty.

"You have been received as an akoluthe?" he added more gently.

"Yes, Brother Johannes."

"And then you pledged your hand and heart to follow the guidance of the Lord?"

"Yes, Brother Johannes."

"Then, my Sister, will you not take this further step in His name?"

What could I say except, "Yes, Brother Johannes."

So on the 11th of January, 1786, we were betrothed; and on the 24th of January we were married by Brother Johannes and were installed by him in the pastorate of Bethabara.

In April Jacob was notified that on the 23rd there would be a reception of akoluthes and the ordination of deacons and deaconesses in Salem. I received a personal letter from Bishop Johannes, telling me to come to Salem at that time to be ordained a deaconess of the Unity of Brethren. With shame I thought of my reluctance to accept the former call he brought me, and was deeply conscious of the grace of God which did not hold that attitude against me but now summoned me to the highest service open to a woman in the church.

Humbly, therefore, I presented myself on the appointed day, and after the akoluthes had been received, two Brethren and five Sisters were ordained by the Bishop. Among the latter were Betsy Colver and I, for she had become the leader of the Single Sisters and was often called to hold services for them. Sweetly the choir sang the liturgy:

Lord, Lord God, Who to each of these whom Thou hast
chosen through the Holy Ghost hast freely given the
talents they will need to lead the sacred worship of Thy
sanctuary. Thou hast desired that these Thy servants . . .
these Thy handmaids . . . in Thy church shall now be
serving. . . . Make them faithful in all things. Let them be
completely God's true children, for every blessed work
prepared.

Then the hands of the Bishop were laid upon the head of each,
and we were ordained and blessed for our sacred task.

Just how sacred the task was I realized to the full at the next
Communion season, when I helped Jacob in the interviews with the
Sisters of our congregation, then sat with him behind the Communion table, stood with him while he consecrated the bread and
wine, and carried the platter from which he served bread and the
flask from which he refilled the cup as we passed from row to row
of the communicants.

23

LIGHT AND SHADE

ETHABARA WAS MUCH CHANGED FROM THE BUSY, OVER-CROWDED
village I first knew. People still came to the tavern, the store,
and the distillery, but the number of permanent residents was relatively small. George Holder, one of the first to live in Salem, had
moved to a farm between Bethabara and Bethania, but sent his
daughter Elisabeth to our Bethabara school. Her escape three years
earlier had become one of the favorite stories of the village, and
she was quite willing to tell me about it.

"It happened three years ago," she said, "when I was seven
years old. One Sunday afternoon in March word came to Father
that fire was threatening our fences, and he hurried out to look
after it, and of course we children went with him."

"I helped beat out sparks for a while, but got tired and sat
down behind a stump to rest, and then decided that I would go
home."

"Didn't you tell the others that you were leaving?"

"After the excitement was over Mother scolded me for not
telling, but somehow I said nothing, just slipped off. Where the
road forked I took the wrong way, and walked quite a distance
before I realized that I did not know where I was. Of course I was
frightened, and when I heard one of the children call me I started
to answer, but a hand was laid on my mouth to silence me. When
I looked around nobody was there!"

"Did that not make you more afraid?"

"No, it seemed quite all right, and a few minutes later I heard the call again, and again was prevented from replying, and then it felt as if a hand were on my shoulder turning me to a low-growing cedar tree where I lay down and went to sleep, and the next thing I knew Father was there to take me home."

"When did they miss you?"

"When the fire was out and they were ready to go; but they thought I had run ahead of them and were not alarmed until they reached the house and did not find me. Father stopped several of the Bethabara people who had been to Bethania visiting and they brought the news here, and some of the men came to help in the search."

"Who had called you?"

"A panther," she said simply. "They tell me now that the cry of a panther sounds like a child calling. They say that if I had answered, the panther would have come and might have killed me, but an angel stopped my mouth and took care of me."

"He will give His angels charge concerning thee," I quoted, and she nodded gravely. I had heard the story at the time, and knew that the child spoke the truth. In spite of the marching and shooting of the war times there were so many panthers about that year that the Assembly offered a bounty for panther scalps, and all Bethabara believed that the angel's care had saved the little girl.

In Salem there was a tragic episode with a less happy ending. Even before the Sisters House was entirely finished and occupied the Single Brethren planned the addition to their house and began work on it, digging the cellar themselves in their spare time.

In the evening of March 24th, after the service, some of them decided to go and work a while, among them Andreas Kremser, a shoe-maker by trade. They had evolved a scheme by which they made digging easier, undercutting a bank and then breaking off a large piece with wedges. That evening one of the Brethren noticed that there was a good deal of sand in the soil, and questioned the advisability of making the undercut, but the others did not agree with him, though they did take the precaution to station a guard at the top of the bank to tell them if it threatened to break of itself.

Dem

lieben und würdigen Bruder

FRIEDRICH WILHELM

von MARSCHALL,

nach zurückgelegten

achtzig Lebensjahren

und

sechzigjährigem

treuem und gesegnetem Dienst

bey der

evangelischen Brüderunität

am 5ten Februar 1801

von

der Gemeine in

SALEM.

SALISBURY, (NORD-CAROLINE.)
GEDRUCKT BEY FRANCIS COUPÉE.

Cover of the six-page ode prepared for the birthday of
Frederic William Marshall in 1801

Original in the Salem Moravian Archives.

Young Ladies Seminary at Salem, North Carolina

SALEM.

Salem, from the Northwest

*From a painting in the office of the Moravian Church Treasurer,
Winston-Salem, North Carolina.*

Half an hour before midnight the warning was repeated, but the Brethren worked on, Brother Kremser on his knees reaching under the bank as he dug. Just at midnight the guard called excitedly, "Look out below there, the bank is breaking!"

There was a wild scramble for safety. Then Joseph Dixon shouted, "Help! Help!" The falling earth had buried him to the armpits.

Quickly they began to dig him out, when someone stopped, exclaiming: "Where's Kremser?" and they realized that he was completely buried.

One man ran for Doctor Lewis; another summoned the rest of the Brethren, who had gone to bed; it was not long before both men were free, though it was apparent that Kremser was badly hurt. Brother Lewis had his lancet ready, and Dixon recovered quickly after being bled, but from Brother Kremser no blood flowed, and two hours later all was over.

"Our Saviour allows nothing to happen to His children except what is best for them," said Brother Koehler to the shaken and distressed group assembled for the funeral. "The fate and unusual departure of our Brother Kremser makes us very sad, but without doubt it was best for him, for his heart was so that he was ready to enter into eternal salvation."

Two weeks later the cornerstone of the addition to the Brothers House was laid, and by the middle of October it was ready for occupancy.

As the Conference of Country Ministers supervised the activities of the country congregations of Friedberg, Friedland, and Hope, so the Board of Elders had charge of the town congregations of Salem, Bethabara, and Bethania, the ministers and their wives of all three places being members of the Board. Jacob went to most of the meetings, and I went with him as often as I could. As the Elders were members of the Helpers Conference and of the Congregation Council of Salem we were kept in close touch with all that went on.

When the Single Sisters moved into their own house it was

agreed that the girls school should stay in the Congregation House, and use the southeast room, Sister Utley taking the former school-room. Brother Koehler took one of the rooms, as he needed more space; and another room was set apart for the use of the married Sisters between services, and we had many a pleasant chat there.

The housing of our members was always a problem, and when Gottlob Krause asked to rent my house I had no objection; but I will not say how I felt nine months later when Jacob came back from an Elders meeting and told me that he had agreed to sell the house to Gottlob. "But Jacob," I cried, "I cannot stand it to have that house sold! As long as it was rented we could go back to it."

"Now, now, Cathy," he said soothingly, "we do not need it, and if we ever return to Salem some arrangement will be made for us."

"But Christian built it for me," I sobbed, "and I was so happy in it!"

Jacob looked a little worried and a little annoyed, for as my husband he had a legal right to dispose of the house, but all he said was "I am sorry you do not like it, but I gave my consent and it is all arranged." It was a hard blow, but even this turned out for the best, and it is in that same little house that I write this story of my life.

This was the most serious disagreement Jacob and I ever had, for in most things we felt alike. I was interested in his occasional visits to families living on Deep Creek beyond the Yadkin, where his preaching was welcome. We agreed in dreading the time of corn-huskings, with their temptations to our Brethren to late hours, levity, and drinking. With all the Elders we agonized over Brother Lewis when he drank more and more, and finally must be told that he and his wife could no longer live in Salem. They went to Pennsylvania, where he, poor fellow, soon passed away, deeply repenting his wasted opportunities.

Highway robbery and the stealing of horses seemed to increase, and the Elders approved the forming of an anti-theft society by our neighbors, and encouraged some of our Brethren to join it, hoping that united effort might put a stop to the evil and give greater protection to our property.

In all our congregations the reaction from the years of war began to manifest itself in a tendency toward what was popularly called "American freedom," which was interpreted as freedom to do as one pleased with little regard for law and order or congregation rules. In Salem the movement took the odd form of departure from our simplicity in dress, the young men especially spending more than they could afford for articles of clothing which were more fashionable. The matter was discussed by the Elders and referred to the Helpers Conference, where the inadvisability of such things was pointed out, and the secretary, Brother Friedrich Peter, was instructed to list the items which were particularly objectionable.

"In the first place," he read, "the desire for fashionable dress is at bottom a wish to wear something different, something new, and so become noticeable and attract attention. Among such things are the big shaggy hats, the hats with drooping brims down which hang cords or a pretty ribbon or an unusual buckle. Colors come under the same heading when they are chosen to strike the eye, or when they are variegated, or when clothing is adorned with silver or gilt or other shining buttons, or when coat and vest and breeches each has a conspicuous color.

"Black buckskin breeches are common among us, and if in summer a man wears white stockings no one objects; but if he wears black velvet breeches with fine white cotton stockings and shammy shoes he shows that he is trying to be different from others and that gives offense.

"Waistcoats with short, or without, sleeves are objectionable, because God gave us clothes to cover ourselves. It is just as bad when Brethren wear waistcoats into the meeting-hall and then unbutton them to show a fine pleated shirt or silver shirt-buttons."

"I'll give you a few more items," said one of the older Brethren, "scarlet waistcoats, large stocks with a silk drape, big buttons, and boots with tops made to hang down."

"All of these prohibitions are aimed at the Brethren," I pointed out. "Are the Sisters blameless?"

We all turned to Sister Colver for the answer. "I think they are modest in their attire as a general thing," she said, "but I wish they would not wear high heels, nor ornament their sleeves with ribbons."

This seemed to amuse the Brethren, but the two items were added to Brother Peter's list.

The weather was unusual during the summer of 1787. On the 6th of May there was a severe thunder-storm in Salem, and a bolt struck the house of Brother Miksch, evidently splitting in half as it struck, for one part broke a window while the other stunned his daughter, who was standing in the doorway, though fortunately it did not kill her. In another storm in July a bolt struck the potter's shop, doing quite a bit of material damage, but the workmen escaped injury.

More unusual was the frost of May 21st, which killed the garden vegetables and they had to be replanted. This was followed by a summer drought, but the harvests were good.

Brother Martin Schneider, pastor of Friedland, was bitten by a rattlesnake which had hidden in his woodpile. He had recently heard that strong salt water was helpful; so he soaked his hand in that until neighbors could kill the snake, put some of its fat on the wound, bind the arm tightly above the bite, and give him a drink made from bitter herbs; and these remedies served to prevent evil results.

In Bethabara our old Brother Matthew Stach passed to his reward, and his long and very interesting autobiography was read to the congregations and then filed in the church archives in Salem.

The main event of 1788 was the building of a new Congregation House in Bethabara, the old one having become ruinous. Brother Marshall drew the plans and came often to Bethabara to consult with the congregation about the plans and with the workmen about the building. The church was in one half of the Congregation House, and in the other half were the rooms for the pastor and his wife and the room for the school, though it was not long until the school was moved to another place.

Jacob was authorized to ask help from our other congregations, and varied his appeal according to circumstances. In Bethania he said: "Brethren, we know you want to help us. How many of you will volunteer to bring your wagons and teams and haul stone for the walls?" In Salem he asked for money in most cases, and secured more than he expected. One old Brother passed away about that time, and his bequest toward the building was gratefully received. Even the weather helped, for a deep snow in January made it possible to pile the stones on sledges and so take them to the building site with a minimum of effort.

In May we had a severe storm, with hail as large as hen's eggs, and some of them pointed pieces of ice. The largest one picked up weighed a quarter of a pound!

Much rain made the roads very bad, and on one occasion, as he was returning from Salem, Jacob's horse stepped into so deep a mud-hole that it fell to its knees and could not rise. Jacob dismounted, and the horse turned on its side, filling one of the saddlebags with mud and spattering Jacob with mud from head to foot.

Another matter in which we were interested was the new Constitution for the United States. A conference was held in Salem and another in Bethabara to discuss the proposed form. "Some of the northern states," Jacob told me, "and also Georgia are in favor of the proposals, but Virginia wants certain changes made."

"What will North Carolina do?" I asked.

"North Carolina usually follows Virginia," he replied; but after the election held at Richmond Court-house we learned that the upper counties of the state opposed the Constitution as it was now drawn, and the lower counties favored it.

In August, George Hauser, Jr., was elected to the Assembly, and served acceptably.

One other organization, of a quite different type, was begun during this year. In Bethlehem the Brethren formed a Society for the Propagation of the Gospel among the Heathen, and sent request that all the ministers in Wachovia, with a certain number of other Brethren, would join and would become a southern branch of their Society. Jacob willingly accepted the invitation, and in the course of the years the organization became a powerful instrument for the promotion of our foreign missions.

In November we moved into our new quarters in the Congregation House, and on the 26th the anniversary of Bethabara congregation was celebrated and the new church was consecrated.

The next two years were trying, hard for Wachovia in general and hard for us. There were no large buildings in process of construction, to offer work to those of our Brethren who must support themselves by their daily wage, and this meant that trade in the stores and shops fell off, and necessary things were bought on credit. There was very little hard money in circulation; the North Carolina currency was of uncertain value and could not be used outside the state. Barter was universal, but even that brought its problems.

"What am I to do?" asked Brother Rudolph Crist, who had taken charge of the Salem pottery after the home-going of Brother Aust in Lititz, Pennsylvania, whither he had gone hoping for relief from a dangerous sore. "I must accept butter, linen, cotton, flax, tallow, etc., in exchange for my wares, and if I try to use them so as to realize their value I am open to suspicion of surreptitious trading." It was suggested that Sister Crist make candles of the tallow for her own use and for sale, but the Elders could lay down no rule as to other items.

Brother Schober had the same difficulty with the sale of his tinware, and for him the matter was complicated by the necessity of finding some way to pay for tin in Philadelphia or other distant place. Complaint was made that he was buying more wax than he needed, and he explained that he was getting it to send to Philadelphia, as it was safer than money. This was approved, but he was warned not to carry on a trade that conflicted with the store. "There is certainly no objection to your accommodating your friends by ordering things for them if you will have place in your wagon," he was told, "but not if you solicit orders and deliver items at a profit."

Our neighbors were in the same plight as our Brethren, for it was impracticable to ship surplus grain or tobacco to the seaport towns. The French Revolution had broken out; all Europe was more or less involved; and export trade was at a complete standstill. If a farmer hauled produce to market he received some things in exchange which his family needed, but he also had to take paper money, sugar, rum, molasses, salt, or iron, and these he must barter in his neighborhood or sell on credit.

Brother Marshall had much trouble with the land belonging to the Unity. Men fell behind in their rent or their installments. "Some would be willing to pay if they could," he told us, "and I have been offered horses, cattle, wheat, cornmeal, and tobacco, but I cannot take them because they cannot be used in our small community. Others make no effort but hide behind a good excuse; if I try to get help through the law the case drags on until the man has abandoned his farm, leaving house, fences, and barn in a dilapidated condition, and has gone to the new land where he can buy new ground cheaply, paying for it with the cattle which he has driven with him. If this happens often, it will gradually become the custom and will no longer be considered infamous, but their need must excuse them."

"What are you going to do about it?" he was asked.

"Wait for times to improve," he said calmly. "We have been expecting this to happen, and even now much is left for which we can thank the Lord."

Our correspondence with Europe was still uncertain, but letters which came through aroused our sympathy with news of the home-going of various leaders of the Unity, including Bishop von Watteville, the Countess Benigna, and the wife of Bishop Spangenberg.

In Salem, Brother Nissen passed away, and the church board took over his house as a residence for widows, Sister Nissen continuing to live there. My house was handled in the same way, for Gottlob Krause decided to move to Bethabara and begin a pottery there, and the Supervisors relieved him of my house and used it also for several widows.

In the August election George Hauser, Jr., was chosen as one of the delegates to the Constitutional Convention which met at Fayetteville in November, and there North Carolina ratified the Constitution of the United States and took her place as a full part of the new nation, of which General George Washington had been unanimously elected president.

Mid-summer had brought a rich harvest, but an early frost in October injured vegetables, tobacco, and late corn.

In November Jacob went to Deep Creek again, but the attendance on the preaching was smaller than usual. "The Baptists, Methodists, and Lutherans were all holding meetings in the neighborhood," he told me. "It is a pity that such meetings cannot be held at different times, since none of the groups have settled pastors, but it seems that as soon as one denomination announces a service the others haste to fix a meeting for the same day."

"At least those who came to hear you came because they wanted to, not out of idle curiosity or the lack of something else to do," I suggested, "and that has its advantage."

In December the schools for boys and for girls were combined, and Jacob undertook to teach them, though he was far from well. Podagra continued to trouble him from time to time, and when an attack made him too lame to go into the church one of the Brethren from Salem would come to hold the service for him.

It was a relief when Wachovia again had a competent doctor. Brother Samuel Benjamin Vierling arrived in February, 1790, took over the house and apothecary shop of Brother Bonn, and soon married Brother Bagge's daughter, Anna Elisabeth. He had been in Salem less than a week when he was hurriedly called to Friedberg. One of the Sisters there was critically ill but he saved her, though the little daughter was still-born.

Jacob continued to have attacks of podagra, and finally became so lame in hands and feet that he was helpless as an infant. We considered going to the hot springs on the Peedee, but heard that in Rockingham County, about sixty miles from Bethabara, a Doctor Coxe had established himself at some mineral springs. Brother Vierling kindly agreed to go thither and investigate, accompanied by Brother Samuel Kramsch, who had come to Wachovia to teach in the Salem boys school. "Doctor Coxe seems to be a man of considerable experience," Brother Vierling reported. "He has provided accommodations for a number of patients, and I believe it would be worth while for Brother Ernst to try the cure."

"But could he stand the trip, and how could I manage?" I asked.

"It should be possible to make him comfortable on a deep bed of hay in the wagon. Johann Samuel can drive, and Peter Shore can go to wait on him, taking Brother Stair to help until you have him under the Doctor's care."

These suggestions were followed, and we spent nearly a month there, during which time Jacob improved considerably and regained the use of his feet, though his hands remained lame. He and Doctor Coxe became good friends, and a month after our return the Doctor came to visit him, just to see how he was getting along.

Jacob's illness interfered with our attendance on the meetings of the Elders, but through the Brethren who came to Bethabara we kept in touch with what happened. Perhaps the most important event was the journey of Brother Koehler to Pennsylvania to receive consecration as a bishop. He left Salem on April 6 on horseback; was consecrated bishop in Lititz on May 9; and reached Salem again on May 19. Brother Joseph Dixon also went to Lititz, where he remained to practice as a surgeon.

Later in the summer Brother Friedrich Peter was called to the pastorate of Graceham, Maryland, to our great regret, for he had been the leader of our music, having much talent both as a director and as a composer.

On the other hand, Brother Benzien and his wife, who had been our delegates to the General Synod of the Moravian Church, returned from Europe after nearly a year's absence; and Brother Christian Stauber came back from Pennsylvania where he had been studying the art of making paper at the Ephrata Cloisters, near Reading. Brother Schober was planning to build a paper mill near Salem, and had sent Brother Stauber north to learn the trade. The mill was placed on the Petersbach, west of Salem, where a dam was built to furnish the needed water-power.

As so often happened the fruit was injured by a late frost, and in May the wolves became so troublesome that two wolf hunts were organized, some of our Brethren and some of the neighbors taking part in them, with reasonable success. The grain harvest was good.

By October we had received the minutes and resolutions of Synod, and were interested in the information concerning certain changes.

"The instructions as to the use of the *lot* in marriages are important," said Jacob.

"Does it alter our procedure?" I asked.

"Not greatly, for Brother Marshall's clear mind had already seen the difficulties of enforcing its use in our country congregations, and had met them on his own responsibility."

"Then where do we stand now?"

"In Salem there is no change, and communicants are expected to be willing to ask and receive the direction of the Lord. In the country congregations it is to be used only by request; otherwise consultation with the pastor and his wife and the approval of the parents is to be considered sufficient. In Bethania each case is to be treated according to circumstances. Bethabara will probably follow the custom of Salem, since our numbers here are so small and we are so closely associated with Salem."

"Who is to perform the marriage ceremony?"

"For the present the ministers will serve if the *lot* has been used; in other cases one of our justices of the peace. That will emphasize the difference between the two methods."

"Are there any new suggestions?"

"Probably the one which will touch you most deeply is the recommendation that we wear the surplice for the administration of the Lord's Supper and in giving adult baptism."

"Will I wear one?"

"Certainly. You are a deaconess, and will wear one when you assist in the Communion." This was news indeed and it was almost with reverence that I bought the white linen and took my needle in hand to make the surplices; our communicants told us that their use made the service doubly impressive.

24

SUPERLATIVES

———

IN THE EARLY SUMMER OF 1791 SALEM HAD HER MOST DISTIN-
guished visitor. Lawyers and judges were no novelty in
Wachovia, and colonial governors had come and gone; Governor
Thomas Burke, escaped from the British, had come to the second
meeting of the Assembly in Salem; and Governor Alexander Martin was our very good friend, often going out of his way to spend
the night in Bethabara or Salem, or coming to attend the early
service on Easter morning. But to hear that the honored and beloved George Washington, the great general of the successful
revolution against Great Britain and now the President of the
United States, would spend the night in Salem was thrilling indeed!

Realizing that the states of the new union had each its tradi-
tions and its problems, President Washington had decided to visit
them in turn for personal acquaintance with their needs. In the
spring of this year he set out on his southern tour, and in March
the Brethren in Salem became aware that he would pass through
Wachovia on his return journey, and began to make their plans.

The first step taken was an attempt to secure good music with
English words. This was not a new idea, for on several occasions
inquiry had been made in Bethlehem, or someone had tried to trans-
late German stanzas so that they could be sung in English, but
neither had been very successful, and this effort also had little
result. Fortunately music is independent of language, and the
eminent guest was equally pleased whether a melody had a German
title or an English one. When he heard the old tune *O Deus Optime*

played by the trombones he asked what words we used. "In colonial days we called it "God save our gracious King," said Brother Marshall, "but now we have named it 'God Save Great Washington,'" and the President smiled.

As the time drew near, orders were given to repair the roads, especially the one between Salem and Bethabara, as it was believed that he would proceed north through our village.

"Shall we go to Salem to see the President?" I asked Jacob.

"No," he said, shaking his head. "I am afraid to undertake to stand in the street to see him arrive; and besides, Cathy, they say he will pass through Bethabara on his way north, and we should be here to greet him if he chooses to stop."

This sounded sensible, but it was a great mistake, for at the last minute the President decided to visit the Guilford battle ground before turning northward, and we missed our chance of seeing the most notable man in the country.

In Salem there was no disappointment. Knowing that the President did not wish to be entertained in private houses, the northeast room on the second floor of the tavern was made ready for him. When word was received that he had left Salisbury the Brethren Marshall, Koehler, and Benzien rode out to meet him; and as he approached the town several tunes were played, some on trumpets and French horns, some on trombones.

In his company were only his secretary, Major Jackson, and the necessary servants. As he descended from his coach he greeted in a friendly manner those who stood around, showing his good will especially to the children.

He had planned to leave the next morning, but when he was told that Governor Martin desired to wait upon him he decided to stay over, and a messenger was sent express to inform the Governor, who was at his estate on Dan River.

The next morning and afternoon were given largely to a tour of the town, inspecting its shops and schools, the Brothers House and the Sisters House. The President was pleased with all he saw, especially with the waterworks. Opportunity to see him was given to all who came. Toward evening Governor Martin arrived, and he and the President and Secretary Jackson attended the song service for which a special program of hymns, choir anthems, and instrumental music had been arranged.

At four o'clock the next morning, June 2nd, the company departed, the Brethren Marshall and Benzien accompanying them to the boundaries of Wachovia.

On the preceding evening Brother Abraham Steiner, the Bethabara store keeper, had come to us with a long face.

"Just look at the note I have received from Brother Kramsch," he said mournfully. "He writes that we will not have the honor of being visited by our illustrious President, because he has decided to go to the battle ground of Guilford."

"Oh, that is just too bad," I exclaimed. "I wish we had gone to Salem." Then seeing Brother Steiner smile as he read the rest of the note I asked, "What is the joke?"

"When the President came into the boys school, Brother Kramsch writes, they were having a reading lesson from Noah Webster's American Spelling Book, and when the President told them to continue, the boy who was reading labored through the next sentence which chanced to be 'A cat may look at a king.'"

"Well, of all things!" I exclaimed, laughing in spite of my chagrin at what I had missed. "What happened?"

"Brother Kramsch says that the President turned to him with a twinkle in his eye, and a glance at the awe-struck small boys, and remarked: 'That is what they are thinking now.' The boys did not catch the significance of what had been read, and were not embarrassed."

"I wish I could have heard the address which Brother Marshall presented in the name of the Brethren, and the President's answer," said Jacob, to whom Brother Steiner had handed the note. And this desire at least was fulfilled in part, for a few days later Brother Marshall brought to Bethabara a copy of his address and the original of the President's answer, and read them to our congregation. He then took them on to Bethania, where he did the same.

"Life would be more pleasant if everybody were as thoughtful as our Brother Marshall," I remarked to Jacob; and Jacob replied: "He means as much to Wachovia as President Washington does to the United States."

During March there had been much sickness in Wachovia, largely an epidemic affection of the chest, and in Bethania Brother Valentine Beck had been called home. This necessitated changes in the ministerial ranks, and resulted in a rather general shift of pastorates. Jacob and I were appointed to Friedland, and on June 7, Brother Michael Vogler and the Brethren Jacob and George Lagenauer came with their wagons and took our things to Friedland. There we found several Sisters cooking our supper for us, and soon other members came to welcome us.

Since I had formerly lived in Friedland there were not many new acquaintances to make. Some had passed away, some had married, some babies had been born, but to these changes we quickly became accustomed. John Vogler had grown into a sturdy boy of seven years, rather homely but with a bright eye and pleasant manner. With him I soon made friends, and was glad when he began to attend school so that I could see more of him. The next year he lost his mother and went to live with his maternal grandparents, Brother Friedrich Kinzel and his wife, who were very kind to him. I tried to give him added attention, which he repaid by calling me "Mother Ernst," a title the other children picked up so that it soon became of rather general use.

This transfer threw us back into the membership of the Conference of Country Ministers, which meant at least a monthly visit to Salem. The works for a town clock had been ordered from Europe, and when they arrived they were placed in the bell-tower on the Square, where the hours could be struck on the bell without demanding the constant attention of Brother and Sister Marshall. The clock needed to be wound every day, and got out of order now and then, but it was a great convenience to everybody in town and Jacob always checked his watch by it.

It troubled us to notice that Brother Marshall's hearing was becoming affected. "It is very annoying," he told us, "especially when I need to go to the county seat on business. Brother Benzien knows much about the land affairs, for I have been training him to assist me, but when we must both be away things stop at home, yet he must go to be ears for me."

Brother Benzien's attitude was different. "It is a privilege to work with Brother Marshall," he said, "and nothing that I can do for him is too much trouble. I am happy that he will allow me to 'be ears for him' as he calls it, and hope the arrangement will continue for a long time."

In August Jacob decided that he would be benefited by another visit to the springs in Rockingham County. John Hein went along to drive for us, and we had a pleasant stay of ten days, finding Doctor Coxe as friendly as ever. In the last days of October Jacob began to teach the school, which was attended by both boys and girls from the Friedland settlement.

When we went to the December meeting of Conference we met two newcomers, John Gambold and Christian Thomas Pfohl. Brother Gambold came as business manager for the Single Brethren, relieving Brother Stotz who took the same office for Salem congregation. Brother Pfohl was called as head teacher of the boys school and assistant preacher. In the following years both of these Brethren were ordained and gave fine service, Brother Gambold in the mission to the Cherokee Indians and Brother Pfohl as a pastor in the home field. Although these Brethren reached Salem in November their baggage did not arrive until the following July.

During this second stay in Friedland I twice touched the lowest depths of my experience, both physically and emotionally. All my life my health had been good, except for several severe, long attacks of illness, two in Pennsylvania, and one in Bethabara during my first marriage; and twice during this fourth marriage I was critically ill, so that doubt was felt whether I would recover. Both times it took a long time to regain my strength, and I often felt very despondent. Jacob, too, had recurring attacks of his podagra, his hands remaining lame, and it made my condition doubly trying when I was not able to give him the care I knew he needed. "I told Brother Johannes you ought to have a younger wife to wait on you," I told him more than once; and more than once he answered: "But I wanted you, Cathy." He was very patient with me, and always found something comforting to say, and I came to lean on him more and more.

The year 1792 did not begin badly, for the school was so well attended that the members decided to build an addition to the schoolhouse. At Jacob's request one of the Brethren estimated the number of twenty-four-foot logs that would be needed, and most of the members brought four each as their contribution. Before work had been finished the dreadful throat epidemic broke out among us, coming perhaps from Salem where it had prevailed since the first of the year. From April to October it raged through our settlement.

"Jacob Lagenauer has gone down with the disease," said Jacob, anxiously.

"He was helping lay beams here yesterday!" I exclaimed.

"That seems to be characteristic of this epidemic," said Jacob. "I must go to see him." We had been doing such visiting ever since the disease made its appearance, but now I was down with it myself, so that Jacob must go alone. Only too well I knew what Brother Lagenauer was suffering, for the pain in the swollen throat was terrible, and nothing seemed to give relief. Jacob had sent for Brother Vierling to prescribe for me, so that I had medicine on hand, which he put in his pocket as he started out.

"He has a bad attack," he told me on his return. "I asked his wife what they were doing for him, and she said that this morning she had gotten an emetic for him from Mary Schmid, but he vomited without it. I should think the thought of it would have been enough, for the emetic was compounded of indigo, blue-stone, and camphor! I advised her to send to Salem for the doctor, but she said that would do no good."

"The doctor seems to be able to give little help, truly," I moaned. "Did you give him some of my medicine?"

"I gave him twelve of the pills, and left seven for him to take tomorrow if these do not have a good effect." In the afternoon his son brought word that the pills had done little; so Jacob gave him sixteen more, to be taken that evening and in the morning, and told him to send to Salem for some China Drops.

Mollie Vogler, John's mother, was one of those who died as a result of this epidemic; others slowly recovered. Apparently if one outlived five or six days, recovery could be expected, for the end came quickly in the case of those who departed this life.

In Salem there were cases in nearly every house, with fifteen departures. "The town has never before found itself in such troubled circumstances," said Brother Benzien. "Led by fear everyone has been avoiding the town and our commerce has suffered. Already we were short-handed, and now so many, especially Sisters, have been taken that we hardly know what to do."

"The Saviour must be our comfort and help, individually and as congregations," said Jacob, which was what he had told me over and over since I had been stricken, and it was indeed our only resource.

In December word reached Salem that our dear old Brother Spangenberg had passed to his reward on the 18th of September. For fifty-eight years he had served the Lord in the Unity of Brethren, and from childhood he had been my ideal hero of the Cross. "He and Count Zinzendorf were very different," I told Jacob, "and I have never been able to decide which was the greater."

"Perhaps they were made to supplement each other," he answered, and doubtless with truth; but I was no good judge, for all my life I had admired Brother Joseph and had loved him with the love that one gives to a strong, wise friend.

After the new year had come, Jacob commenced school again, but at first only fifteen came. "The trouble is that many of them have neither shoes nor stockings," said Jacob, and this gave me an idea. A few days later I began to teach some of the older girls to knit, and to this I added lessons in sewing; the school also doubled in size. We had a lovefeast for the children when the winter school closed on February 22nd; the summer school commenced on the 3rd of April.

Our pastoral work was varied, and one episode still amuses me when I think of it. One married couple did not get along together, and neighbors told of quarreling and nagging, the intimation being that the fault was mostly on the wife's side. One day they came to Jacob with the amazing request: "Pastor, we want you to separate us."

"But," said Jacob, turning to the man, "when you came to see me the other day you told me that your wife had left you and had taken all her belongings; so what does this mean? I did not unite you and I cannot separate you."

"You told me to let her alone and she would come back to me," said the man, "but she is not willing to do that. We cannot get along together, and you must give us a paper showing that we are free of each other."

Jacob tried to explain the impossibility of doing what they asked, but they insisted, and he finally drew up a contract, which they both signed.

"Now," said Jacob sternly, as they rose to go, "remember, you are not to have anything more to do with each other, and that means that you are not to say one word about each other to anyone. And remember further, in the sight of the Lord you are bound so long as you both live, and neither of you dare marry anyone else."

A few days later Jacob came in chuckling. "That contract settled the case," he said. "I am glad I slipped in that provision of silence. Evidently if they could not gossip about it there was no fun in separation, and they are living together again and peaceably at that!"

The year 1796 was noteworthy for two reasons: the twenty-fifth anniversary of the organization of Salem congregation and the

January flood. That flood will go down in history as the worst in Salem's history because of its tragedy, worse than any broken mill-dam.

It happened on Sunday, the 17th of January. For several days it had rained, and the stream at the foot of the Salem hill was very high and far out of its banks. Brother Stotz and others were worried about the mill, for a horn had been heard from that direction and it was feared that the mill-dam was in danger.

"I will go and see," volunteered William Hall, one of the younger Brethren.

"You cannot get there!" exclaimed several of the others.

"O yes, I can," he replied. "I will go on horseback; and if the ford is too deep we will swim for it."

Protests were numerous, and he was reminded that the water would be icy cold, but when William Eldridge offered to go with him nothing could stop them, and some of the Brethren went with them to the ford to see them make the attempt, for the bridge was under water and worse than useless.

Eldridge succeeded in swimming his horse across, though with great difficulty, took the horse to a stable on a farm near by, and returned to find that Hall was in grave danger. He tried three times to swim to help him, but became so chilled that he could do nothing and went back to the farm, not knowing until the next day what had happened.

Hall was caught by the swift current and was forced against a submerged fence, in which his horse became entangled. Twice he dismounted and freed the animal, but the third time he became alarmed and shouted, "Come and save the horse." Brother Joshua Booner plunged in and rescued the horse, but did not realize that Hall, who was a good swimmer, was also in need of assistance, and by the time Booner reached the bank he was faint with cold and had to be supported to a place to rest.

Meanwhile Hall was swept down stream, finally catching the limb of a tree, but too stiff with cold to climb upon it. Hanging half over the limb he shouted, "Help! Help!"

By this time the news had reached the town and practically all the Brethren hurried thither. "Let me try to reach him," offered Brother Schaub, hastily stripping to his linen under-drawers. He succeeded in reaching and climbing the tree, but he was so cold by that time that he could not lift Hall from the water. All he could do was, by various means, to hold up Hall's head so that he should not drown. As Brother Schaub reached him Hall said, "God will not forsake us!"

"There is no rescue for us now; we must think where we are going," answered Schaub, tying himself and Hall to the tree with a grapevine he found there, so that their bodies might be more easily recovered.

"Hurry, hurry!" he shouted; and a few minutes later the message was: "William Hall is dead and if you do not come quickly I will go too."

Meanwhile the Brethren on the bank worked with all their might to build a raft, and the Negro Peter tried three times to swim to the stranded men, but could not make it. Brother Christoph Reich also tried but got a cramp in the leg and had to be helped back.

When the raft was finished the Brethren Welfare and Christopher Vogler got on it, but it sank with them, and they had to swim back. Then they tried to go supported by a plank apiece, but the swift current tore the planks from them.

"Get a large tub from the still-house," cried someone, and Brethren raced after that, nailed boards to the bottom to keep it from upsetting, fastened a rope to it by which they could steady it, and finally got it into the water. Isaac Booner and the Negro Peter got into it and set out in the name of the Lord.

After indescribable effort they reached the tree, and Brother Schaub began to sing at the top of his voice:

Now thank we all our God,
With heart and hand and voices.

When an effort was made to lift Hall into the tub the Negro Peter, brave so far, fainted from the shock of finding him dead, but Schaub and Booner succeeded, and with much more effort the tub was brought to land, Brethren rushing waist-deep into the flood to help.

"It is barely possible that we can save him," said Brother Vierling, and all night men worked, rubbing him with hot cloths, knowing that he had not drowned, and hoping that he might be resuscitated, but it was in vain. Brother Schaub revived, but was sickly for a long time; and thereafter men compared every flood with the one in which Brother Hall lost his life.

In the spring of 1798 Jacob and I were both sick again, and we greatly missed our Sara, who had moved to Salem the previous year. Her mother passed away when Sara was but a year or two old, and in response to her dying request Jacob's first wife took the child to bring up; when I married Jacob her care fell to me. Now, as a young woman of nineteen years, it had seemed best that she should live in the Sisters House, and when we needed help we must call on one of the Friedland Sisters, as we did from time to time.

When Sister Koehler came to see me and found me so weak and miserable and Jacob lame and feeble, she readily agreed to pass on to the Elders my feeling that we ought to be allowed to retire.

"Certainly I will tell them," she said, "but you know how short-handed we are, and I fear it will not be possible to arrange for a new pastor at Friedland. Even if you are not able to do much, your being here is worth a good deal to your members, for they can come to you even if you cannot go to them."

So for two more years we did our poor best, but when Jacob had to go to bed again with high fever, and remained very weak even when the fever broke, he finally dictated a letter for me to send to Brother Marshall, asking for our retirement. "We are both old and feeble," he told me to say, "and we ask the consideration of our Brethren. We know that the going of the Brethren Koehler and Schroeter to the General Synod has further reduced the number of ministers in Wachovia, and we regret that we are no longer able to serve, but indeed, Brother Marshall, we can do it no longer, and we ask your help."

Tears filled my eyes as I wrote, for the saddest part of growing old is that we are obliged to give up the work we love. But I knew that Jacob was right, and I could offer no argument against it, for I too was ill and must spend many a day in bed.

The answer that came surprised us both—it was a call to go back to Bethabara. "What will that help?" I groaned, but when Brother Pfohl came from Salem to see us it did not sound so bad.

"They are asking only that you live in the Bethabara parsonage," he told Jacob, "and hold the week-day services when you feel able. Perhaps you can teach the few children who go to school there. You need not visit, and the Brethren from Salem will take turns coming to you for the Sunday services, so that you will not have them on your mind."

Jacob looked at me for answer, and I said, "That does sound possible. The rooms there are comfortable and we can arrange them so that we have no stairs to climb." In the beginning of November we made the trip, which seemed endless in my feeble condition.

Wearied by the journey I was not able to go to Salem on the 9th to the dedication of the new church; still worse, I was unable to attend the Communion service on November 13th to which all communicants in Wachovia were invited. With some difficulty I persuaded Jacob to leave me and go, and he reported the two occasions as successful and inspiring. Not to have shared in that Communion seemed my crowning disappointment, but on the 16th Brother Stotz came to hold the services; he gave Communion to the seven of us who had been unable to go to Salem, and I was comforted.

25

THE TURN OF THE CENTURY

THE CLOSING OF THE EIGHTEENTH CENTURY AND THE BEGINNING of the nineteenth seemed to coincide with changes in the life of Wachovia, particularly in Salem, where old leaders were passing away and younger Brethren were taking their places.

Even the landscape was changing. The countless hills were still forest-clad, green in spring and summer, flaming with red and yellow in autumn, while in winter the pines and cedars held sway and whispered to each other about the departed glories of oak and chestnut. Clear little streams continued to run through the many valleys. After every hard rain our Muddy Creek justified its name. The Yadkin River rose and fell, now a raging torrent, overflowing its banks and flooding the lowlands on either side; now a subdued river, showing its sandbanks and rocks and permitting travelers to ride or drive across the Shallow Ford. From the northwest old Pilot watched the changing seasons as he had done for ages uncounted.

But man had come into the forests of piedmont Carolina. On the first day of January, 1754, eleven Moravian Brethren were occupying a one-room log cabin in Wachovia, their nearest neighbors miles away and few in number. On the first day of the new century there were six organized Moravian congregations in Wachovia, with a membership of 1,147, men, women, and children, not counting the hundreds of neighbors and friends who attended our services from time to time or to whom our ministers proclaimed the Gospel at various preaching places.

There was still much vacant land, but farms had been developed here and there through all the country from the Catawba River to the Virginia line; homes had been built; streams had been utilized to furnish power for the mills to which the farmers brought their grain for grinding.

In the center of this development stood Salem, with its increasing importance in many lines and its growing number of buildings.

After the addition to the Brothers House was finished a suitable building had been erected for the boys school, so arranged that a few boys could room there under the care of their teachers, and, if necessary, cooking could be done for them, though it was preferred that they should take their meals with their parents and sleep in the schoolhouse.

While the workmen and their equipment were available it was decided to finish the outside of the Congregation House, which would greatly improve its looks. "We have decided to cut back the wide eaves and remove the narrow roof between the stories," Brother Stotz told us, "and to cover the outside with plaster."

"That will certainly be a great improvement," said I, "and it ought to make the house last much longer. Will you color the plaster?"

"It is to be light yellow, marked off in blocks with white," he replied, and this proved a pleasing combination.

In 1798 Salem's most ambitious project had been undertaken —the building of a church with a commodious meeting-hall. The original plan had been to place it on the east side of the Square, but the space between the Congregation House and the Sisters House proved to be rather too small and it was finally decided to move it north a little and place it diagonally across from the northeast corner of the Square. Brother Marshall drew the plans, and I am glad that he lived to see the completion of this his crowning work, and that he could share in its consecration on November 9th, 1800, when a great congregation filled the church to overflowing and forced the chapel servants to cut in half the buns provided for the lovefeast. The impressive Communion which followed on the 13th (which I missed), must have filled his heart with great joy, and it must have thrilled him through and through to see so many, many souls gathered for such a service on the site which he helped to select in the center of Wachovia, for the city that was to be. I hope he thought of that, and not of the faces no longer there, for few remained of those who had helped to build that city.

In April Salem had had an epidemic of some disease of the chest, and one of those called home had been our Brother Traugott Bagge, who for more than thirty years had served as merchant, and during the Revolutionary War had been our ablest Brother in public affairs. In his place Brother Conrad Kreuser was called from Nazareth, Pennsylvania, much to the disappointment of Charles Bagge, who had hoped to succeed his father. The Elders thought Charles too young and inexperienced, though he had been a good clerk under his father's direction, and they made no objection when he proposed going to Pennsylvania to see whether his prospects would be better there. He found nothing that he liked and came back to Salem. Then he married the daughter of Brother Charles Holder and moved to the Friedberg settlement, where he opened a small store.

As Brother Bagge's name will always be associated with the era of the Revolution, so a story that I heard from Sister Maria Barbara Boeckel reminded me forcefully of the pioneer days. Sister Boeckel and her husband, Valentine Boeckel, had moved from the Friedberg settlement to Bethania while we were in Friedland, and during my third stay in Bethabara I met her more often and was greatly interested in her account of her coming to America.

"I was two and a half years old," she said, "when my parents and some of their friends decided to emigrate to Pennsylvania. I remember little about it, but my mother told me that there were thirty children on the ship when we sailed, and that the voyage lasted twenty-six weeks."

"A voyage of more than six months is hard on adults, and must have been doubly hard on little folks," I remarked.

"It was more than that. Because of the stale water and impossible food, I suppose, an epidemic broke out among the children, and one and another passed away and must be buried in the sea. They told me that out of thirty children who sailed I was one of three who landed in America."

"Twenty-seven child funerals in one voyage!" I exclaimed. "That is the worst I ever heard."

"I have always been glad that I was too young to know much about what went on," she agreed, and I who had had no children felt sorry for those bereaved parents even though their sorrows had long since ceased to trouble them, for after sixty and more years probably few of them were left in this vale of tears, as some people call it.

Another of our greatest had passed away late in the preceding year, but it was not until January, 1800, that we heard that George Washington was no more; and with the news came the call from Congress that the nation should observe his birthday, February 22nd, as a day of remembrance. No direction was given as to how the day should be observed, and after due consideration the leaders in Salem decided on a song service, much like the one President Washington had enjoyed when he visited Salem. It was an impressive and beautiful service, and the ode was filed in the archives. "Do you suppose anybody will ever look over those papers when they are old?" I asked Jacob, and he said he thought they would be considered of value in some distant day. "We owe it to the future to keep the record of the present," he said.

Ever since I have known the Moravians they have kept a diary of the daily happenings of each congregation, and at the close of the year have compiled a summary of the most notable events, the *memorabilia* of the current year. In the year 1783 we had two Memorabilia, one for that year and one summing up the eight years of the Revolutionary War. It has become customary for the leading minister in Salem to compile the Memorabilia for Wachovia, which is not only read in Salem on the last night of the old year but is sent to all the congregations to be read in the closing services of each, and in the last night of the last year in the century the one written by Brother Benzien seemed doubly impressive.

"We are one period nearer the return of our Lord, and perhaps it is very near, for the signs of the times are unusual," so he wrote, but "of that day and that hour knoweth no man," and only the new century can tell whether it is very near or not.

The first year of the new century was signalized by the beginning of a mission to the Cherokee Indians. Brother Spangenberg had told us of the purpose of the first Moravians in Georgia to preach the Gospel to the Indians, and the early settlers in Bethlehem had made such missionary work their first concern, even when it meant such tragedy as the massacre which Brother David Zeisberger so narrowly escaped. Here in North Carolina there had ever been the desire to begin mission work among the Cherokees, our nearest red neighbors, but Indian War and one thing and another had prevented. Now at last the way opened, and after a preliminary visit by Brother Abraham Steiner and Brother Gottlieb Byhan, Brother Byhan married and he and his wife and Brother Wohlfahrt left Salem to make a small beginning as messengers of peace to the red men in the Cherokee Nation's territory.

Another forward step was the use of cowpox to anticipate smallpox.

"We are informed," said Brother Vierling, "that a new kind of smallpox has been discovered in England which is much lighter than the ordinary kind, and that a doctor in Raleigh has secured some of the necessary material to produce it."

"Does it prevent the ordinary kind, and is it safer?" he was asked.

"So they say, and apparently with truth," he replied.

"Would you advise trying it?"

"Yes. There has been no epidemic of smallpox for fifteen years, and all the young people who have grown up in that period are in constant danger. If this does what is claimed for it, we owe them the protection," he said very positively.

"We cannot force parents to permit it."

"Of course not, but we can recommend it," said Brother Vierling.

"I am much in favor of trying it," said Brother Schober, "and I will get the material and instructions for its use and give it to Brother Vierling."

This was done, and so far everybody has been much pleased with the results. If the scourge of smallpox has been conquered the new century has begun with a great blessing to mankind.

Still another sign of progress was the establishing of a regular post. Wachovia, like all the rest of the country, had been obliged to send letters by chance travelers or by our Brethren as they went and came, but in 1794 the United States government gave us a regular, bi-monthly post, and Brother Schober was appointed postmaster. Our correspondence with Bethlehem was much facilitated, and letters came and went much more rapidly. If it was more expensive, it was worth it for important letters, and others could still be sent in the old way.

One of the oddest accidents of which I have heard happened at the Brothers House in June. "Jacob Krause, one of the older boys, has often walked in his sleep," said Brother Pfohl in telling us about it, "but he had not done it recently and the Brethren hoped he had outgrown the tendency. One night recently it was quite warm and a window was left open in the sleeping-hall. One of the Brethren waked just in time to see Jacob poised on the window-sill, but before he could get to him the boy jumped."

"Jumped three stories!" I exclaimed.

"Jumped three stories, and landed on his hands and feet, clear of the barrels and a wheelbarrow that stood near the wall of the house. The Brethren at the window saw that he moved and rushed down stairs and picked him up, after they carried him into the house he waked and asked what had happened."

"How did he escape death?" I wondered aloud.

"No one can answer that, but he was not badly hurt though he was stiff and sore for two weeks."

"Years ago the Brethren would have said that the angels protected him," I said, remembering many instances when escape from death had been ascribed to their protecting care.

"The angels are still the messengers of God," replied Brother Pfohl gravely, "and I erred in saying that I did not know how Jacob escaped. Either through the agency of the angels or in some other way the Lord spared his life."

While young Jacob Krause escaped as by a miracle, one of our older members was taken home; in August Brother Adam Spach, the pioneer of the Friedberg settlement, entered into the joy of his Lord in his eighty-second year, and Brother Pfohl held his funeral.

On the 5th of February, 1802, the Conference of Country Ministers met in Salem, and all the ministers and their wives were invited, since it was the eighty-second birthday of our dear Brother Marshall. For two years he had been subject to attacks of severe pain and oppression in the chest, which often lasted three hours, and two such paroxysms had come only a few days before his birthday, but that day he seemed bright and strong; Conference expressed its affection for him in a poem composed for the occasion.

We all ate dinner together, and during the course of it conversation drifted to several episodes which recently had brought much distress to Salem. One young Brother had asked the advice of the Elders as to his marriage, but counsel had to be refused because investigation showed that he had already made all his plans, and the use of the *lot* was out of the question under those circumstances.

"It looks as though the younger people were rebelling against the leadership of the Lord," said one Brother.

"It is dreadful to think of acting exactly contrary to the express wish of the Lord," said another, referring to two of our young people for whom the negative *lot* had been drawn, in spite of which they had decided to marry and with that in view had severed their connection with the congregation.

Brother Marshall evidently sensed that something was disturbing us, and asked Brother Benzien what the trouble was. When he heard, a look came into his face that I had never seen before, a sort of rapt look such as one imagines upon the face of one of the prophets of the olden days, and he raised his hand as though commanding the silence that fell upon us.

Then gravely and sweetly he spoke. "My children, when one is old and the hearing greatly impaired one thinks much, and sees that which before was hidden from view. Be not troubled concerning the guidance of the Lord, He is still the Almighty, and still the loving Father of His followers. Of old He led Israel for forty years by means of the pillar of cloud and of fire, and then it was withdrawn but He did not leave them. For well-nigh twice forty years He has led the Unity of Brethren, making known His will for it through the *lot*, but that method too will cease. When a high privilege becomes merely a church rule then it dare no longer be called imperative. You have seen changes made in its use, and you will see more, but be not affrighted; God will find other means whereby to make known His will to those who seek it."

Tears of love filled many eyes as we listened to this and more from this godly man. Comforted and reassured, we joined in a happy lovefeast with him and his grandson, Fritz von Schweinitz, who had come to him after the home-going of his wife, and had cared for him with the tenderness of a son.

It was the last time we saw him, for five days later another attack came on, and from that he did not recover. Because of the distress in breathing that the attacks brought he feared a struggle at the end, and asked that no Brethren should be called; so only Fritz, Brother Benzien, and Brother Vierling were with him when the summons came. He need not have feared. The Saviour did not permit that which he had dreaded, but gently and sweetly as a tired child he fell asleep in the midnight hour, as Brother Benzien laid his hand upon the venerable head repeating:

> The Saviour's blood and righteousness
> Thy beauty was, thy glorious dress,
> Thus well arrayed thou need'st not fear
> Now in His presence to appear.

For sixty-one years he had served the Lord in the Unity of Brethren, showing himself ever a man gifted with unusual grace and wisdom.

Everybody who could come gathered for the funeral, some ten or twelve hundred persons, and the church could not begin to hold them all, for many living outside the town honored him greatly and considered him "the father of the settlement," through whose service a wilderness had become a fine community, inside and outside Wachovia, and they were right.

On April 18th, we prayed the Easter liturgy on our God's Acre, and asked everlasting fellowship with those of our Brethren and Sisters who had fallen asleep since the last Easter Day, and especially with those faithful servants of the Unity who had rested from their labors, Brother Christian Gregor in Herrnhut, Brother John Ettwein in Bethlehem, and Brother Marshall in Salem.

Brother Benzien took up the work which Brother Marshall laid down; and on May 30th Bishop Carl Friedrich Reichel and his family arrived from Pennsylvania, Brother Reichel having been called to take the place of Brother Koehler, who was to become pastor of a European congregation instead of returning to America.

While I had regained my strength Jacob remained feeble, and it was only at intervals that he could go to Salem to the meeting of the Elders, but in April we did attend and took the opportunity of renewing our request for retirement. This brought up the question of where we should live, as I knew it would, and I begged as earnestly as I could that we might return to my former home, where two widows were living.

"It will require a little time to find other rooms for them," said Brother Stotz, "but we will do our best to arrange it for you." When word came in June that we were allowed to move to Salem, it was into my old home that we were taken, no longer mine in law, but mine for the rest of my life I was assured by Brother Benzien, and without charge in view of the years of service which Jacob and I had given.

"Have you enough to live on?" he asked us kindly. Consideration showed that our income would not suffice, and he asked Jacob what disposition he proposed to make of his property in his will.

"After certain smaller bequests and after providing that Cathy should have the interest as long as she lives I planned that the principal should go to the church," said Jacob.

"Then," said Brother Benzien, "I suggest that we arrange an annuity bond which shall pay ten per cent as long as you both live, and six per cent for the lifetime of the remaining one of you." This made everything easy for us, and we gladly accepted the suggestion.

I had hoped that the moving to Salem and the release from all responsibility might benefit Jacob, but during the rest of the year he gradually failed. He did not suffer much, only grew steadily weaker, and when he was asked whether he thought he would soon go home he did not reply except with a gentle smile. On the 4th of December he entered into the joy of his Lord, after thirty years of faithful service in various Wachovia congregations. I would gladly have taken care of him for a longer time, but I could not begrudge him the escape from weariness.

On the 31st of October an important conference was held in regard to a shift of pastorates, and Brother Simon Peter came to tell me about it, knowing how interested I would be to hear that he was to move from Bethania to Bethabara, and that Brother Pfohl was to follow him at Bethania. "Another thing was decided that may have a far-reaching effect," he said. "You know that for ten years parents have been asking that we would add a boarding department to our girls school, so that their daughters might be brought here to share in the advantages of our girls."

"Yes," I said, "I have often heard that wish expressed, as far back as the days when it was my duty to look after ladies visiting our town."

"We have had no suitable building, and no one to put in charge of a boarding school," he said, "but now the Lord has pointed the way. Brother Kramsch and his wife have had experience in the boarding schools of Europe. Brother Pfohl has been giving advanced lessons to some of our older girls, and by the time a house can be built they will be ready to teach."

"Then it has been decided to arrange for boarding pupils?" I asked.

"Yes. Brother Kramsch has been called to Salem from Hope and for the present will look after the boys school and help with the preaching, but he has also been called as Inspector of a boarding school for girls to be established as soon as arrangements have been made."

"Where will the new house be placed?"

"That is not yet decided definitely, but probably on the east side of the Square, between the Congregation House and the Sisters House."

"That street is coming to have a row of imposing buildings," I remarked. "With Brother Vierling's large brick house just completed, and this planned, it has even more than the main street."

"Had it been possible to carry out the original plan for the town," he said, "they would all have been grouped around a large octagonal Square."

"Christian said the plan would have to be changed when this site was selected," I said, "but I suppose this arrangement serves just as well."

The incidents of 1803 are too recent to need recording; so I mention but two. My little friend John Vogler has come to Salem as a permanent resident, and has become a member of the congregation—it is hard to realize that this is the infant whom I held in my arms, the sturdy lad of seven years, the growing boy of twelve who was so anxious to move to Salem but must await the proper time. Now he is a young man, living in the Brothers House and learning gunsmithing from his uncle, Christoph Vogler. It is good to see him pass my window nearly every day and to get his cheery greeting.

The other event of which I wish to record a few notes is the recent celebration of the jubilee of Wachovia. Because of our large church it was decided to hold the anniversary services here instead

of in Bethabara, and much was the interest and many the conferences which preceded it.

"Sister Ernst," said Sister Reichel, "will you give me some help
in planning the decorations? I am a newcomer, and you will know
better than I on whom I can depend for help."

"Have you decided what you want to do?" I asked, much
pleased at being consulted.

"Partly. I have thought that under the canopy above the minister's chair we might have the inscription of the Daily Text for the
day on which the first Brethren arrived in Wachovia: *I know
where thou dwellest*, with the date 17 NOVEMBER 1753, in a
half oval with a jet-black ground and with large, golden-yellow
letters."

"Ask Friedrich Meinung to do the lettering for you."

"Son of Brother Ludwig Meinung?"

"Yes. I understand that he is good with his pen and pencil,
and I feel sure he will feel complimented at being asked and will
do his best to please you. I suggest that you also have the figure 50
made in large numerals, and hang it at the center of the arch of the
canopy."

"I think we will put that number on a dark blue oval in gold
figures, and festoons of evergreen and flowers can be arranged on
both sides of the canopy."

"I fear there will be no flowers in November."

"We can make them, if we can get enough help. My daughter
Dorothea learned the art in Nazareth and can show them how."

"Ask Sister Benigna Benzien to appoint enough of the Single
Sisters and older girls to give you the help you want. She will know
which of them are most deft with their fingers."

"Many thanks. That gives me a start, and I will probably
consult with you again."

When the day came the decoration pleased everyone. In addition to what was planned that first time, there was an inscription
in front of the minister's table, giving the Text and the date of
November 17, 1803; there were more festoons and flowers, which

looked well against the white cloth covering the table and platform steps; and across the table were ribbons in the colors of the Choirs, cherry, pink, light blue, and white—I had worn them all except the cherry, for I was no longer a girl when I joined the Unity.

When the great day arrived, a wagon was sent to Bethabara and Bethania to bring Brother and Sister Johannes Beroth and others who had been among the first colonists in Wachovia and might now join in this beautiful day of thanksgiving and jubilee. With rejoicing hearts and tongues we brought to our dear Lord, to His and our Father, and to the Holy Ghost, our praise and honor, glory and adoration, for all that He, the Triune God, had done for his humble Brethren in Wachovia.

At what better place than this could I end the story of my life? I am seventy-seven years old and cannot know how many or how few my remaining days may be. As I look back over my journey through time I am conscious of many things in which I have been remiss, but the dear Saviour has ever shown me grace and mercy. Now I am well content to sit beside my window and watch life go by until it shall please Him to take me to Himself.

POSTSCRIPT

———

WHEN ANNA CATHARINA ANTES KALBERLAHN REUTER HEINZ-
mann Ernst laid down her pen it did not mean that she ceased
to be a vital part of the life of Salem and of Wachovia.

When a vacancy occurred in Friedland she was called to go
there for the third time, keep the parsonage open, and give pastoral
care to the women of the congregation, which she did for more
than three months.

Her home was always shared with some other widow, and
when Brother Steiner, pastor of the Hope congregation, wanted to
send his little son to school in Salem, arrangements were made that
the boy should room in the schoolhouse but take his meals with
Catharina and her companion.

From her window and as she crossed the Square to church she
watched the progress of building the house for the girls school. By
her door passed the leading men of North Carolina and adjoining
states, bringing daughters to the boarding school in Salem; and
from friends she learned their names, as well as the arrangement of
classes. The older girls from town and the boarding pupils were
placed in groups according to age and ability, while separate classes
were held for the smaller day-pupils, though all in the new house.
Their Christmas dialogues, their public "Examinations," were her
delight, and she never missed attending when she could.

For the children of the town she had a special fondness, which
they reciprocated in full, and she gave them many a happy hour
with some small treat in her room.

In 1808 Brother and Sister Michael Rank and Brother and Sister John Beroth gave a lovefeast in Bethania in celebration of the jubilee of their marriage, and Sister Ernst was an honored guest, the only other person still living of the sixteen who had been wedded in Pennsylvania fifty years before.

Brother Lewis de Schweinitz and his bride made a perilous voyage across the Atlantic just as the War of 1812 was breaking out, and time after time she held her breath as she listened to the thrilling story of their experiences when they came to America so that Brother de Schweinitz might take the place of Brother Benzien as representative of the Unity in Wachovia.

John Vogler remained attached to "Mother Ernst," dropped in now and then to consult her about his plans, and made up his mind that when the time came he wanted to take her house.

Considering her advanced years her health was good, and she was able to attend the lovefeast held on February 19th, 1816, fifty years after the first Brethren moved to Salem to make a real beginning with building the central town. As she looked at the fifty candles arranged in a pyramid before the minister's table, and at the fifty more placed along the edge of the two galleries, she thought of the past and of the future, and as she scanned the earnest, intelligent faces of such younger men as Friedrich Meinung, Benjamin Reichel, Lewis de Schweinitz, and John Vogler she thanked God and took courage, seeing in them representatives of the new leaders of her church and her community.

ANNA CATHARINE ERNST

Daughter of

HENRY ANTES

Born Pa. Nov. 19, 1726

Leader in Church and
Community service in
Bethabara, Salem, &
Friedland, N. C.

Entered into rest, Mar. 9, 1816

A life spent in the service
of others

313
34